D0585551

 Ch Crackley Superb 1927

Crackley Supremacy 1928

 Ch Eden Aristocrat 1928

Ch Crackley Surething 1934

Coleg *LLYSFASI*	
Coutts	**Date** 8/11
Accession No. [barcode] 12350	£ 10 -00
Boo	**Class No.** 636.755 CHA

KINGDOM

© Kingdom Books 1996. All rights reserved.
No part of this publication may be
reproduced, stored in a retrieval system, or
transmitted in any form or by any means,
electronic, mechanical, photocopying,
recording or otherwise, without the written
permission of the publisher.

Designed by Add Graphics
PO Box 15
Waterlooville PO7 6BQ
England

Kingdom Books is an imprint
of T.F.H. Publications

Photo: Robert Smith

Published by Kingdom Books
PO Box 15
Waterlooville PO7 6BQ
England

THE
World of Dogs
fox
TERRIER
Diana Chads

CONTENTS

This is a guide for the Fox Terrier fancier. Having owned and loved Fox Terriers for over 50 years I felt it was time to share the fun that they bring to any owner's life. No one book can cover all aspects of Fox Terrier ownership, but a great deal can be learned from exchanging experiences with other people and by reading various books and articles in dog papers such as *Our Dogs* and *Dog World* and similar publications in many countries around the world. These contain mainly show reports, but there are also interesting articles on such topics as breeding and remedies for various problems. There are other magazines in which information is exchanged among pet owners. Still more can be learned through the Breed Clubs, and the names of Breed Club Secretaries can be obtained from The Kennel Club (see Appendix A: **Useful Addresses**).

This book is written as a tribute to the Fox Terrier, and I hope it will encourage people to have one (or two) as a pet. He is a typical Terrier, so an understanding of the Terrier type is helpful in training. He is affectionate, friendly, lively and interested in everything, always on the look-out for the next bit of fun, be it a walk, a meal, someone to play with, or a cat to chase. A farm is a particularly good home for him, as he loves to sniff out rats and mice. In the house he enjoys his creature comforts. He is out for anything he can get: petting, a comfortable chair, your bed, food or anything else of interest, even some television programmes. One of mine likes giving clarinet lessons. When he starts going into a crescendo (howling!) they all join in. The youngest puppy is surprised at first, but he soon succumbs to his 'musical' instincts.

Fox Terriers are very jealous and if anyone else, human or animal, seems to be getting attention they are quick to make it clear that they want some too. They may sit on the visitor's knee, come and nudge you, or simply sulk. Sometimes they even stage a 'dirty protest'. I have come to the conclusion that punishment is not always the answer where jealousy is the underlying problem. The dogs are intelligent and, if punishment is given, they get the 'attention' they want. I therefore tend to ignore them. They often defy a serious scolding at the time, but a marked improvement can be seen afterwards. Usually they are very happy to co-operate, and it is on this that I base my training.

Care of the coat of the Wire Fox Terrier might worry some people, but it does not take a lot of time, determination or skill to keep the dog looking reasonable for normal purposes. Preparation for the dog show is another matter: that takes time, skill and experience. Time taken for routine daily or weekly grooming is well spent, however, as it serves both to give the dog attention and, by keeping the coat clean, to help avoid problems from dust, fleas, and other skin irritants.

I trimmed my first dog myself, knowing nothing about it at all. No-one having told me differently, I used scissors (strictly forbidden!). On one occasion, to make him really smart, we took him to a 'Professional' groomer. He came home totally unrecognisable. He was extremely upset and self-conscious about his appearance. He was aware he looked awful and did not want to venture out on his nice walks until his coat had grown and he looked like the fine chap that he was. From then on I vowed I would do the job myself, although I was not yet even into my teens. The dog was happy about this and so was I. Fox Terriers are very aware of their appearance and

INTRODUCTION

like to look nice. However, once they are beautifully clean and trimmed, they nearly always go and find something really smelly to roll in; that way, they think they have the perfume to match the appearance.

Fox Terrier activities are really great fun. The amount of time they take up depends on what you want to put into your hobby and how many dogs you have. The Local Authority guideline is usually not more than two breeding bitches (six months to the end of a dog's life) and not more than five animals in total. After that you need a breeder's licence. This means your kennels will be inspected on a regular basis and must conform to Local Authority standards. The Local Authority has no right of access to the private owner with just a few dogs.

To own Fox Terriers is a wonderful, uplifting hobby, whether you breed them, show them or simply keep them as pets, and I have many a tale to tell. For instance, there was the time the Vicar said he would leave some apples and Devon cream in the front porch when he returned from holiday. I found the apples but no cream. I was afraid it would be ungrateful to ask what had happened to it. I had a friend staying with me at the time and she had not seen it either. I made the dreaded phone call and was advised that the cream was left with the apples. I looked everywhere but found nothing. Next morning I went to work and, on my return, was told that Mischief had buried the cream pot in the garden and had his second helping that morning. There were no tell-tale signs and he got away without a scolding.

Christmas parcels are another target. One year I decided Belgian chocolates would make good presents and bought and wrapped up several boxes costing not far off £20. Dear Traffy found them and did not leave one. He was not even sick afterwards but spent the night on my bed as if he had done nothing wrong.

Life with a Fox Terrier, then, is anything but predictable. In this book I shall describe in some detail the history and general management of these charming Terriers, and hope that I shall encourage you to get to know them better.

Astona Didgery Doo: a fine example of a Smooth Fox Terrier. Photo: Diane Pearce.

I should like to thank everyone who has helped me with this book. The task has proved far greater than I ever imagined, but has been made all the more rewarding by these kind, helpful people, many of whom I should not otherwise have met. It is not possible to list everyone by name, but I should like to make special mention of the following:

Mrs Sheila Alcock for allowing me to use material taken from her 'Feminine View' column in *Our Dogs*, a very useful column for the dog owner.

Mrs Grethe Bergendahl (Marstens) for loan of photographs and a considerable contribtion to the text.

Mrs H Bradford (Flyntwyre) for help with text and some good photographs.

Mrs P Broom (Roxway) for help and the loan of useful books.

Mrs E Cartledge for the loan of her books and for allowing me to use photographs from a screen depicting early champions (see end papers).

Mr Collins (Yiriwyre) Australia.

Miss Paddy Cutts for advice about writing pet books and photography.

Mrs Cherry Davies (Mosvalley) for illustrations and notes on trimming the Smooth Fox Terrier.

Mr M Hibbit (Sufredon) who has done so much research for me about the Smooth Fox Terrier to include in the text. Also for the list of Champions.

Mr A Hunt (Dominus) for advice on trimming and for the loan of many historic books.

Mrs Jan Kennedy (Sceftesbr) who researched the pedigrees of the Wires for the List of Champions, made corrections, and sent historic photos from the Linda Beak collection.

The Kennel Club for use of the library and for their help.

Mrs Ruth Libner (Libwyre) for photographs and information about showing in the USA.

Mr George MacLeod for allowing me to use material from his *Homeopathy For Pets*.

Mr Axel Möhrke (von der Bismarckquell) for notes about dogs in Germany and for photos.

Dr D B Morton of Birmingham University for his contribution about frozen semen used in dogs.

Mr Brendan O'Loghlen (Extreal) for pictures and a considerable contribution about dogs and dog shows in Australia.

Dr A J Raw who kindly read the proofs and suggested improvements.

The Smooth Fox Terrier Association for permission to print in full the A-Z Fox Terrier poem by Rev Dr Rosslyn Bruce on Page 73 and for all their help and co-operation.

Mrs Rose Turner (Rotur) for the loan of historic books and photos.

Mrs E Winstanley (Boreham) for help, advice, encouragement and loan of photographs.

Last but not least, I should like to thank the many friends who have made helpful suggestions and corrections to the text, and my publisher's editorial and design staff, who have worked closely with me throughout.

Many thanks also to everyone who has lent photographs for this book, and apologies to those whose photographs have not been used for technical or copyright reasons. My special thanks go to the following:

Mrs Lynn Bell (Belyndi).
Mrs M Bird (Marick) for 'Fun Day' photographs.
Mr Martin Booth (16825 Mayfield Road, Livonia, Mich. 43134, USA).
Mrs Ursy Burnand (Burnand Photography, Field Place, Hungerford, Berkshire).
Mr Dave Freeman (photographer).
Mrs E Geddes (Gedstar).
Mrs Ruth Libner (Libwyre) for photographs from the USA.
Mrs Geraldine Limburn
Mrs Sarah Osborne
Ms Diane Pearce
Mrs Anne Roslin-Williams
Mrs A Somers
Mr Robert Smith
Mrs J Spackman for domestic photographs.
Mrs B Spagnoletti
TFH Inc for allowing Isabelle Français's pictures to be used.
Mr T Ward of **Bonhams Auctioneers** for permission to use the Arthur Wardle Fox Hunting picture.
Mr P Winfield (Riber) for use of photographs from Australia.

Photo: Isabelle Français.

FOREWORD

It has been some 30 years since anyone in Great Britain has written a book on the subject of the Fox Terrier, and this one by Diana Chads most certainly fills the gap. She has undertaken an enormous task and I feel that her book is much more comprehensive than many published, as it is entirely unbiased. It covers most aspects of this 'dog game', and is targeted at everyone: the pet owner who knows nothing, the 'back-yard' breeder, the serious breeder/exhibitor and the professional.

Diana Chads is no novice to Wire Fox Terriers, as she developed a serious interest in them some 50 years ago and did a little pet trimming during the Second World War. She is completely devoted to the breed and to criticise it in front of her is tantamount to a declaration of war. She has bred and owned two English Champions, Parkside Regale and Parkside Vanity Fair, and bred one US Champion, Parkside Whitehall at Nethertonion, who has recently returned to Great Britain to join her kennel.

The earlier part of her life, although she always maintained an interest in Fox Terriers, was taken up with her careers, firstly with the Forestry Commission, then as Personal Assistant to a senior manager at British Airways, and finally with the Probation Service. Latterly, since her retirement, she has pursued her passion for breeding and showing good Wire Fox Terriers, also giving music lessons and, of course, tackling this mammoth undertaking. I am sure this book will do much to help readers in their understanding of the breed, and we wish her well.

Maurice Marshall
Whittingford Wire Fox Terriers
November 1995

Photo: Anne Roslin-Williams

fox
TERRIER

CHAPTER 1

History
& **Development**
of the Fox terrier

The early days

Man has always been a hunter and used dogs to help him in this activity. They have been used to hunt deer, game and vermin including foxes, badgers, rats and rabbits. As the smaller dogs were found to be good at going to ground and to have the courage needed for fox hunting they were selectively bred to improve their hunting skills. The Latin word for earth is *terra* from which the name Terrier is derived.

When Julius Caesar invaded Britain in 54 BC the soldiers reported seeing 'strange appearing dogs which followed their quarry into the ground'. This may be the first written reference to terriers.

Marco Polo mentions that in the thirteenth century the Grand Khan had 5,000 hounds of different types. He goes on to say our Roman conquerors had little shooting dogs that were too small to fight in the arena.

In 1409 *The Mayster of Game* was published. This is the oldest book in English devoted exclusively to sport, and was written by Edward, Duke of York, grandson of Edward III. In it he translates from a work by Gaston de Foix (1387) and gives a list of breeds including 'terriers, teazers and kenettes'. It gives advice on treating sick dogs and deals with the character of hounds, the working qualities of many dogs, and kennel management. Another early reference to terriers is in 1486 when Dame Juliana Berners, the Prioress of Sopwell Nunnery, published her *Book of St Albans* in which she mentions her 'terroures' as being 'so bold with a heart that harbours no care'.

In 1557 Dr John Caius, a Cambridge University professor, founder of Caius College, Cambridge and physician to Edward IV, Mary and Elizabeth I, published his *Englishe Dogges* in Latin, and it was translated into English by Abraham Fleming and printed by Rychard Johnes in 1576. Fleming divides the breeds into categories, and terriers are listed under 'hounds', which include 'harriers, bloodhounds, gasehounds, greyhounds, lyemmers, tumblers and stealers'. A description was given of a 'Terrarius' hunting foxes and badgers. It was reprinted by L V Gill in London in 1880. A small extract reads:

Another sorte of hunting dog there is which hunteth the Foxe and Badger or Greye onely, whom we call Terrars, because they (after the manner and custom of ferrets in searching after Conneyes) creepe into the grounde and by that means make afrayde, nyppe and byte the Foxe and the Badger in such sort, that eyther they teare them to pieces with theyr teeth being in the bosome of the earth or else hayle and pull them perforce out of theyr lurking angles, darke dongeons and close caves, or at least through conceved feare drive them out of their hollow harbours, in so much that they are compelled to prepare speedie flyte, and being desirous of the next (albeit not the safest) refuge, are otherwise taken and intrapped with snares and nettes layde over holes to the same purpose.

Jacques de Fouilloux published a *Book of Hunting* in France in 1560. This was translated in 1576 by Turberville and the following description is an extract from it:

A Lorde or Gentleman whiche will follow the pastime should have half a dozen mattes to lie upon the grounde on, as theye hearken to the terriers; some use to carrie a windhead which is made of leather strongly sowed on all the foure sides, and having a Pype at one of the corners to blow it as you woulde blowe a Bagg-pype, and when it is blown full of wind, to stoppe it up and lie upon it on the ground; but this were too greate a curiositie and yet a Lorde or Gentleman cannot take the greate heede of the colde and moysture of the earthe for there be many therebye take sundrie diseases and infirmities.

In 1591 Sir Homas Cockaine's *A Short Treatise on Hunting - Compiled for the Delight of Noblemen and Gentlemen* offered advice about training terriers and, in his *Sir Tristram's Measure of Blowing*, tells how the terrierman should be summoned:

Where the Foxe is earthed, blowe for the Terriers after this manner. One long and two short, the second winde one long, and two short. Note this, for it is the chieftest and princinalest poynt to be noted. Every long conteineth in blowing seuven quuvers, one minome and one quatter.

In 1600 Gervase Markham also wrote a piece about terriers, and *The Gentleman's Recreation* published in 1667 by Nicholas Cox told of two varieties of small dog who went to ground after game, one with rather crooked legs and a short coat, the other with straighter legs and a long coat. These dogs bore no resemblance to the modern terrier. In the *Complete Sportsman* of 1718 Jacobs gave a similar description of two sorts of terrier. In about 1760 Daniel also described the work and colour of rough- and smooth-coated terriers in his *Field Sports*. About this time many French writers mentioned the work of terriers in general. In 1781 Peter Beckford published *Thoughts on Hunting* in which he described his black and black-and-white terriers running with the hounds.

Mr John H Walsh, editor of *The Field*, frequently wrote about dogs and hunting under the pseudonym 'Stonehenge'. His book *The Dog in Health and Disease* was published in 1859, 1872, 1879 and 1887, and each edition paid considerable attention to the use and breeding of terriers. He was also a judge at the first organised dog show, held at the Town Hall in Newcastle on 28-29 June 1859. In his *The Dogs of the British Islands*, written in about 1890, he includes a letter dated 16 August 1617 from James I. It starts:

To our right truest friend the Laird of Caldwell [asking him] to search out and to send us two couples of excellent terriers or earth-dogs, which are both stout fox-killers and will stay long in the grounds.

He goes on to say that he had some of these dogs which he lost but he has heard that the Earl of Monteith has some good dogs and he is sure he will let him have some. It is thought that these dogs were of varying colours, weighing 9-13.5kg (20-30lb).

Thomas Bewick has a good picture of a typical terrier in his *History of Quadrupeds*, dated 1790.

Ch Dusky Siren, b January 1903. Bred by F Redmond.
From a painting by Maud Earl. Photo: Lynn Bell.

The *Sporting Dictionary* of 1803 states:

Terriers of even the best blood are now bred all colours - red, black, with tan faces, flanks, feet and legs; brindled, sandy, some few brown pied, white pied and pure white; as well as one sort of each colour rough and wire haired, the other soft and smooth.

This description covers nearly every variety of terrier and from then on the separate terrier breeds evolved: the Irish, Airedale, Welsh, Lakeland, possibly a brindle Bull Terrier, and the others. It seems clear that Smooth and Wire Fox Terrier could be recognised by then. *The Sporting Dictionary* goes on to state that these dogs were so popular they were seen in the stables of most country gentlemen, who paid four or five guineas for a good one.

HISTORY AND DEVELOPMENT
OF THE FOX TERRIER

In 1840 Blaine published his *Encyclopedia of Rural Sports*, stating that:

... there are two prominent varieties of terrier, rough and smooth, the former appear to have been more common in Scotland and the north, the rigours of a more severe climate being favourable to a crisped and curled coat.

In 1881 Mr Vero Shaw wrote 26 pages about the breed in the *Illustrated Book of the Dog*, and he included a *Scale of Merits* written by Mr Francis Redmond. The old *Kennel Encyclopedia* also gives some information on the breed.

In his book *The Fox Terrier*, published in 1889 (the fourth and last edition coming out in 1902) and illustrated by Mr Arthur Wardle, Mr Rawden Lee (Kennel Editor of *The Field*) gave a detailed account of the evolution of the breed and the top winners of the day. While writing this book he had in front of him a copy of an old engraving of 'King James, hawking' with four terriers at his feet, one of which was almost white in colour.

The first edition of *British Dogs* by Hugh Dalziel came out in 1881 and included an article on Fox Terriers by Mr T H Scott (*nom de plume:* 'Peeping Tom') In 1892 Mr Dalziel wrote *The Fox Terrier*, which ran to six editions.

In his *Modern Terriers* (1894) Mr Rawdon Lee supported his view that the original Fox Terrier was black and tan by referring to a painting by de Wilde, dated 1806 and called *The Fox Terrier*, which he describes in detail:

Ch Donna Fortuna, bred and owned by Mr Francis Redmond. One of the 'Totteridge Eleven' in Wardle's picture of that name. From a contemporary painting. Photo: Lynn Bell.

The dog is distinctly black and tan, perhaps somewhat ragged in coat, which although inclined to be wavy is in reality as smooth as are the coats of many of the ordinary fox terriers of the present day. He has drop-ears, a docked or shortened tail, capital legs and feet and nice bone: about eighteen pounds in weight, lacking character somewhat but bearing in all but colour a resemblance to the fox terrier of the present day.

Left: Edward VII photographed with Caesar.
Above: Caesar being led in Edward VII's funeral procession.
(Contemporary postcards from the collection of
Mr and Mrs Philip Wright of the Yockley affix.)

He also tells us that the Duke of Beaufort had these dogs at his Badminton home.

In the January 1899 *The Stable* went into circulation. To increase its appeal they started to include articles about dogs. The first such article was about the Fox Terrier and starts 'No one will dispute the right of the Fox Terrier to figure first in the ranks of popular breeds'.

Mr Sydney Castle's *Monograph on the Fox Terrier* first appeared in 1910 and it was published again in 1916 having been re-written by Messrs Theo Marples and Sydney Castle. In 1908 Tinne wrote about the breed in Vol II of *The Kennel Encyclopaedia*. Cassell's *New Book of the Dog* (Vol III: 1912) gives details of the later stages of the Fox Terrier origins in eight pages written by Desmond O'Connell.

Viper: copied
from a 1796
painting by
Sartorius

In 1925 The Rev A J Skinner wrote *The Popular Fox Terrier*, which was updated by The Rev Dr Rosslyn Bruce in 1950. Other writers include Mr Pardoe, Mr Stanley Dangerfield, Linda Beak, Elsie Williams and Lindley Wood. There are also 22 volumes of *The Fox Terrier Chronicle* from 1883-1905.

The Royal family have had an interest in the breed over the years. There is a picture of Caesar, a Wire, who was led in the funeral procession of Edward VII, his royal master. Queen Victoria had a Smooth, and Edward VII sent two of his bitches to be mated to Mr Curl's dog Oxon. In 1910 Sandringham Peg visited Dr Rosslyn Bruce's Ruby Galliard and in 1924 Sandringham Lucy visited Ch Kinver.

Early paintings

The first picture of a Fox Terrier as we know it today was painted by Hamilton, a Dutch artist, in around 1700 and was seen in Vienna by Sir J A Doyle in 1880. The painting is of fruit and flowers with a dog in the foreground which, to Sir J A Doyle, looked like the Wire Fox Terrier of his day both in colour and shape.

HISTORY AND DEVELOPMENT OF THE FOX TERRIER

Three Fox Terriers at a Fox Hole, by Arthur Wardle. Reproduced by kind permission of W & FC Bonham & Sons, Ltd.

Sartorius painted a picture of Viper in 1796. Viper was a large and rather ugly white dog with black patches, a thick white neck and long back. The painting was discovered in 1896 by Captain Keene. Another picture by Sartorius depicts two terriers, one all white and the other with two black patches and tan around the right eye. Much later on, in 1929, Mr L W Lucas painted a picture of the famous Int Ch Barrington Bridegroom.

Arthur Wardle painted numerous animal pictures and was particularly good at capturing the Fox Terrier on canvas. He painted the well-known picture *The Totteridge Eleven*, showing Mr Redmond's 11 Smooth Fox Terriers, all fine examples of the breed. This painting was given to Mr Crosthwaite and is now owned by The Kennel Club. Mr Wardle also painted *An Ideal Fox Terrier (Smooth-coated)*, which is reproduced on the front of the *Smooth Fox Terrier Association Year Book*. His painting *Three Fox Terriers at a Fox Hole* was sold at the Bonhams specialist 'Dogs and Cats in Art' sale in January 1995. On the front of the Fox Terrier Club's *Jubilee Year Book* of 1926 is Lionel Edwards' *The Terrier Man*, showing a brace of Smooths straining at the lead. The Smooth Fox Terrier Association over the years has reproduced pictures of most of the old important dogs.

Crossing breeds

Hunting earlier in history was mostly for deer and hare. Later, when fox hunting became a favourite sport, the need for a dog that would go to ground was identified. Smaller hunting dogs with rough coats were selected for the work. Many of these first terriers used for fox hunting in the late seventeenth and early eighteenth century were black-and-tan or even fawn in colour and slightly larger than they are today. They needed to be small enough to go to earth but to have long enough legs and sufficient stamina to follow the hounds. Sometimes they looked so similar to the fox that they were killed by the Foxhounds by mistake as they came out of the earth. Suitable terriers were crossed with Foxhounds and Beagles to induce the qualities required. It is believed that, to introduce more white colouring into the terriers, they were crossed with the Old English White Terrier and the Bulldog. These crosses produced the smooth-coated dogs, the rough coats belonging to the original terriers with which they were crossed. Some undesirable traits followed and these were gradually bred out.

Trials and errors in breeding

Various crosses were tried to improve the terrier. These resulted in some benefits and some problems. It is thought that the cross with Foxhounds or Beagles produced the smooth-coated dogs with longer legs, the cross with the Bulldog increased the courage and produced wide fronts, and the cross with the Bull Terrier produced the white coat. Wire and Smooth coats were crossed to reduce size and to get a coarser rough coat.

Ch Cackler of Notts, b August 1898, bred and owned by Her Grace the Duchess of Newcastle. From a picture by Arthur Wardle. Photo: Lynn Bell.

Between 1872 and 1880 not many Wires were being shown. The best dogs came from the Hunt Kennels, especially from the Master of the Sinnington Hounds in Yorkshire. Mr Kendall bred Old Tip who is the first known Wire. His pedigree is not known and he was used solely for work. He is the founder of the breed and sired three champions, Pincher being one. A mating with his daughter produced Old Jester, who was shown at dog shows when he was five years old. He produced many winning dogs, the greatest being Young Jester. Malton in Yorkshire also produced good dogs.

The best dog at this time was Venture by Old Tip from the Sinnington hounds. He was sold to Mr Holmes of Beverley for 70 shillings, a very low price for a dog described by Mr Rawdon Lee as being 'of good coat, built on proper lines and without the slightest particle of bulldog appearance'. In 1872 his half-brother Tip was born, weighing about 9kg (20lb): a very powerful dog, with a short head, small ears and a dare-devil expression. From Tip all the Cackler of Notts dogs were descended. The pedigree ran as follows: Tip in 1872, Pincher, Old Jester, Young Jester 1884, Knavesmire Jest 1885, Meersbrook Bristles 1892, Meersbrook Ben 1894, Ch Barkby Ben 1897, Ch Cackler of Notts 1898.

HISTORY AND DEVELOPMENT
OF THE FOX TERRIER

Mr Wooton of Nottingham owned the notable Smooth, Jock, a nearly-all-white dog weighing about 8kg (18lb) and born in 1859. Mr Rawdon Lee describes him as rather long in the leg, with well sprung ribs, heavy shoulders and neat ears on a long, lean head. For two seasons he proved his worth with the Grove hounds and then he went on to win consistently in the show ring from the first classes at Birmingham in 1862 until he was 11 years old, and he died two years later. Mr Murchison was his eventual owner, but he changed hands several times, once for as much as £100.

Tartar (not Jock) produced the most notable Smooths: Tartar in 1862, Grove Willie, Grip, Old Foiler, Hognaston Willie, Hognaston Dick, Dickon, and Ch Splinter in 1880. By this time the breed was improving, with longer heads and better ears and style.

Old Trap was descended from the black-and-tan English terriers and was strongly marked himself. His pedigree is in the 1880/81 Stud Book.

In 1877 Mr H Gibson held a sale of 40 Smooth Fox Terriers at Brockenhurst. They ranged in age from eight months to a year and fetched from £3 to £75. Most were daughters of Foiler, a founder of the SO Line, and sired by Boxer or Bitters (Boxer's sire). Mr Gibson always made a short statement about each dog, and made it clear no dog was sent on approval. He advertised his stud dogs for two guineas; one had won a second prize and another only a fourth prize. However, these were the top dogs in their day.

Next down the line came an attractive hound-marked dog Meesbrook Bristles who, having sired a number of winners, was bought by Mr Keyes from the USA for £500. While the show dogs were developing the farmers had their own agenda for a good working Fox Terrier. Here both the Smooth and the Wire were rather shorter in the leg, but very game dogs. They did not have to run as fast as they were carried by the mounted terrier man.

Parson John Russell (1795-1883) from Devon bred hardy working Fox Terriers with dense wire coats from about 1812 to 1873. These were longer in the leg than those described above. In May 1819 he purchased a dog called Trump whom he saw on a passing milk cart, and from this beginning he established his own strain of terrier. The Queen has a water-colour painting of Trump at Sandringham, and this was reproduced in *The Kennel Gazette* in May 1959. The painting is by Mary Palmer and is dated 18 January 1820, eight months after Jack Russell had bought the dog. The Prince of Wales owned the painting by 1876-1878. Trump was smart in appearance, being entirely white in colour except for a patch of dark tan over each eye and ear and a small dot of tan at the root of her tail. Her jacket was thick, wiry and weather-resistant. She appeared to have cropped ears and a slightly low set docked tail (according to current fashion) and her stifles appeared over-angulated. Mr F Jackson quotes Mr Davies' accurate description that her legs and feet were perfect and 'the loins and conformation of the whole frame indicative of hardihood and endurance'. She was said to be the size of a grown vixen fox, which suggests that she was about 35cm (14in) tall and weighed about 6.3kg (14lb).

The Parson Jack Russell breed was not recognised in the show ring until 1991, when they were offered four classes at Crufts. Mr Russell became a member of The Kennel Club on 13 March 1874 and he judged Fox Terriers at The Kennel Club Show the following year. If you go to a country terrier show today the show dog will not stand a chance against the farmer's working dog (as seen by the judges from the farming community) as I learned to my surprise. That is not to say the show dog cannot do the job; in France and elsewhere in Europe it is part of their qualification. England was noted as specialising in the breeding of farm animals, the noblemen and gentlemen seeking perfection in all farm stock. To this end a *General Stud Book* was started to improve horse breeding and the Masters of Foxhounds copied the system for the breeding of dogs. The *Kennel Club Stud Book* was started in 1859 and from 1860 the winning Smooths are all recorded in it.

Before 1882 the breeds were known as Fox Terriers and Wire-haired Terriers. Indeed, until 1878 Fox Terriers were regarded as 'sporting' and Wire-haired as 'non-sporting' breeds. The term 'Smooth' was first noted by The Kennel Club in the 1883 Stud Book.

Three early dogs. From the left: Old Jock, Grove Nettle and Old Tartar.

In 1879, 16 Fox Terriers were registered and only one Wire-hair Terrier. The following year there was a massive increase to 116 Fox Terriers and 21 Wire-hair. Included in this list is Mr W Carrick's Viper (Venture ex Nettle), and Mr J H Murchison's Jock, Trimmer and Vandal. It was noted 'the late Duke of Beaufort has kept up a breed of black and tan fox terriers and excellent dogs they were'.

Treadwell, a Berkshire huntsman, had several good dogs, notably Tip, who was descended from Charley, a black and tan dog of the Cottesmore Hunt whom he had owned 25 years earlier. Charley was bred by Mr Canverley of Greetham, near Oakham, whose family had already been breeding terriers for 100 years. Mr Treadwell's dogs were tough and weighed 4.5-7.2kg (10-16lb). Belgrave Joe, Brockenhurst Joe and Mr Burnam's Trimmer all sired champions.

In 1905 Bruce Lowe wrote *Breeding Race Horses*. The Rev Dr Rosslyn Bruce applied the system to Smooth Fox Terriers. It was then adopted by Mr Asa Lees, who has all records dating back to 1860. It was found that nearly all winning dogs were descended from Belgrave Joe and Ch Splinter, a few being descendants of the Wire-haired Old Tip. Any dog going back to him is known as a T wire.

Belgrave Joe (1868 to 15 January 1888) had a tan head and white body. His descendants are known as the J line. His skeleton was preserved at The Kennel Club. Two of his descendants, Ch Result and Ch Dominie, were so important that they too needed a letter and became Jr for Result and Jd for Dominie. The only known descendants of these dogs today are in America and Australia. The last known winning descendants in this country were Ch Avon Snowflake (1925), Ch Solus Smasher (1949) and Ch Dinah of Notts (1948).

The S line came from the Grove Kennels, specifically from Grove Tartar, an all-white dog weighing 7.7kg (17lb). Through him came Foiler (1871), who carried on this line to Ch Splinter (1883), who unfortunately died of rabies in October 1885. Foiler's pedigree is oustanding because he had Grove Willie and Grove Vixen as grandparents on both sides and his only great-grandparents were Grove Tartar and Grove Nettle. There is a picture of his head in *The Smooth Terrier Association Year Book* of 1938.

HISTORY AND DEVELOPMENT
OF THE FOX TERRIER

Tracing pedigrees can be difficult because people often used the same name for successive generations. To make things more confusing, if the dog changed hands its name often changed also. Thus in the records changed names are sometimes recorded, but 'pedigree unknown' is occasionally shown against the new name. As the problem of finding unique names increased, The Kennel Club suggested using an affix which could identify a common name with many different breeders.

The breed clubs

The Fox Terrier was an established breed by the beginning of the nineteenth century. By the 1870s the Smooth and Wire were recognised as being different species of the same breed, the Smooth being the more desirable dog.

In 1876 Major Harding Cox was having a dinner party and suggested forming a club to improve and maintain the breed. The Fox Terrier Club, one of the first breed clubs, was duly formed in the same year. The Kennel Club itself had come into being in 1873, and the Bulldog, Dandie Dinmont and Bedlington Clubs in 1875. Her Grace Kathleen, Duchess of Newcastle became the first President, and there were 21 other members. The post of Hon Secretary was initially taken by Major Harding Cox; Mr S Dixon, Mr Russell Earp and Mr Reid followed in succession, then Mr Tinne took over from 1881 to 1909 (28 years), handing on to Mr F W Bright on becoming President. Mr Bright stayed until 1920, (11 years) and his successor, Mr Neville Dawson, stayed until 1945 (25 years), when Mr Ludford took over. The members of the Committee changed

Ch Oakleigh Topper, b March 1880. Bred by Mr Lindsay Hogg, owned by Mr Harding Cox and Mr W Wright. From a painting by George Card. Photo: Lynn Bell.

more frequently but some have remained for 20 years or more. One member, Captain Crosthwaite, did a great deal of work in making up a Fox Terrier Club volume, filling in Stud Book information from 1921 to 1932. There is now a membership of 180 with a further 67 overseas members.

The first Fox Terrier Club Show was held in May 1877 at Lillie Bridge. Mr Bassett judged both coats together and he had an entry of 220 dogs. In 1880 the first Committee of the Fox Terrier Club introduced various Stakes classes, including the Derby Stakes for puppies in both coats. The Wire puppy, Dahley Topper, won. In 1882 a separate stake for Wires was created. Fourteen years later the classification was widened to provide a subdivision of the Stakes into Derby and Oaks stakes for Smooths. The Oaks for Wires was not introduced for another year. These Stakes are still being run today for members to show their young hopefuls.

By the 1930s, registrations of Smooth Fox Terriers were going steadily down while the Wires were going up. It was decided that the way forward was to form the Smooth Fox Terrier Association in 1932, on the strength of a Smooth Fox Terrier Register, then in its third year, which listed 268 breeders. The first President was Mr W S Glynn. He was succeeded in 1933 by Dr Rosslyn Bruce. According to Dr Bruce, it was Mr C H Bishop who really got the club going, and this was endorsed by all the past Presidents right up to 1947. Mr Bishop resigned early because of a prestigious editorial appointment, but he did become President in 1944. The President is elected annually, but the Secretaries have stayed much longer. The first Secretary was The Rev Dr Rosslyn Bruce who stayed in office from 1932-1953. Next came Mr John Lowe (1953-1965). Miss Brenda Gough took on the post from 1965-1973; then Mr C N Ripingale (1973-1984); then Mrs Freda Blondon (1984-1995); and Mrs Rose Turner is the current Secretary.

The earliest shows run by the Club were Open shows. The first was in Oxford in 1933 and the judge, Captain Holdsworth, had an entry of 216. The next show was in 1934 at Scarborough and Mr H L Curl had an entry of 130. The following year the show was held at Leamington Spa where Captain Hicks drew an entry of 152 dogs. The first Championship show was in 1936 in London and was judged by The Rev Dr Rosslyn Bruce with an entry of 296 dogs.

The Wire Fox Terrier Association was established in 1913 to further and protect the interests of Wire Fox Terriers. The first President was Mr A E Way; he was succeeded by Her Grace The Duchess of Newcastle in 1916 until 1920, when Mr W S Glynn took over. From then on the President was elected annually. The Association has a President, Vice-President, Hon Treasurer and Secretary and 21 committee members. The membership in Great Britain is around 247, with an additional 135 members from overseas.

Establishing the breed

The first registered dogs were Mr Padwick's five Brooms in 1885. In February 1890 Captain Crosthwaite registered first his Wire Musk and later his Smooth Old Button. In June 1893 The Duchess of Newcastle registered five Smooth dogs.

The bitch Nettle from the Grove Hunt was used to form the standard drawn up in 1876 by the Breed Club. The main difference in type since then is that they are now slightly smaller, more refined and weigh less, the optimum weight being 8.25kg (18lb) instead of the original 9kg (20lb).

Then, as now, the best stud dogs went to the United States of America. In 1889 Go Bang was sold to an American for £500. His brother, Meersbrooke Ben, sired Barkby Ben, who turned out to be a great show dog and a prolific sire. His principal son was the famous Cackler of Notts who sired over 100 winners and eight Champions. 'Of Notts' was the suffix used by Kathleen, Duchess of Newcastle. She bred both varieties, Wire and Smooth, and had some excellent stud dogs. Cackler was said to be large, and Comedian weighed 10.4kg (23lb). Although he was big, a picture of him shows that he was a beautiful dog with good balance and great neck, shoulder, feet and front. His mother was Cobweb of Notts. The Duchess bred from half-brother to half-sister and from father to daughter in her efforts to improve the conformation.

These matings have produced nearly all the ancestry of the present day Fox Terriers and her breeding success would be hard to beat. From Cackler the line continued through Ch Dusky Cackler (from a mating of Cackler to his daughter, who was bred from a Smooth called Don't Go), Morden Blusterer and Catch'em of Notts to the famous Comedian of Notts. Comedian sired Oldcliffe Captain who in turn sired Ch Fountain Crusader, whose son was the beautiful Ch Talavera Simon. The Comedian line also produced Ch Beau Brummel of Wildoaks. Other Of Notts top sires included Collar, Corker, Cracker and Chunky. Ch Chunky and Ch Cocoatina of Notts were mated, and a notable descendant was Ch Crackley Supreme of Wildoaks, who sired the famous Int Ch Gallant Fox of Wildoaks. (See **Dominant Sires and Dams** for further ancestry.)

Around 1929 the very successful International Champion and stud dog Ch Barrington Bridegroom was being exhibited. This famous dog produced

Ch Oxonian, bred by Mr D O'Connell, owned by Mr Reeks. Shown 1904-1905. From a contemporary painting. Photo: Lynn Bell.

Ch Crackley Sensation who was also greatly used for stud. This line continued through Crackley Supreme of Wildoaks (grandson) into Gallant Fox of Wildoaks and followed into such names as Talavera, Epping, Weltona, Cornwell, Watteau and Penda. Ch Crackley Straightaway was the first post-war champion of any breed.

The breed became popular when it was seen that Edward VII owned Caesar of Notts, and that this dog was his constant friend and companion. Caesar was sired by Ch Cackler of Notts and his dam was Caddie of Notts who bred nine Champions.

The Kennel Club beginnings

In 1873 The Kennel Club was founded at the North of England's second Exhibition of dogs at Islington Agricultural Hall, which also became the venue for Cruft's show until it was destroyed during the Second World War. Mr Russell was an early member of The Kennel Club and judged Fox Terriers at their show in 1874.

Dog shows - classes for Fox Terriers

The first formally organised dog show was held on 28-29 June 1859 at Newcastle-on-Tyne. There were three judges to each class and one class per breed. Shows were held at Birmingham, Leeds and Manchester in the following year.

There were no show classes for Fox Terriers at first. The South of England Exhibition of Sporting and Other Dogs held at the Islington Agricultural Hall in June 1862 had the first classes scheduled for Fox Terriers. There were 20 entries, the winner being Trimmer, who did not even have a pedigree. His owner was Mr Harvey Bayley, Master of the Rufford Hounds.

Later that year there were classes at the Birmingham Show, where Mr Wootton won a class of 24 entries with Jock and Mr Bayley came second with Trap, born in 1859 and weighing 18lb. This show was held at the Old Wharf, Broad Street, Birmingham and the class was for 'white and other smooth-haired English terriers except black and tan'. Trap was shown six times and was sold as a stud dog for £25 to Mr Murchison. Jock was a consistent winner for nine years, by which time he was 11 years old and Mr Murchison's Trimmer took the honours. Tartar was another great dog at that time.

In 1873 there were classes for Wires at Crystal Palace with two prizes offered for dogs and bitches. Mr Harding Cox and Mr Wright Nooth were not at all happy with the judging, and they wrote a long letter to The Kennel Gazette:

Messrs Lort and Walker were the judges, and in placing Young Tip over Venture they made a grave mistake. The latter, after being beaten by Nettle - one of the best bitches ever seen on the bench - in 1874 was placed first in the ensuing year, when for the first time the wire-haired terriers came to be looked upon as fox terriers proper, they have hitherto been relegated to the degrading position of non-sporting dogs....

After 1875, Venture was almost unbeatable, his main rivals being Mr Easten's Tip, and Thorn (later called Spike). In 1879 The Kennel Club rules for dog shows were drawn up, and they were revised in 1880. Benching exhibits became the practice at this time. The shows in 1879 were at Alexandra Palace (which was also home to a special Bulldog show), Birmingham, Brighton, Burton-on-Trent, Blagdon-on-Tyne, Belfast and Bristol.

Some shows in the early days lasted up to a week. Exhibitors were not allowed to handle their dogs in the ring, and owners and public were excluded from the building during judging. At The Kennel Club Summer Dog Show at Crystal Palace in 1881 there was a Fox Terrier Derby for Smooth or Wire-hairs born in 1880. The prizes were as follows: First - £50, Second - £20, Third - £15, Fourth - £10. The entry fee was £1, with an extra charge of £2 for the main show.

It was not until 1883 at a show in Oxford that two judges were appointed, one for the Smooth coat and the other for the Wire. This was the first time they were totally separated in their classes.

At the first major show for Terriers in 1886 at the Royal Aquarium in Westminster (the Manager being Mr Charles Cruft) there were 125 Smooths and 50 Wires. However only two years later there was an equal number of Wires in the show ring. Mr E C Ash in his book *This Doggie Business* puts the reason down to exhibitors learning the art of show trimming which makes the Wire a very attractive animal. He tells us that such was the popularity of the Wire that Mr Wootton, acting for

HISTORY AND DEVELOPMENT OF THE FOX TERRIER

Lord Lonsdale, bought a Wire called Briggs from the Fourth Terrier Show for £200. Other dogs were purchased for £105, £100, the cheapest going for £42. On a subsequent occasion Mr George Raper sold Ch Go Bang (one of the top dogs at the 1898 Birmingham Show) to an American for £500 and bought Coastguard of Notts for £150 from the Duchess of Newcastle. These figures are amazing when one takes into account the relative value of money in those days. The Smooth breeders who had previously had more success were astonished at these prices for the Wires. Today show dogs in the ring and Champions might fetch anything from £1,000 to a reputed £28,000, depending very much upon how much the purchaser wants a particular dog. Historically such high prices are regarded with some disbelief.

The Sheffield show in 1888 had 52 classes for Smooth and Wire Fox Terriers, with an entry of 434 dogs. In August of that year the York Fox Terrier Club Show offered Novice classes with an entry fee of 10s and prizes of £4, £2, £1 and 10s. The entrance fee to other classes was 7s 6d, with prizes of £3, 30s and 15s.

Dr Rosslyn Bruce tells us that a list of the first 11 Smooth Breeders was published. These included Mr Clarke, Mr Vicary, Mr Tinne, Mr Redmond, Dr Master, Mr Reeks, Sir James Hosker,

Ch The Sylph, b 1903, owned by Mr Tinne. From a painting by J N O Emms. Photo: Lynn Bell.

Mr Losco Bradley, Captain H T Crosthwaite, Mr Calvert Butler and The Duchess of Newcastle, whose last dog to become a Champion was Correct Wartax of Notts in 1951. Top breeders of Smooth and Wire-hairs since then are listed at the back of the book. These and many other people have played their part in making the breed what it is. The most amazing lady in the breed today is Mrs Constance Wilcox who, with her Lanscove dogs, is still enjoying showing at the age of 93.

The Fox Terrier show record world-wide

In Britain today Fox Terriers are not often selected in the Terrier Group ring; when they are it is usually the Wires. They do better in the United States, but here again the Wires tend to be the more favoured of the two. In Australia they seem to share equal honours, but the Smooths, notably the second and third generations of imported stock, do especially well at All Breed Shows.

Evidence of the interest in Fox Terriers can be seen by the fact that about 50 people from America are members of British Fox Terrier Clubs, 20 in France, 15 in Japan, and nine in Australia.

The rise and decline in numbers

The breed gained enormous popularity and in 1924 the Kennel Club registered 7,156 Wires and 2,573 Smooths. The Fox Terrier is so attractive that in the 1940s the breed was widely used in advertisements. Fox Terriers also became the models for cuddly toys, pyjama cases and toys to sit upon or push.

In 1947 there was a record of 8,227 Wire registrations and 2,338 Smooths. However, numbers gradually decreased as other breeds gained in popularity. By the 1950s the numbers registered were around 1,500 Wires and 750 Smooths. The breed has never regained the original high numbers, but has benefited in quality. Breeds with high numbers of registrations often have associated problems that need veterinary attention.

The drop in numbers of Fox Terrier registrations since 1947 started when the economy of the country began to recover from the Second World War. Food became cheaper and more readily available as rationing was lifted, so more people could afford to keep the larger breeds. At this stage, large breeds had a novelty value, and their profile was further raised by their use in the Armed Forces, in the Police Force, and as guide dogs. Fox Terriers were used in London to lay cables, but that work was neither long-lasting nor so glamourous.

Another factor which increased this trend was the introduction of television into our homes. The 'His Master's Voice' picture on the old records must have been a strong influence in making the Fox Terrier so popular in the early days, but now the rise in popularity of the breeds of dogs used in films and advertising was very noticeable.

When Newmaidley Ursinia won the Southern Television Challenge Trophy in the first 'Dog Beats Dog' inter-town competition she went to the television studios three times. This was followed by Vetzyme advertisements and much newspaper coverage. Miss Howles also had a great actor in the dog appearing as 'Psyche' in the television series *A Life of Bliss*, starring George Cole. I hope there will be some more great acting dogs soon.

Since 1975 the dog scene has changed considerably, especially in the show ring. In the late 1970s, large kennels owned by very knowledgeable breeders dominated the scene. At this time professional handlers only handled for one kennel. This is not the case today; not only may they handle for three or four different breeders, but they handle different breeds also. Competition was keen in the 1970s but there was not any unpleasant rivalry. Dog showing was a pleasant pastime and an enjoyable day out.

In the 1980s many leading kennels disappeared; some owners died, some retired, and some could no longer afford the huge expense of vets bills, registrations, entry fees and travel costs. Because of the expenses involved dog breeding became more of a business than a hobby providing enjoyment and relaxation. With the loss of top breeders there was a fall in the number of knowledgeable judges, some judges having had no previous experience of the breed at all.

HISTORY AND DEVELOPMENT
OF THE FOX TERRIER

Fox Terriers are extremely attractive and most loyal companions. We are always hearing people say 'I have not seen a Fox Terrier for years', or 'My grandfather used to have one of those'. This is where the small breeder of today can enjoy a few good dogs and have the occasional litter to satisfy public demand.

Despite the past losses of great breeders, there are still plenty of dedicated people who are intent on ensuring the standard of the breed is maintained and, although England is reputed to have exported all her dogs, she still has plenty of top quality dogs and the background to keep the standard going.

Keeping the Breed Standard

The Fox Terrier originated in England and has remained much the same over the years. This is because the Breed Standard set in 1876 and later modifications have been agreed by The Kennel Club and accepted by kennel clubs world-wide for breeders to follow.

There are no serious problems with the breed and they are not required to have an eye, hip or personality test before being sold as pets. Indeed they are marvellous companions and excellent with children and will behave impeccably when treated as part of the family.

Breeding the perfect show dog is an on-going pursuit because there are always certain features in different lines that want improving. The breeder looks at his stock and assesses its virtues, noting where certain features can be improved. This may be movement, head, placement of ears, tail set, or anything else laid down in the Breed Standard. With a firm objective in mind he selects a suitable stud dog, having closely examined the good and bad points of its immediate relations.

The modern Fox Terrier is really beautiful compared to the original one and is greatly admired all over the world. People from many nations come to see Fox Terriers at the big shows in this country, especially at the Fox Terrier Association Shows and Crufts. These people travel vast distances to see Fox Terriers in the ring with the idea of taking one or two home. Offers to purchase are often made there and then.

Fox Terriers are game dogs, ready to chase anything, quick with rats and ready to battle with a fox, badger or rabbit. They hunt as a pack, the first one to find the prey barks and the others rush to join in and surround the victim. They sometimes play with the rat or squirrel as if it were a squeaky toy, but if it bites or escapes they quickly kill it and tear it apart, each dog having a helping. They are used effectively today on the farms, especially to kill rats. Temperament, too, must be taken into account in keeping the Breed Standard.

Wires - dominant sires and dams

As stated in the section on History, before the First World War the 'Of Notts' Wire Fox Terriers owned by Her Grace the Duchess of Newcastle dominated the breeding pattern of the time. Ch Cackler of Notts was the sire and grandsire of numerous champions including Ch Briar Cackler, Ch Commodore of Notts, Ch Captain of Notts, Ch Raby Coastguard and Ch Dusky Cracker. If anyone goes back far enough in any pedigree one of these dogs is sure to be found.

Mr S G Filde was another prominent breeder. His Wyche Wires were handled by Mr Cartledge, a professional handler. Ch Wyche Workman was born in July 1917 and he won six successive Challenge Certificates (CCs) when he was three years old. Ch Wyche Workman sired Ch Wyche Wrangler, Ch Wyche Wondrous and Ch Wyche Witchery, the latter producing Ch Wyche Warm. Ch Wyche Warm, born in April 1923, won four CCs in six weeks.

In 1928 Her Grace the Duchess of Newcastle wrote in *The Wire Fox Terrier Association Year Book* about improving the Terrier's coat, feet and hindquarters. She thought the dogs were of high class quality but wondered if they were moving away from the 'old standard' of 'bone and strength in a small compass' and that 'a terrier should stand like a cleverly made hunter'.

Ch Fountain Crusader was another winning dog in London. He sired several champions including Ch Talavera Simon, born in 1924. Simon was the correct size, heavily hound-marked and had a great personality. Mr Holland Buckley, a very respected judge, describes him as being as

Above: Mr J R Barlow (left) with his son Jack and friends. Facing: Mr Barlow, Mr Simmonds and Mr Hughes.

near faultless as possible. He fathered 11 champion sons and 12 champion daughters, the last, the 'ginger' bitch Ch Darrock May Queen, when he was 11 years old.

Elsie Williams had several of Simon's off-spring as a base for her Penda stock. Simon's son Ch Talavera Romulus sired her Penda Pompilius, a large white dog with tan head. He was born during the war and sired two champion bitches from which came Ch Wybury Penda Quicksilver who also had several champions.

Mr J R Barlow, also known as 'Mr Fox Terrier', handled many of Simon's grandsons through the bitch line, including Ch Crackley Startler, a white dog with a black patch at the rear and an unusual ear which was half tan and half white. Ch Crackley Startler sired four champion sons and four champion daughters before Mr Barlow took him to America and brought back Simon's daughter's offspring.

HISTORY AND DEVELOPMENT
OF THE FOX TERRIER

In 1934 Ch Talavera Simon's daughter, Int Ch Gains Great Surprise, was thought to be the best-ever show bitch. She produced the two great dogs Int Ch Gallant Fox of Wild Oaks (born in 1929 and owned by Mrs Bondy), who sired 15 champions, and Ch Beau Brummel of Wild Oaks (born in 1928), who sired 13 champions. When Mr Barlow took Ch Crackley Startler to America he brought back these two dogs and Ch Bobby Burns of Wildoaks, another of Simon's grandsons. Two other Talavera dominant sires were Ch Talavera Nigel and Ch Talavera Jupiter, who sired 16 champions.

Mr Barlow handled his own and other people's dogs. At one show he handled a small dog of his own and a large one for a client. When asked which was the correct size he replied 'the one you own'. The same can still be said for size today; sometimes the small dog wins, sometimes the large.

I will now write a brief resumé about Linda Beak because she has played such a big role in breeding Smooths and Wires in the last 50 years.

Linda Beak was born in 1907 and started showing in March 1933 when she took Newmaidley Shock into the ring and won fourth prize at Reading. She bred from this bitch and her sister Newmaidley Wonder, using good stud dogs whose progenitor was Ch Barrington Bridegroom. Newmaidley Rex won two Reserve Challenge Certificates (RCCs) in 1938 and the first CC in 1939 under Mrs Barber at Birmingham. She gained four more RCCs before war broke out. There were no

Miss Linda Beak with Ch Newmaidley Verdict, winning BIS. Judge: Mr S Dangerfield.

Ch Newmaidley Dancer.

shows then but Linda Beak line-bred to her own stud dogs, thereby creating the Newmaidley strain, paying particular attention to good temperament and quality.

The first Wire champion was Ch Newmaidley Hob, born in 1948 and gaining his title in 1951. Cleopatra also became a Champion that year, and Dancer followed in 1952. Then came her daughter Treasure in 1957 and Verdict in 1963, and others followed.

Linda Beak showed Wires until her sister Brownie died and she could no longer do all the show preparation, and judged at home and abroad up to her eighty-fourth birthday. She was still breeding litters of Smooths and showing them until 1991 when she was 84 years old. By this time she had a pacemaker and was in very poor health, but such was her enthusiasm that if the driver was not going fast enough she would suggest that 'we will never get there at this rate'. She died on 30 January 1992 and will be remembered for the many lovely dogs she produced, both for show and as pets, including my lovely Mischief about whom I have written elsewhere. Her best dog was probably the Brazilian Ch Newmaidley For'ard, with 50 Best In Show (BIS) wins.

Mr H Hingle of the Easternvale affix had his first champion in World and Int Ch Croyland Chantress of Wildoaks (Ch Gallant Fox of Wildoaks ex Int Ch Crackley Supreme). In 1936 she won the Kennel Club Cup for the Best Exhibit in Show at The Kennel Club's All Breeds Championship Show. She was bought by Mr Bondy from the Wildoaks Kennels in America. After the war he continued breeding his special lines and a dozen or more champions were made up in Australia and five in England.

Ch Crackley Straightaway was the first champion to be made up after the war. In 1946 Colonel Phipps of the Talavera affix judged him at the Wire Fox Terrier Association Show, reporting that he was one of the best dogs he had ever seen. He sired Ch Polo Fireaway and Newmaidley Ceasar, thus influencing that line.

In 1947 Ch Clarington Contender, Ch Holmwire Hyperion, Ch Crackley Sailaway, Ch Travella Strike and the light-coloured dog Ch Weycroft Woolcomber were all made up. Ch Travella Strike (1946) was descended from Ch Gallant Fox and could be traced back to Ch Travella Simon through the bitch line. He became a Champion the day after his first birthday and went on to sire 14 Champions, including Harrowhill Strike Again. There were many other Travella Champions at these kennels in the 1950s when they had enormous success in the ring. Strike had a beautiful head and a lovely neck and shoulders. He put his stamp of quality on many successful exhibits at home and abroad. Mrs J Creasy of the Roundway Kennels was one of the first to benefit from using Strike, and she made up several champions.

Eden Autocrat sired Ch Waterton Maryholm Wendy in 1948 and he also sired Ch Wycollar Duchess, whose head and body, most unusually, were black.

Mr A Churchill of the Weltona affix made up 10 champions between 1946 and 1975. Weltona Exelwyre Dustynight had a great influence on the breed. He sired Ch Madam Moonraker who won several Best In Show (BIS) awards at Championship shows before going to the USA. He also sired Elsie Williams' Ch Penda Peach who was BIS at the Fox Terrier Club Show in 1956.

Mrs Dorothy White bred Ch Wyretex Wyns Tuscan in 1945. He was a good dog, not too large, and he sired Ch Weltona What's This, Ch Wyretex Wyns Wunder, Ch Penda Callern Melody and many others abroad. Ch Penda Callern Melody was interesting in that she had rich tan markings (no black) and was the only 'ginger' bitch to become a champion since Ch Darrach May Queen 20 years earlier.

Hazel Bradford of the Flyntwyre affix has bred many ginger Wires who have had some good wins over the years and up to the present day. Her first ginger came from Mr Wally Prizeman's Arklow kennels and his dogs came from Mrs Josephine Creasey of the Stocksmoor affix.

Ch Wyretex Wyns Wunder was born on 4 May 1955 and was sold by Mrs Williams to Mrs White at five months as a show dog. She tells us that he was a large white dog with a good head, neck and shoulders, a good coat and excellent movement. He sired five English champions and many more overseas. He is also the grandsire of Ch Zeloy Emperor who sired 23 Champions (13 dogs and 10 bitches) which had a lasting influence on the breed.

HISTORY AND DEVELOPMENT
OF THE FOX TERRIER

In 1950 Mr C H Burton bred Ch Burtona Betoken. This dog was sold to Mr J H Pardoe of the Cawthorne affix and sired many champions under that name, including an all-white dog called Ch Cawthorne Climax. This dog in his turn sired several champions, including Ch Penda Cawthorne Cobnut, whom Elsie Williams bought in 1958 after judging him at the Fox Terrier Club Show where he was placed second. He went on to sire some good dogs, including Ch Baros Jewel, Irish Ch Baros Cobbler, Ch Wyrecroft War Bonus and Ch Penda Peerless. The line continued with Peerless siring Ch Penda Daleskirk Caress, who was BIS at Bath and had other major wins, in 1960 and Ch Penda Tavatina in 1961.

In 1956 Ch Crackley Standard, a nice, hound-marked dog, was made up and he sired Ch Crackwyn Cockspur, winner of 22 CCs under the expert handling of Mr Barlow. Ch Crackwyn Cockspur won BIS at Cardiff Championship Show and Birmingham Championship Show and was the Supreme Champion at Crufts in 1962. He was then owned by Mr H L Gill who sold him to M Lejeune of Belgium. He went on to win Best Terrier at the International Championship Show in France, Best of all Breeds at the International Championship Shows in Belgium, Holland, Italy, Germany and Luxembourg, and Best in Show all Breeds at the Swedish Kennel Club Show in Stockholm. Ch Crackwyn Cockspur was an outstanding dog, of correct size and beautifully hound-marked, with a long head, short back, and superb legs and feet. His wire coat went right down to his feet, which was rare in those days.

The dogs bred by Mr Cyril Whitham and his wife Edith with the Townville affix were another great influence. Mr Whitham had previously kept Alsatians and then Bullmastiffs. He used to do some work for Mr Harold Shepherd (Tolhill), a Wire breeder, and in March 1956 he saw and admired a bitch called Tolhill Treacle. Mr Whitham was working late one night when Mr Shepherd came to see how the job was going. Mr Shepherd was very upset because a dog was barking, and said that that dog would have to go; he would advertise it in *Our Dogs* the following day. On asking which dog it was, Mr Whitham found it was Treacle, and offered to take her straight home and save the cost of advertising. From then on he never looked back.

He mated Treacle to top winning dogs of the time, including Ch Caradochouse Spruce, and he kept three bitches from a litter of seven puppies. He bought Tollhill Masterpiece for stud, breeding his stock until he had 22 dogs in all. Then disaster struck. A nine-month-old puppy brought into the kennel for re-homing was found to have distemper. The puppy died at once - and within two weeks all his dogs had died except for Tolhill Masterpiece. Cheview Candida had been sold as a puppy to a Mr Snow, and Mr Whitham went to see him about buying the bitch back. He did so, and of course she was mated to Masterpiece. He bred Townville Trinket, who was a superb brood bitch. From her came the first champion, Ch Seedfield Ernley Empress, born 5 September 1962.

Ch Wintor Statesman was a superb stud dog handled by Mr Ernest Sharpe. Mr Whitham used him to produce his famous Ch Townville Tally 'O in 1967. Ch Wintor Statesman features on numerous pedigrees today. He won his first CC at just 12 months and his third was given to him by Linda Beak amid congratulations all round to owner/handler/breeder. He went on to sire nine champions.

Ch Townville Tally 'O in his turn went on to sire many champions, including Ch Sunnybrook Spot-on, who fathered Ch Brookewire Brandy of Layven. This dog, bred by Mr F Robinson, won 13 CCs from 1972 to 1975 and became the 1974 Crufts BIS winner before going to Italy. Tally 'O also sired Miss Evelyn Howles'

Ch Harrowhill Huntsman, Crufts BIS winner in 1978. Ch Cripsey Townville T'Other'Un was a great dog, BIS at Blackpool when only eight-and-a-half months old and going on to win many more top awards. He was bought by Mr Binelli of Italy, and Albert Langley handled him to Bests all over Europe.

Ch Townville Tobias got BIS at the WFTA Show and went to Mr and Mrs Libner in the USA. There he sired America's 'Dog of the Year' of 1977, English and American Ch Harwire Hetman of Whinlatter, who later became America's all-time top sire.

Ch Townville Tradition became a champion in 1980 and he produced Ch Townville Texan and the beautiful English and American Ch Penda Precision. In 1982 Ch Treasure of Townville (bred by Pauline Fox) was made up and later sold to a kennel in the USA. He was followed by Ch Townville Tassie and then Frank Kellett was asked to handle Ch Townville Taveta.

Ch Harrowhill Huntsman, Crufts BIS 1978. 16 CCs, 15 BOBs, 4 Groups and 3 BISs. Bred, owned and handled by Miss E Howles.
Photo: Anne Roslin-Williams.

Mr and Mrs Whitham have had 25 Champions and their dogs have sired a further 42. Many of their top winning dogs were exported, gaining top awards all over the world. In 1988 Townville Tarique won 11 CCs, seven BOBs and 11 RCCs. In 1989 Townville Tradesman was the top winning Wire Fox Terrier, gaining 10 CCs, seven BOBs, Reserve Terrier Group SKC and BIS at the Fox Terrier Club Show. These two dogs went to Japan to continue their show careers and finally returned to England to become top stud dogs and continue the Townville tradition of fine dogs.

Ch Seedfield Meritor Superflash was another great stud dog, who sired nine British champions and many more abroad.

In 1969 one of his sons, Ch Tavabob (Ch Seedfield Meritor Superflash ex Tavaclaire), went to America and subsequently sired 15 American Champions.

From the Harrowhill kennel, other influential sires apart from Ch Harrowhill Huntsman include Harrowhill Huntersmoon and Harrowhill Concorde.

In 1986 Ch Easternvale Echo (son of Harrowhill Huntsman) was the top winning puppy in breed and won the Pedigree Chum Puppy of the Year Contest. He became a champion the following year. Ch Easternvale Envoy (Blackdale Patrol ex Easternvale Suntan) won the same prizes in 1987 and his litter brother Int Ch Easternvale Ensign gained numerous top awards in 1989 including four BISs, two RBISs and 14 Group wins. Emblem and Exalt (also Blackdale Patrol ex Easternvale Suntan) both became champions. In 1989 Blackdale Prospect became Top Stud.

Fox Terriers from the British Isles have had a considerable influence world-wide. In Argentina English and American (Eng/Am) Ch Townville Tristanian (born in 1967) won eight CCs and multiple US and UK BISs and Specialities. He has sired many English, US, Canadian, Brazilian, Ecuadorian and Argentinian champions and is owned by Ruth and Robert Libner in the United States of America. Am and Int Ch and Argentine Grand Ch Cefbryn Kibella was Best Dog of All Breeds in Argentina in 1981.

Blackdale Stargazer was exported from Ireland to Argentina in 1984. He soon became Argentinian Grand Champion, Uruguayan Champion, South American Champion and Champion of the Americas. He attained five BISs, 13 Best of Groups, two Reserve Best In Shows and five Reserve Best of Groups.

Mr and Mrs Baxter's Killick of the Mess (Ch Sylair Star Leader ex Molmik Cinderella) had a great year in 1987. He won the Pedigree Chum Champion Stakes Final in January, and was RBIS at Crufts in February. In April he won the Canine Supporters Charity 'Contest of Champions', with other prizes to follow. His wins include six BISs, four RBISs, nine Terrier Groups, 21 CCs and 20 BOBs, before he went to America to continue his career. He was handled by Mr L Snow. Ch Blackdale Stardust won nine All Breed Shows, 30 Groups and Specialities and is the sire of several Champions.

Albion Land Junior Huntersmoon (Ch Harrowhill Huntersmoon ex Ch Cefnbryn Megan) has sired Chilean Ch Albion Land Busy Body and five other champions.

Wires from Scandanavian countries have also been influential. Wiredresst Wait and See from Denmark was a top show winner and a top stud dog in the USA. Geir Flyckt-Pedersen of the Louline affix has bred many beautiful champions in Sweden, the UK and America. Ch Louline Pemberton was out of Ch Penda Passion at Louline. Ch Louline Heartbreaker and Head Over Heals both went to America and were professionally handled by Mr Wood Wornall and Mr George Ward respectively. Head Over Heals won 75 Groups and 18 BISs. Ch Louline Pickled Pepper was used at home for stud. Int, Eng, Norwegian and Swedish Ch Aywire Adam became Terrier of the Year in Norway in 1985.

Ch Louline Lord Fountleroy won 14 CCs and 11 RCCs. He came back into the ring in 1988 as a veteran and won First in Veteran and RCC at the Fox Terrier Club Show, and was Best Veteran in Show at Leicester Championship Show. He has sired several English and American champions.

Elsewhere in Europe, Supercrack Show de L'Abbaye du Gard from France must be one of the top dogs. Int Ch Ted v d Bismarckquelle from Germany has won several awards, including Danish Champion, Dutch Champion, Spanish Champion and Sieger (Germany) three times.

Valken Downtown Boy was a more recent big winner, gaining 18 CCs, 10 BOBs, seven RCCs, four Reserve in Group, two BISs and is the sire of 11 UK Champions. Wyndam the Boss gained 11 CCs with 10 BOBs before going abroad.

Top champion bitches are hard to identify as they are usually sold abroad either just before or just after they are made up and we do not hear any more about them.

In 1934 Int Ch Gains Great Surprise (sired by Talavera Simon) was regarded as one of the best bitches ever and, as stated earlier, she produced the two top dogs of the day, Gallant Fox of Wild Oaks and Beau Brummel of Wild Oaks. Blackdale Cindy was one of the top winning bitches with 20 CACIBs. Another good bitch was Ch Castlecroft Content (sire Beau Brummel) and she produced Castlecroft Contender.

Penda Peach tended to have large dog puppies, but when mated to Penda Cawthorne Cobnut she had two boys and two girls. The white son, Penda Peerless, was BOB at Crufts in 1961. She was the first bitch in history to produce three English champions, and she produced some foreign champions also.

Ch Gosmore Kirkmoor Tessa won the CC, BOB and BIS in the Novice class at the Manchester show in 1963. She went on to win a record 19 CCs, three BISs, three RBISs and in 1964 she won the Terrier Group at Crufts.

Louline Hell Cat won 12 CCs in Sweden in 1982 and produced Ch Greenfields Hell's Angel who became the top bitch in the breed's history.

In the last 15 years there has not been a particularly dominant sire or dam because they are usually sold abroad and it is not possible to keep track of their records. Our overall record in recent years must therefore stay with Ch Killick of the Mess who was the top winning dog and sired four Champions before going to America. For other top dogs see the World-wide section.

It is interesting to see that looking at the breeding of 200 Champions from around the 1950s, 121 (60.5%) had Champion sires, 65 (32.5%) neither parent was a Champion, nine (4.5%) both parents were Champions and five (2.5%) only the dam was a Champion. In the last 15 years the record shows 78 (60%) of all Champions had only a Champion sire, 29 (22%) had no Champion parents, 21 (16%) both parents were Champions and only two (1.53%) had only the dam as a Champion. These figures are rather misleading because many of the dogs became Champions in other countries later on. However it is interesting that so few Champion bitches have been used for breeding.

Photo: John Hartley.

Ch Sufredon Inkling, sire of more than 40 champions in this country alone.

Smooths - dominant sires and dams

Smooth Fox Terriers were bred to hunt and the painting *The Totteridge Eleven* by Arthur Wardle (now owned by The Kennel Club) shows them as a hunting team. The Terriers in this group were all top winning Smooth Fox Terriers, several being champions. Mr Wardle did a lot to improve the breed because his paintings enhanced the appearance of the dogs he painted, and photographers followed this idea by 'touching up' photographs to make the dog look perfect.

Over the years there have been several sires with the ability to produce show winning stock. Unfortunately these dogs have only sired effectively for one or two years. Looking down the list of Champions it will be seen that sires like Ch Newmaidley Whistling Jeremy, Ch Riber Ramsey, Ch Sirandra of Maryholm and Ch Boreham Blueblack have regularly sired champions. Seldom do we find a dog which has made a real impact on the breed, lasting for as many as nine or 10 years. An exception to this occurred just prior to 1975 when Ch Watteau Snuff Box dominated the Smooth scene. He was probably the most successful sire of all time. Another is Ch Sufredon Inkling who has sired over 40 Champions in this country and many more abroad since 1984. His pedigree includes Ch Newmaidley Whistling Jeremy, Ch Riber Ramsey, Maryholm Stockmark and Boreham Blueblack. Most of the present day winners include Inkling in their pedigree.

HISTORY AND DEVELOPMENT
OF THE FOX TERRIER

From the early history it can be seen that Francis Redmond bred 10 champions, and Her Grace Kathleen Duchess of Newcastle, after breeding Wires, then bred nine 'Of Notts' Smooth Fox Terriers. She was also President of the Fox Terrier Club for some years. She showed her dogs on a long, loose lead. When judging she paid attention to legs, feet and coat, preferring the cobby type to the bigger and longer dogs even if they had long and lean heads.

Mr F Reeks bred eight champions and his daughter bred a further three.

Mrs Blake bred Ch Watteau Midas and has made up a remarkable number of champions since.

Above: Ch Boreham Briar Rose.

Facing: Int Ch Boreham Bernadette.

Ch Watteau Snuff Box, born in 1962, was special, winning 19 CCs.

Captain Tudor Crosthwaite and Mr Tinne each bred four champions in the early days of the breed.

Dr R M Miller bred Ch Boreham Bisdon in 1931 and ever since the Boreham dogs have been highly regarded, many becoming champions.

In 1934 Miss Kathleen Emery won the Fox Terrier Club Gold Cup with Ch Hermon Conversion Loan. In 1956 she won it with Ch Hermon Palmist, in 1961 with Ch Hermon Card Trick and finally in 1962 with Ch Hermon Blacklands Sophia. Ch Hermon Parthings Loyal Lad won seven CCs and sired numerous superb champions at home and overseas. In 1956 Ch Hermon Rebel was born and she won 11 CCs. Other good bitches followed including the lovely Ch Hermon Carick who was born in

Ch Boreham Blueback.

1958 and won 13 Challenge Certificates. Mr T George bred Ch Lethal Weapon who won the Gold Cup in 1946 under the ownership of Mr Leo Wilson, an all-round international judge. Ch Lethal Weapon sired many champions including Ch Boreham Bendigo and Ch Harkaway Lili. Ch Laurel Wreath went on to sire such dogs as Maryhold Spun Gold and Ch Watteau Midas.

In 1953 Mr F Taylor handled seven-month-old bitch Gosmore Rosemorder Fireaway. Mr W Burrows was the judge at Leeds where she won all her classes and the championship also. From this CC to the next Leeds show she won 22 CCs and then went to Italy for a four-figure price.

Mr Herbert Johnson, a championship show judge, had some successes under the Brooklands affix from 1946, making up 11 champions and exporting many fine dogs. His Ch Brooklands Present was bred by Mrs Blake and sired by Ch Watteau Chorister.

Mr Clanachan had many champions, starting with Ch Maryholm Spun Gold in 1948. In 1949 Hampole Truering was made up and Elizabeth Lindley Wood followed with four more.

Many Smooth champions have been very white dogs. More black gradually came into the breed, making it more popular. The experts were inclined to think it was hard to breed a top-quality black and white terrier, but such a dog usually has a better head and expression. Such dogs are also inclined to have 'Huntly' spots on their legs, named after the Marquis of Huntly, a famous hunting man of his day. Smooths should be all white, tan and white or clear black and white. Breeding from brindles and dull tan colours leads to a problem that is hard to eradicate; brindle, red or liver markings are described in the Breed Standard as 'highly undesirable'.

Ch Lanneau Jewel, Mr J Lowe's first champion, was born in 1947. In 1949 she won nine CCs within seven months and also had a litter later that year. She was a real show girl, knowing when to turn on the charm, and she moved on a loose lead, refusing to leave the ring until she had received the claps and pats she felt she deserved. She ruled over all the bitches at home and thought the 'boys' were perfect. She lived to be 14 years old.

Ch Selecta Rich Reward was bred by Mr P Davenport and later purchased by Mr H R Bishop who added his affix 'Selecta' to the name in 1949 when Ch Selecta Rich Reward was five years old. He sired many champions and made his mark on the breed.

In 1954 Ch Lanneau Jeremy was born and he won five CCs two years later. In 1957 he was exported to Rhodesia, increasing the popularity of the breed there.

In the 1960s it was recognised that to improve the quality of the puppies produced it was essential to improve the bitch line in the kennel. It therefore followed that the bitch out of every litter to be kept had to be an improvement on the last one.

Linda Beak's first champion was Ch Newmaidley Jehu who was born in 1960. Linda Beak had a marvellous kennel of Smooths and Wires, but particularly excelled in the Smooths she produced.

Miss B Stapley had a top sire in her Ch Harkaway Lancashire Lad who became a champion in 1965 and went on to produce 10 British champions. Mrs Blake's Ch Watteau Madrigal sired three champions in the 1960s and Mr Ken Dickenson's Ch Ellastone Firecrest, a particularly nicely marked dog, sired five champions in the early 1970s.

Mrs M D Gabriel, wife of show judge Mr Malcolm Gabriel, started with a white bitch Ch Gabryl Greta who became a champion in 1972. They too went on to breed more fine dogs.

Mr W Browne-Cole's Ch Smooth Touch at Travella, a son of Ch Sufredon Inkling, became a champion in 1988. He did well in 1989, gaining 13 CCs, nine BOBs and one BIS.

A full analysis of Wire and Smooth champions and their breeding can be made from **Appendix C: List of Champions**.

Travel to shows

Until the late 1950s and 1960s not many people had cars, so most enthusiasts travelled to dog shows by train. This meant that ways and means had to be found to get from the nearest station to the show ground. The show societies would lay on 'suitable' transport which often comprised a fleet of vehicles as diverse as buses, cattle trucks, dilapidated ex-army trucks and coal carts. At the station the porters would take the dogs to the exit where quite often the owners could not be found. This was all part of the day's work. In and around London taxis were used to take exhibitors to the shows. Taxi drivers were generally helpful and happy to take the dogs and the gear. No matter what problems arose, the handlers would find ways and means of getting there somehow.

The advent of the motorway has made driving to shows much quicker and easier. Many more people have cars and the large estate has become the boon of dog showing. Everything can be put in the boot, which can be extended up to the front seats if required.

From the onset of the 1980s it has become common for Championship Shows to last three days with entries of 14,000 dogs. The caravan and camper have therefore become useful conveniences which can be parked next to the show ground.

The most pleasant means of transport today is undoubtedly by air. You park your car at the car park, take a courtesy ride to the terminal with the dogs, have breakfast on board and get a taxi to the show. Win or lose, you have a meal and a drink on the way home and rest until your arrival at the airport.

Whilst this sounds good there are snags: the first flight may not arrive early enough; there is always the possibility of delay; dogs will not always be carried (it depends what other livestock is booked); and goodwill is needed on the part of baggage handlers and taxi drivers.

Exports

In recent years the Fox Terrier has gained enormous world-wide popularity as other countries build up their dog show calendars. This has led to the widespread import and export of dogs between many European countries and across continents. This has only become possible with the faster journey times available through air travel, and serves a useful purpose in expanding the breed lines available in those countries. Each country has its own regulations for import and export and these have to be checked through first.

This world-wide demand for Fox Terriers has become a profitable proposition and it frequently happens that as soon as a dog becomes a champion (often sooner) it is sent abroad. Many potential stud dogs and top winning sires have been lost to

Great Britain because of this. The good bitches have gone away too, sometimes in whelp, so that British records show few Champion bitches as bearing Champion offspring. Whilst the Smooth coat can do well in most countries the Wire does sometimes find hot climates uncongenial. It can be seen clearly here on a hot summer day which dogs like the heat and which find it too much. Some dogs really suffer from the heat, just as we sometimes do. This is not a breeding problem; just a fact of life. Some like to bask in the sun (or next to a radiator) until they get too hot, but this is their choice. I would therefore hope that the dog's disposition to a different climate is given full consideration before any export takes place. Also it is important in such countries that the dog is well housed in suitably air-conditioned premises.

Hopefully if the dogs are taken to shows in hot climates their needs are taken into consideration. If there is a traffic jam on the motorway on a hot sunny day the dog quickly pants and it is not always easy to reach the dog to give him water or cool him off with a wet towel.

There have been a few dogs who have had great show careers at home and abroad, eventually returning to their country of origin. This happened to Ch Townville Tarique and Ch Townville Tradesman who returned to Great Britain from Japan in 1993, and Am/Can Ch Burrendale Escort of Purston and Am Ch Parkside Whitehall at Nethertonion, who returned to this country in 1995 to continue their show careers.

The strict import laws in Great Britain make imports very expensive, taking into account the cost of dog, travel and quarantine. It was estimated that a dog imported from Australia recently cost a total of £5,000 by the time the owner could take it home. Exporting dogs is much easier, as other countries do not have such strict laws. The main importing countries are: The United States of America, Japan, Sweden, Norway, Germany, Holland and Finland. We also export dogs to Brazil, Argentina, Hong Kong, Gibraltar and Spain.

The most striking dog to be exported in recent years was Mr and Mrs Baxter's Ch Killick of the Mess who won 16 Challenge Certificates (CCs) and 14 Best of Breeds (BOBs) in 1986, surpassed only by Ch Gosmore Kirkmoor Craftsman who won 22 CCs in 1969. He had sired four champions before going to America.

Frozen semen

In about 1986 Leicester University perfected the technique of freezing semen for use in artificial insemination. The reasons for acquiring this technique were many and varied, and not least to preserve rare species. As a result of this technology, the loss of the services of a top stud dog can now be avoided by freezing his semen for use in later years. It was not known how this would be viewed by kennel clubs throughout the world. The Kennel Club will only agree to register puppies sired in this way after considering all the reasons given for such action. (See section on freezing semen in Chapter 6.)

This new procedure was soon taken up in Europe because of the ban on showing docked dogs, and became the only way Scandinavia could use English stud dogs. They have also used this technique successfully in Australia. (See Chapter 2 **Australia** and **Norway**.)

Docking Law

In 1991 the Government amended the Veterinary Surgeons Act, prohibiting the lay person from docking puppies' tails, with effect from 1 July 1993. This meant that even breeders with 40 or more years experience could no longer dock their own litters. Following the new law the Council of The Royal College of Veterinary Surgeons ruled in 1992 that docking was unethical 'unless for therapeutic or acceptable prophylactic reasons'.

A general anti-docking fever resulted and, despite early warnings of the consequences experienced in Scandinavia, the law was passed. Vets prepared to dock were faced with the threat of disciplinary action and the possibility of being struck off the professional register. The Council of Docked Breeds was formed to help vets who were prepared to dock in any legal matters, and to provide breeders with lists of vets in their area who are prepared to dock. The RSPCA took some people to court but were unsuccessful.

Although some undocked Fox Terriers seem to have no problem, it has been found generally that the undocked tail is lifeless, curled onto the back and unable to wag in the way it did. The risk of damage to the tail is more likely, and it restricts the working terrier going down a fox hole. The ban came into force in Sweden in 1989 and that year 38% of dogs in one breed alone had tail injuries before they were 18 months old. By 1991 the number of injuries increased to 51%. The practice of docking was instituted 450 years ago for good reasons; it would appear the same reasons exist today.

A head study of Gold Cup winner
Boreham Ballet Star painted by
Brenda Gough.

2

Fox terriers
World-Wide

The Fox Terrier Breed Standard is similar world-wide. It was set in England, and The Kennel Club has reciprocal agreements with other canine clubs throughout the world. There are minor differences in wording (various ways of describing 'movement' for example), but the ideal is the same.

All the dogs abroad are descended from British stock, and top winning dogs from Britain continue to be taken abroad for showing and to improve the local stock.

Argentina

British people (among others) have been farming in Argentina for many years; what better dog than a Fox Terrier can you have on a farm?

In 1974 the imported dog Jarken Jethro became an Argentinian Champion, and in 1978 he went on to become Best Fox Terrier. His son, Albion Land Busy Body, also became a Champion in Argentina and was subsequently sold to Chile, becoming a Chilean Champion and sixth in All Breeds in 1984.

Jokyl Carefree from England became an Argentine and South American Champion and in 1979 was Best Fox Terrier and Best Terrier. She arrived in Argentina already in whelp to Eng Ch Harrowhill Huntsman and had two puppies. Her son was Grand Champion Mina's Favourite who in 1982 was Best Fox Terrier and Best Terrier.

Am Ch Cefnbryn Kibella was bred in Wales and exported to the USA. After showing in the USA he went on to do the rounds from his home in Argentina. He won numerous Best in Shows (BISs), the highest prize being when he won the Challenge Cup for winning BIS three times running at the Federaçion Cinologica Argentina. He is now American Champion, International Champion, Argentinian Grand Champion and Champion of the Americas (a FCI title). He was also Best Dog of the Year All Breeds in 1981, and his picture is on the front cover of *The Fox Terrier* by Elsie Williams.

Penda Premium became Argentinian and South American Champion in 1982.

Cefnbryn Megan was mated to Harrowhill Huntersmoon and was exported to Argentina in whelp. She was the Top Wire Bitch in 1984.

Int Ch, Ch of America, Argentine Grand Ch, Ch of Uruguay, South American Ch Blackdale Stargazer arrived from Ireland in 1984. In 1985 he won five BISs, 13 Best In Groups (BIGs), two Reserve Best In Shows (RBISs), five Reserve Best In Groups (RBIGs) and in 1986 he was Best Dog All Breeds.

Australia

The Australian Fox Terrier Club was formed in Melbourne in 1878, and the Southern Fox Terrier Club shortly afterwards. These clubs had ceased to exist by the time The Fox Terrier Club of New South Wales was set up in 1910. Mr Hamilton was the first President, serving for 28 years. The Fox Terrier Club of New South Wales represents both coats, with a dominance of Smooths at present.

The Smooth Fox Terrier Club in Melbourne has a greater membership and is supported by Mr Bob Musket and Mrs J E Braithwaite, both breeder/judges. (The club, and the breed, suffered a sad loss in the recent death of the Rev Keith Braithwaite, husband to Mrs J E Braithwaite.) Melbourne is the area where most Fox Terriers are bred, the Smooth stock being largely influenced by the imports from Watteau and Brooklands. There are about a dozen Australian members of breed clubs in the UK. Numbers are increasing and there are some good quality dogs coming out.

Most shows are held in the capital cities and once a year each State holds a Royal Show. The shows in the country towns are relaxed and informal outings for dogs and owners alike.

The first Smooth import was in 1868: a bitch called Careless. The first Wire was Nell, who arrived in 1876 from Parson Jack Russell. She won the Sydney Royal Show in 1878 and 1879. It was at this show in 1937 that the breed was at its most popular, with an entry of 369 Smooths and 169 Wires.

Mr Cameron E Milward set the standard of Smooth presentation in the last 50 years. Although there are not so many dogs as there were in the 1930s to early 1950s, there is still a good entry at the Royal shows. Among the many exhibitors are the aforementioned Mrs J E Braithwaite of the Optimo affix, M Prendergast (Ambeth), B Larkin (Kenilglen), H P Luyten (Rama), J S Rowles (Graebrook Kennels), and B Mushet (Teshum). The many other affixes include Ecirp, Springfox, Cindisue, Mirolinda and Ttarb.

Christmas down-under.

There have not been many Smooth imports to Australia in recent years, probably because the home kennels are so strong. One recent one is Rotur Revelation, owned by Mrs M Prendergast. He was born in September 1987, and is by Eng Ch Riber Mint Imperial ex Rotur Rowanberry, a daughter of Riber Danny Boy. Another recent import is Mrs J E Braithwaite's bitch Bothwell Foxtrot, by Eng Ch Sufredon Cracknell ex Eng Ch Bothwell Snowdrop.

It is certainly fair to state that Smooths dominate the Fox Terrier scene in Australia at present. At the Royal Melbourne Show in 1994 there was an entry of 81 Smooths (32 dogs and 49 bitches) compared to 19 Wires (6 dogs and 13 bitches). However, there are many good representatives among the Wires.

Aus Ch Extreal Select Edition.

Mr Brendan O'Loghlen, to whom I am indebted for much of my information about the Fox Terrier scene in Australia, inherited the Extreal affix from Mr Syd Mallam in 1982. His home-bred Aus Ch Extreal Select Edition (Aus Ch Extreal Royal Flush (bred by Syd Mallam) ex Eng/Aus Ch Kilnhill Kate of Purston) was born in January 1987, and is grandson to Ch Townville Tradition and Ch Townville Texan. Mr O'Loghlen has also sought to strengthen the breed in Australia by importing semen from Eng/Nor/Swe/Int Ch Aywire Adam, owned by Grethe and Hanne Bergendahl, Norwegian pioneers in the use of frozen semen. In February 1991, Eng and Aus Ch Kilnhill Kate of Purston produced a litter by 'Adam', among whom were Extreal Adams Ace and Extreal Adams Angel, who have subsequently played an important part in his breeding programme. Mr O'Loghlen has also stored frozen semen from Aus Ch Extreal Special Edition for future use.

Eng/Aus Ch Kilnhill Kate of Purston. Photo: Peter Winfield.

The late Miss Barbara Withers, of the Cadbury affix, was very influential in the development of Wires in Australia. She concentrated on British bloodlines and stock with Worsbro breeding, and among her imports over several decades were Eng Ch Penda Pied Piper (winner of many BISs), Eng Ch Sarabel Penda Polly Perkins, Worsbro Wink, Townville Tana and Penda Pepo.

Shirley Goodwin and Ernie Parker of Victoria are also recent importers of Wires. Among these were Eng Ch Blackdale Ambassador (who has subsequently achieved many BIS and Group wins), Penda Pollyanna, Penda Pastel and Blackdale Accommodator. They are now showing the progeny of some of these imports.

Among numerous other Australian breeders and exhibitors of Wires are H P Luyten of the Rama affix, M Clark (Cooniwire), L Walmsley (Coolaney), L Coyle (Wyrecourt), J and D Collins (Yiriwire), Mrs Attrill (Attline) and Messrs Lee and Hodgkins, who have enjoyed great success with Aus Ch Chaduna Lovem'n'leavem. Two more recent enthusiasts are Brian Fanning of Queensland and Wendy Brown of New South Wales.

Among other imported dogs was Ryandos Real Star, from New Zealand, who was bred from Harmil Howzat and Bothwell Bluebell - a round-the-world influence of UK originating stock.

Anyone visiting Australia will be daunted by its size. To keep Terrier people in touch in such a large country there is a publication called *The Terrier Down Under*. It is not unusual for dogs to travel 600 miles to go to the right stud dog, or to travel by

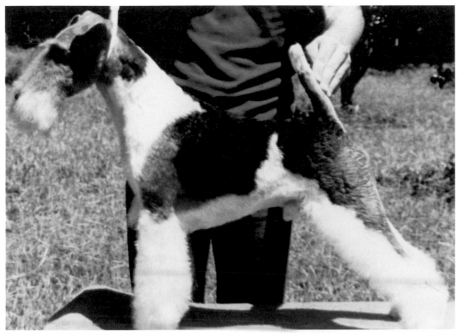

Brazilian Ch Newmaidley For'ard: a very successful British import.

air for five and a half hours (for example, Perth to Melbourne) into a different time zone, show, and return home next day - a very exhausting journey for dog and owner/handler.

Brazil

The Brazilian Kennel Club was founded in 1922. The first Fox Terriers to arrive came from England, France, Germany and the USA. Breeding came through the lines of some top dogs like Barrington Bendigo, Barry Brigadier, Crackley Sensation, Eden Aristocrat of Wildoaks, Talavera Simon and Gallant Fox of Wildoaks. Am Ch Crackley Polly Girley (Beau Brummel ex Crackley Skylight) was the top winning bitch.

After 1945 a few breeders imported dogs from England, including Newmaidley Tipstaff, Onlooker and Pickles, Penda Prestige and Dominus Deal Dulcie. Shoeman's Laster arrived and won 50 BIS titles. Newmaidley For'ard gained 50 BIS titles All Breeds, and was Top Dog in Brazil All Breeds in 1982. The other high ranking dogs are Int Ch Harvey v d Bismarckquelle, with 13 BIS All Breeds and Fourth Top Dog Brazil All Breeds in 1985. Brazilian Ch Crizwood Silver Fox from the USA won 11 BIS All Breeds. Lastly, Int Ch Greenfields Hell's Angel (by Galsul Excellence ex Louline Hell Cat) was All Breeds Top Winning Bitch in the breed's history in 1990.

Winners have been sired by Champions including: Townville Tobias, Newmaidley Tipstaff, Harrowhill Huntsman, Penda Worsbro Weasel, Penda Premier, Penda Precision, and Galsul Excellence all from the UK. The main kennels are in Rio de Janeiro and Sao Paulo. One kennel uses the affix Brasmaidley as a tribute to Linda Beak who had the Newmaidley Wire and Smooth Fox Terriers.

There are no specialist pet shops in Brazil, and show and grooming equipment is not readily available. This makes presentation of the Wire a hard and laborious finger-and-thumb job. Specialist materials have to be bought in the USA, and not everyone can afford to do that.

Most dogs in the city areas of Brazil are kept as guard dogs, behind very high railings topped with barbed wire. This applies especially to the new development areas outside the main city centres.

Canada

The Wire Fox Terrier Club of Canada was formed in 1984. The first general meeting was held at The Caledon Championship Dog Show. The membership stands at about 50, but it was found that in such a large country it was difficult to attend shows and meetings because of the vast distances involved. A quarterly newsletter called *News Wire* was therefore started and five regional directors were appointed to send in news from their respective regions.

Mr Ormsby formed his kennel in 1919. Mrs Irene Webster bought dogs from England and bred the By Town dogs. Mr Beer bred Smooths in Toronto in the 1930s. Mr Scarpa of Quebec was showing in the 1930s and exhibited the dog Starting Event of Wildoaks, son of Crackley Startler and grandson of Ch Gains Great Surprise of Wildoaks, born in 1933 and bought from Mrs Bondy.

Mr Ward (Albany) had a great influence with his dogs. His son, George, went to the United States where he became an outstanding handler. Some of the more recent leading names are Foxlington, Halfmoon, Trollhattan, Wyndfyre and Wirehill. To these can be added Foxbar, Maluzo, Runwyre, Plawsworth.

Holmwire Vitoka Vanessa left the shores of the UK for Canada, where he became a Canadian and Am Champion. Am Ch Worrindale Wavesong also went to Canada to collect his title there.

A considerable amount is done in Canada to make people aware of the attractions of the Fox Terrier, and special shows are held in each region to promote the breed. At these shows they give displays about the Fox Terrier, supplying information, pictures, leaflets and lists of breeders, and answering any queries. They also have a rescue service to find homes for dogs left in animal shelters.

Chile

Although I have been to Chile many times I have never seen a Fox Terrier there. Even the big show in Vina del Mar at Easter did not attract any. There are few pedigree dogs of any breed in Chile, so most show dogs have to compete against dogs of other breeds. Showing dogs is very much a minority interest but those that do go enjoy it; there is a pleasant, relaxed atmosphere around the arena, something like a village fête.

Dogs for pets can be bought very cheaply, and most run loose or sit at the side of the road. Numerous mongrels can be seen as a result of this. Occasionally you get to hear of a stud dog who has overstayed his welcome in an area. I have yet to see a pet shop; most people feed their dogs on scraps from the table, though tinned foods are available in the supermarkets. It is virtually impossible to find grooming tools, although grooming salons have them. Most people would have to make a trip to the USA or Europe to buy them. The Argentine import Ch Albion Land Busy Body became a Chilean Champion very quickly and in 1984 was Sixth Dog All Breeds.

Denmark

At the beginning of the 1980s there were not many Fox Terriers in Denmark and dog showing in general was in its infancy. However, by 1987 there were 17 Championship shows during the season, at which time half the winning stock was imported, mostly from England, but also from Eire, Holland, Germany and the USA.

The Danish-bred Starups Merry Clayton did well in Europe, gaining RBIG and becoming Top Winning Terrier in 1985. Ted v d Bismarckquelle was exported to Denmark and toured Europe, winning everywhere. Among his many titles are Wire of the Year, Terrier of the Year, Dog of the Year and Fourth All Breeds. He won 11 Best Of Breeds (BOBs), 15 Best Dog and seven Groups, being placed each time in the final four for BIS.

Blackdale Contessa was the first Danish-owned bitch to become a Dutch Champion in May 1986. Wiredresst Wait and See became an international champion under Mr H Hingle in 1988. He was also the Top Stud Dog in the USA, and was already a US, Canadian and Dutch Champion. He went on to get the EUSG and BDSG.

At the shows in Denmark every exhibitor is handed the judge's report as they leave the ring after each class. At the end of the show the exhibitor may ask the judge further questions about his dog. BOB winners gain points and there are certain shows where extra points may be gained.

Eire

The first post war champion was Ch Reaghcastle Roberta out of an arbitrary mating to Hartleydene Hi Flight while she was on the way home from an unsuccessful attempt to mate her to a planned sire.

Mrs Williams' Ch Penda Oregan Witchcraft came out of an Irish dog Ch Kenelm Supremacy. Mr Alex Barrett bred good Wires winning many BIS in Eire. Ch Dunwyre Countess was home bred and Ch Dunwyre Criterion was produced from an imported dog.

Mr O'Donoghue bred Lakeland terriers first and then started to breed Wire Fox Terriers. Int Ch Blackdale Starbright was one of his first successes (going to Sweden) followed by Blackdale Consort, and Blackdale Aristocrat (son of Starbright). He came to Crufts as a veteran and still looked magnificent. Next came Blackdale Prospect, who proved to be an excellent sire, and then many more.

Fairwyre Ballerina was the top winning Wire in Ireland in 1988. Michael Kirby bred Int Ch Wonderwyre Bunratty Bouquet, and more recently Mr Stanfield of the Fairwyre Kennels bought Burrenedge Marksman from the breeder Mr Thompson, showing him extensively in the UK.

Finland

The Finnish Terrier Club's Annual Special Show and the Finnish Fox Terrier Association Show are the main events for the breed. Finnish Fox Terriers do well in Groups at International and National Shows. The Smooth Fox Terrier Dk Ch Gainsay Guess My Name has won Groups and has been placed in the BIS ring. The SF Ch Starring German Gold has been placed in Groups, and Norwegian Ch Gainsay Holeproof qualified for the Champion of Champions Show. Wires took part in the World Winner Show in Copenhagen. Guess My Name won the Open Class and Challenge Certificate (CC) and became a Danish Champion.

France

Ernest Sharpe took Ch Drakehall Dairymaid to Paris for the first show after the Second World War when she had just won RBIS at Crufts.

Weltona Readicut went to France in 1954 and won the CACIB and BOB. In 1956 Weltona Glannant Gaylord and Bancross Bridesmaid dominated the show scene, and in 1982 Poumy de Lamasquère was twice Best Terrier at Barcelona.

Ch Flashman and his son Ch Cripsey Captain Poldark were followed by Supercrackshow de L'Abbaye Du Gard, who won 14 CACs in 1985. In 1987 he won eight CACIBs, two RCACIBs and 12 CACs. Another dog from this kennel, Glanrob Bayly Comet, won 9 BOBs in 1991 and was surpassed by his rival Blackdale Cindy who won 20 CACIBs, two BIS All Breeds and 10 Best Terrier awards.

In 1989 Glanrob Bayly Comet won 9 BOBs.

English handlers are often invited to handle dogs at the big shows in France and English judges are in demand too. The most recent example of this is Mr Frank Kellett, handling Erica des Caussières, who won RBIS at Chateau Roux in 1992. It is interesting that in France the dogs have to show their hunting skills and the Best 'Complet' (Show and Fox Hunting) at Alençon Nationale d'Élevage in 1993 was Cannelle de la Barrière Rouge.

Germany

In 1989 and 1990 the Top Wire was Flash v d Bismarckquelle. Also that year, Int Ch Easternvale Ensign from the UK won four BISs, two RBIS, and 14 Groups.

The year 1992 brought great wins for Walzerkönig v d Bismarckquelle (15 CCs, 13 BOBs, and five BISs). Meanwhile his rival Hazel v Vorsterfeld became World Champion and Germany's Top Wire with 70 CACs, nine BOBs, five BIS. Luigi v Vorsterfeld also became a World Champion that year. Another top dog was German, Luxembourg and Europe Champion Kilja v Vorsterfeld.

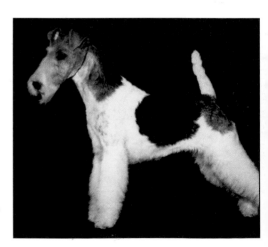

Above:
Ger/Am/Dan/Dutch/Lux/Int Ch Flash v d Bismarckquelle: Top Wire 1989, Top Fox Terrier 1990.
Photo: Herr Möhrke.

Left: A future German Smooth Champion?
Photo: Herr Möhrke.

Right: Ger/Danish/Int Ch Serina v d Bismarckquelle: Top Fox Terrier in Germany 1993.
Photo: David Dalton.

Gibraltar

Gibraltar is so built up that there is little or no space for a dog to have fun. However there are some Wires there (pets and show dogs) and they do have some success. Valken Double Strike is the most recent arrival, winning his first CAC Excellent, and Fourth in Terrier Group at Zafra, Badajoz in Spain.

Holland

There are some real enthusiasts in Holland, and for them importing dogs from the UK is cheap and easy.

Ch Townville Tieve Tara won the bitch CACIB and Ch Townville Toastmaster the BOB and BIS at their first show. Brittlewire have been making the most wins in Holland with Primary Girl, Shotgun, Felicity, Sundance, Cadans, Ursa Major, Caprice and now Passionate.

Italy

The Italian top Wire in 1991 and 1992 was Ch Seawire Silver Bell with 10 BOBs and three BISs.

Japan

Several Fox Terriers have been exported to Japan. Townville Tarique (1988 top winner in the UK with 11 CCs and seven BOBs) went on to win four BISs in Japan. Townville Tradesman (1989 top winner in the UK with 10 CCs and seven BOBs) went to Japan. After showing there both dogs returned to the UK.

New Zealand

Pandora of Summerplace from Australia went to New Zealand to become a Champion, then returned home. Ch Fairwyre Ballerina from Ireland became a New Zealand Champion in 1989.

Above: Five pups from frozen semen (Ch Sylair Star Leader ex Int/Norwegian/Swedish Ch Marstens Tricky Miss Smidth). Breeder: G Bergendahl.
Below: Norwegian/Swedish/Int Ch Marstens Puppet on a String; an undocked Champion (docking is forbidden in Norway).

Norway

Norway is a wonderful country for Fox Terriers and there are some lovely dogs there. They first arrived in Norway from England around 1893. In 1902 the Smooth and Wire were divided into two breeds. Imports came from England, Sweden, Denmark and Germany. Several Wires came from the Oldcliffe Kennels and, in 1916, the first of many Wires came from Mr Butler of the famous Watteau Kennels, now run by Mrs Blake and Mrs Thornton. Epping and Talavera Kennels also exported dogs to

Norway. In 1930 a Norwegian-bred Smooth out of an English import, Siguls Sparknekt, was exported to the UK, gained his champion status and was returned to Norway.

After the war the Watteau Kennels were exporting Smooths, and dogs from Brooklands, Hampole and Stockmoor also started arriving. It was in 1965 that the first Newmaidley Smooth arrived, and dogs from Lanneau and Sidewater. A very important bitch for the breed was Int Nordic Ch Sidewater Cornish Pisky, owned by Berit Foss of Bajas Kennel. She produced many Scandinavian Champions. GB Ch Shaftmoor Bellechien White Heather was also imported from the UK.

Ch Pittlea Chortle arrived in 1973 and was BIS at his first International Show. Although, sadly, he died soon after this show, he was so striking that several Pittlea dogs were imported.

GB/Int/Norwegian/Swedish Ch Penda Passion at Louline. Breeder: Elsie Williams. Photo: A Konda Midttun.

Berit Foss imported Ch Watteau Chief Barker in 1974. He won several groups and did a lot to improve the breed in Norway, Finland and Sweden where he ended his days.

The Bajas kennel imported Newmaidley Eden and dogs from the Riber Kennels who made a great influence on the breed. There are very few Smooths now in Norway and only one breeder. They are, however, strong in Sweden largely as a result of the Bajas Kennel.

After the war Wires were imported from Wyretex Wyns and Kirkmoor, and also from Sweden. In 1955 the all white Swedish Gårdskals Master Gunner won many BISs but had little influence on the breed.

At this time Grethe Bergendahl (Marsten) imported three Roundway Wires and Burntedge Baritone who later sired many Champions, one of which was sold to Mr Geir Flyckt Pedersen (Louline) who was then in Norway. A Penda bitch arrived at this time also.

In 1962 Nordic Ch Tydfil Trader arrived and was winning BIS until 1967. R Kjølstad and Grethe Bergendahl imported from the St Erme Kennel and these dogs greatly influenced the breed.

Ch Gosmore Kirkmoor Satisfaction arrived in 1967 to become No 3 Top Dog the following year and No 2 Top Dog in 1970. He was owned jointly by the Silverling and Marsten Kennels. He sired 22 Champions. Ch Kirkdale Pirate came the following year and had some good wins.

In 1975 R Kjølstad and S Kolstø (Silverling) and Grethe Bergendahl (Marsten) imported Nordic Ch Willbe of Worsbro who became No 4 Top Dog in his first year. He sired the 1979 Top Dog, Ch Silverlings Sun Dancer. Jarken Mimosa also arrived now to the same three owners, becoming not only a Champion but also a Norwegian Hunting Champion. St Ernie Tucker, another import, was a BIS winner and sire of 15 champions.

A Steenersen (Hearty Vision Kennel) started her kennel with Int Ch Arklow Amaryllis, who was the dam of many Champions. In 1980 Irish Ch and Ch Blackdale Starbright was imported by Mr Pedersen to Sweden. He soon became top dog in Norway and Sweden.

Ch Aywire Adam was imported by the Bergendahls in 1983, was Top Terrier in 1985 and sired 12 champions. He won his Huntingtrail CC, and his final claim to fame was having his frozen comon sent to Australia.

Drakehall Dainty Miss became an International Champion but she only had one live puppy: Marstens Tricky Miss Smidth. The latter made history in 1988 by becoming the dam of the first litter in Norway from frozen semen, donated by Ch Sylair Star Leader. There were five puppies, four going on to become Champions. This was a remarkable event, bearing in mind that frozen semen has to be very carefully monitored and that her mother had had such difficulty in producing.

Int Nordic Ch Little Big Man (grandson of Adam) was sired by Ch Zino v d Bismarckquelle and was Top Terrier in 1988.

In 1989 Int Ch Baxee Killick Seaman (son of Killick of the Mess) was Top Terrier. He won six Terrier Groups and was placed every time in the BIS ring.

Next came Int Norwegian and Swedish Ch Louline Head for Heights, who became Top Terrier and No 3 Top Dog in 1990. He has sired many champions.

The year 1990 saw the arrival of the beautiful six-year-old Int Ch Penda Passion at Louline, and in 1991 she became Top Dog in Norway. She had already had several litters in England; now she was mated to the stunning Eng and American Ch Louline Heartbreaker to produce six puppies. The five surviving puppies, one of whom was Ch Marstens Boomerang, all became (undocked) Champions. They all also won CCs from the Puppy class. In 1992 the undocked Int Norwegian and Swedish Ch Marstens Puppet on a String was Top Terrier. Her wins included several BISs and BIGs in Norway and Sweden. She is the daughter of Louline Head for Heights and grand-daughter of Ch Aywire Adam.

Last but by no means least, in 1993 that superb dog Int, GB, US and Swedish Ch Louline Heartbreaker (b 5 April 1986), as a veteran, won five BISs and 11 Groups in only 16 outings. He was Top Terrier and No 3 Top Dog.

Other breeders in the country include Ann Steenersen, (Hearty Vision); Silva Kolstø, (Silverling); Ingeborg Utnes, (Mulegården); Hanne Bergendahl; Grethe Bergendahl (Marsten); Ole Jørgen Sørlie, (Hunterfield).

Wires have now been Top Terrier for six consecutive years which is a great achievement. There are no Smooth breeders now, but one person breeds pets without registration papers.

Norway has done a considerable amount of work using frozen semen for artificial insemination. This has now been used legally for some years. In 1986 the first terrier litter was born in this way from an English dog. The semen was frozen by Dr Morton of the University of Leicester; eight months later, the litter arrived. In 1987 some frozen semen from Ch Killick of the Mess was purchased from Mr and Mrs Baxter, and it has been used to produce several litters. This is a costly procedure, providing some amusement. For example, it is often carried in something looking like a thermos flask, and some passengers have been heard to remark on coffee being carried. Some imported frozen semen has not been successful, due to the lack of expertise outside the country to freeze it correctly. However, in Norway it has been 100% successful.

The import of frozen semen is a complex process: the dog must be selected, the owner's agreement procured, and all the paper work completed. (In one case it took six months because they also had to wait for space in the freezer at the Norwegian Kennel Club!) The frozen semen is preserved in liquid nitrogen. During the freezing process the semen has to be constantly tested because it is not always of adequate quality to freeze successfully. Once thawed, it only lives a few hours, so artificial insemination has to be done exactly on time. This requires daily visits by the vet to check on the bitch.

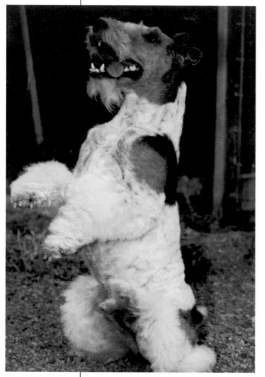

A happy boy:
Eng/Am/Int Ch Louline Heartbreaker.
Owner: G Bergendahl.
Photo: H Bergendahl.

On 1 July 1988 the docking law was passed in Norway and Sweden. This was a disaster for the breed; several breeders gave up and now only 25-30 Fox Terrier puppies a year are registered with the Norwegian Kennel Club. No dog born and docked after 1988 may be shown, regardless of country of origin, so there is no point in importing dogs to improve the breed. Two un-docked Wires have done well: Int Ch Marstens Puppet On-A-String and Ch Marstens Boomerang.

On 1 May 1994 Norway and Sweden opened the borders for dog showing from EFTA countries. The rules are that the dog must have its ear tattooed, a rabies vaccination, and four months later a serum test to check its effectiveness. (Difficulty arises here because there are not many places where the check can be undertaken.) Then follows a vaccination against leptospirosis, distemper and hepatitis, an import licence from the Government to take the dog home, and a final veterinary health check to get a certificate which is valid for 10 days only. All this costs about £200 for a weekend.

Romania

Ch Cid Grand Prix won the Budapest and Moscow titles and BIS All Breeds at the Timisoara Show. James of White Joker won the Junior Warrant in 1989 and four CACs.

Russia

The big show in Moscow attracts around 3,000 dogs from all over Europe. Ann Arch judged the Fox Terriers at the 1988 show and Cid Grand Prix from Romania was the winner, Excellent II, and Anja of White Joker winner, Excellent I.

Singapore

Ch Harrowhill Superman won seven CCs and BOBs, seven Terrier Groups, two BISs and two RBISs in his first seven shows.

In 1986, Singapore, Aust and NZ Ch Cefnbryn Celtic Consort of Classicway won RBIS and Terrier of the Year at nine-and-a-half years of age. He was New Zealand's Top Terrier in 1981.

Spain

A dog has to be 15 months old to win a CAC. There are four classes:

- Puppy - five to nine months
- Junior - nine to 15 months
- Open - 15 months onwards. The National Challenge Certificate (CAC) is won from the Open class, which is followed by:
- Champions

At International Shows the CACIB is awarded to the best of sex between the winners of Open and Champions classes. To be a Spanish Champion you need four CACs from three different judges: in addition your dog has to attend the National Terrier Championship Show of Spain and win at least an 'Excellent'. One of the CACs has to be won at the Kennel Club of Spain International Championship Show in Madrid, held in May and November each year, where the competition is particularly tough. Like everything else in Spain, shows are run in a relaxed way, often running late, with plenty of time to chat and make new friends.

The Club Espanol de Terriers is for all Terrier breeds and was set up by British enthusiasts. The El Sevillano Kennels specialise in well-presented dogs and perform a professional handling service for owner/breeders. They are also interested in exchanging information about the breed.

There have been Fox Terriers in Spain for many years. Dog showing started when Cripsey Carlos and Newmaidley Leader arrived. They won several BISs and interest in the breed grew, presentation being helped by English professional handlers.

In 1984 Ch Sandwyre Smuggler was the top winning dog. In 10 shows he won 10 BOBs, nine Groups, seven BISs, and one RBIS. Ch Ted v d Bismarckquelle arrived from Germany and other Champion dogs from Holland and Italy followed. Ch Blackdale Contrast and other Blackdale dogs were campaigned.

Spanish-bred dogs are descended from such names as Blackdale, Cradleydale, Penda, Panfield, Harrowhill, Baxee and Maryholm. In 1990 Zamborino Starfighter was the top winning Fox Terrier in Spain and Portugal. Zamborina Starlight (Blackdale parents) had some good wins in 1992 in Spain and Portugal including Terrier Group winner (Puppy Class) at the Valencia World Show. Zamborino Moony Lass won the Wire bitches (Young Class) at the same show.

Sweden

In 1978 the Swedish Wire Fox Terrier Club was formed. It has a magazine which appears four times a year and holds two open shows a year. The first real major open show was in August 1982, where Mr Ernest Sharpe gave the BIS to Ch Blackdale Commander and BOB to Ch Alkara Anna Marie, out of a large entry of 43 dogs.

Most of the shows in Sweden are Championship shows with CCs freely on offer. It is not unusual for a Swedish judge to withhold a CC if he feels the winner is not worthy of being a Champion.

Judging in Sweden is based on the same lines as in Norway and Denmark. There are five classes: Junior, Youngster, Open, Champion and Veteran. The age varies slightly according to country and breed. Every dog gets a written critique from the judge.

In Junior and Youngster you get a 'quality' prize, and several dogs can be of the same quality: First, Second or Third. A First in quality entitles you to compete for five placings in the class. If a dog is awarded a Prize of Honour in Junior he joins the dogs from Open when competing in the Winners class.

The Open class has the same quality prizes (you can get First, Second, Third or untypical O). The First prize winners will then compete in the Winners class together with the juniors and youngsters that have the special honour prize. The winner of this class can win a CC (if good enough) and the second best dog can get the RCC (if good enough). The next male can get a CK if he is of CC quality.

The Champions class is only for Champions and there will be No 1, No 2, No 3, No 4 and Reserve placings. CK prizes will be given to as many dogs as the judge sees fit.

The Veteran class has a quality prize First, like the first three classes. First winners can go on for competition in the class. CK can be awarded to as many dogs as the judge sees fit. A very well kept Veteran not quite of CK standard can receive a Prize of Honour if it has a first in quality.

In Norway and Sweden all the dogs winning CC, RCC, or CK compete to be placed No 1, No 2, No 3, No 4 and Reserve Best Dog, and they are followed by the bitches. At the International Shows they can compete for CACIB and RCACIB for each sex if the judge thinks they are of extremely high quality. At the end the best dog and best bitch compete for BOB and BIS (provided they have each won a CK at least).

In Denmark all the dog and bitch CC, RCC or CK winners compete together (sometimes a very large class) to be placed No 1, No 2, No 3, No 4, or Reserve BOB. At International Shows the judge will award the CACIB and RCACIB to each sex if they are of extremely high quality. CACIB is awarded at the International shows. Four of these in three different countries are needed to become an International Champion, with at least a year between the first and last win.

In Sweden the Fox Terrier needs two CACIBs in two countries and has to pass a working trial. To win a CACIB the dog should be of a quality that would win a CC in its country of origin. There are no restrictions on how many times a judge may judge in any one year.

In Sweden (and also in France) the hunting competition is again based on quality. A First class will allow further competition, and if the dog is of very good quality he can get a CK and then go on for the competition for best dog/bitch.

To become a Champion you need three CCs. In Norway one of these has to be at the Kennel Club Show.

Ch Wiredot Whisper came from England in the early 1970s and produced Ch Jaravallen Playboy who was one of the best ever Swedish Wires and a prolific sire. Whisper also produced several Champions.

Ch Jokyl Debutante went to Sweden in whelp to T'Other'Un and five out of six in the litter became champions, as well as others in subsequent litters.

British dogs that have been shown in Sweden include Arklow Aramis, Ch Jokyl Sandwyre Solomon, Ch Seawire Successor, Ch Gregdon Cora, Ch Penda Precision, Ch Twynstar Accurist Again and Ch Bodium Bizzie Lizzie.

Ch Layven Lacy Girl, Ch Harrowhill Honey, Ch Harrowhill Hyperion, Ch Cefnbryn Cracksman of Gwenog and Ch Blackdale Starbright are all part of the background of winning dogs in the country. Louline have made a marked impression in Sweden, the UK and America with beautiful dogs superbly presented. In 1991 Scanwyre Knock Out won seven CCs, five with a BOB.

The law prohibiting the showing of any dog with a docked tail came into effect from 1 January 1989. This greatly reduced the number of dogs imported from England because, since they were still being docked, they could not be shown in Sweden.

Above: Ch Townville Tristanian, imported from Great Britain by Libwyre.

Left: Ch Libwyre Legend (Ch Townville Tobias ex Ch Holmwire Vitoka Vanessa), Libwyre's first homebred multiple BIS, handled by George Ward. Photo: Martin Booth.

United States of America

The American Fox Terrier Club was formed in 1885 at a meeting held during the Westminster Kennel Club Dog Show. Warren and Rutherford Smooths were the start of the lines. Their first show was in 1886 when Mr Francis Redmond went over from England to judge 75 Smooths and four Wires. Warren Remedy won BIS at Westminster three years running from 1907. No Smooth has won this show since.

Ttarb The Brat became a notable top winner and won a Group in 1982.

In 1882 Tyke became the first Wire to be shown. This was at the famous Westminster Show where he came first in the Miscellaneous Class. He had just arrived from England and was bred by Mr Carrick. By 1887 the Wire entry was up to 24.

Until the 1940 there were no separate classes for Wires and Smooths. When they were introduced only one dog could

GB/US Ch Townville Tobias. Photo: Martin Booth.

go forward to the Group. It was therefore necessary to identify them as two separate breeds so that there could be two winners in the Specials to go on to represent the breed in the Terrier Group. In 1984 the two Breed Clubs submitted new breed standards which were approved by the American Kennel Club, and by 1985 the Smooth and Wire coats were regarded as two separate breeds.

Eng/US/Can Ch Townville Tristanian, top producer of Champions in the USA.
Photo: Martin Booth.

People into dog showing in America today are real enthusiasts and travel vast distances to show and to see dogs at home and abroad. Breed shows like the Wire Fox Terrier Specialty Shows are held in each State.

After a great BIS win at the 1936 The Kennel Club's All Breeds Championship Show, Mr Hingle's World and Int Ch Croyland Chantress of Wildoaks was bought by Mrs R C Bondy of the famous Wildoaks Kennels and was later featured in the publication *Champion Dogs of the World*. Other UK imports followed, including Mr Whitham's Townville dogs, Miss Howles' Harrowhill and Linda Beak's Newmaidley. Later Blackdale and Louline also influenced the breed.

In 1969 Tavabob (Ch Seedfield Meritor Superflash ex Tavaclaire, sister of Ch Penda Tavatina) went to America and sired more than 15 American Champions.

Ch Killick of the Mess, superb top winning dog and RBIS at Crufts, also went to America. Losing such a fine dog made the possibility of freezing his semen an interesting point of conversation and exploration. Ch Baxee Jimmy the Won also went to America to gain his American and Canadian titles.

In 1985 Ch Townville Tristanian (having won eight CCs, seven RCCs, and BOB at Crufts) went to America to win BISs, BOBs and BIGs in the USA, Canada and South America. He sired Champions in England, USA, Brazil, Ecuador and Argentina.

Ch Libwyre Crime of Passion.

In 1987 Libwyre's Blackdale Stardust won nine All Breed BISs and 30 Groups and Specialities. He also sired several champions.

In 1989 Am Ch Sunspryte Peter's Piper went to Denmark to be serviced by her great-grandsire ASm, Canadian, NL, Int, EUSG, BDSG Ch Wiredresst Wait and See. At the two shows she went to she won BOB each time. Ch Sunspryte's Prime Contender won the Best American Bred Dog in 1988 and 1989.

By 1989 Am and Eng Ch Louline Head Over Heals had won the Reserve in Terrier Group Crufts 1988, and went on to win 75 Groups and 18 All Breed BISs. He is an excellent sire, one example being Ch Albany Guywire To Redoak, who gained his title at only one year of age.

The most recent winning stock from the UK includes such dogs as Ch Louline Stringalong, Ch Louline Peterman and Louline Pemberton, the latter gaining BOB at the Hatboro Kennel Club Show on Montgomery Co Weekend, handled by George Ward. Also doing well are Ch Davwin Danny Boy, Ch Burrendale Escort of Purston, Ch Rayfos Secret Service and Ch Casper Libra.

Ch Registry's Lonsome Dove, an American-bred Wire, is the top winning Terrier of all time, with 212 BIS wins.

The year 1992 brought many Group wins to Libwyre Spy Master. Ch Redoak's Lancelot (by Ch Louline Head Over Heels) has won many groups and some BISs in 1993. American Ch Rayfos Secret Service

Ch Libwyre Midnight Marauder (Eng/Am Ch Louline Pemberton ex Ch Libwyre Crime of Passion).

Am/Can Ch Holmwire Vitoka Vanessa.

won the Breed Class at the Montgomery Show from an entry of 105 dogs, and he also won Group 3.

The competition in America is extremely keen and the standard of presentation excellent. An owner or handler has to have a particularly outstanding dog and do a superb job of training, conditioning, grooming, presenting and handling to stand any chance of beating the professional handlers.

Exporting dogs

Considerable stress and neglect can be suffered by dogs travelling long distances, especially by air on longhaul flights. Sometimes young dogs are shipped with little or no experience of the outside world, to be faced suddenly with a different language, climate and surroundings.

The dog is boxed two hours before departure. There can easily be an hour's tarmac delay for technical reasons, and on arrival the authorities can take three hours or more going through the formalities. During all this time the dog may not get any water and may be left out in the heat.

My recent experience in this connection was when I flew my dogs to Scotland for the show at Ingliston. It was a very hot sunny morning and the dogs were left on

Wires sometimes experience more difficulty than Smooths in adapting to climatic changes. It is obvious that, as far as this one is concerned, all that is needed is a refreshing nap.
Photo: Animals Unlimited.

the tarmac in the sunshine. The baggage handlers were not working because it was a Saturday. The area was out of bounds and I could do nothing to get the dogs moved into the shade or collect them. It was a very distressing situation.

When working with the airlines I saw many statistics about animal casualties in flight and the neglect they suffered at transit stops. The problems did not only arise on the tarmac: animals have been frozen to death in-flight and water has been found to be frozen hard. (I have known the passenger water also to be frozen, but this is more exceptional.) Whilst more care is taken these days, I think there is still some reason to be apprehensive for the dog, especially on longhaul routes. In particular, it would seem to be a good idea to take care, if possible, not to send the dog by air when the weather is likely to be excessively hot, cold or windy, so that there is less chance of further discomfort and delay occasioned by unscheduled stops.

There was one occasion when a dog was found in the cockpit with the captain on a cargo flight. When going through the list of animals on board it was found that no dogs were listed; it was a wolf!

Fewer problems arise on board modern air liners and more care is taken generally. Nowadays there are companies which specialise in the safe international transportation of animals by air and will take every care of your dog during his or her journey. There was a recent case of a passenger liner making an unscheduled and expensive stop because the cooling system in the hold was faulty and a live dog was being carried.

Dogs do not hate all forms of international travel. The carriage of dogs across the Atlantic reminds me of an American dog that went sailing with his owners in the Adriatic. He seemed to enjoy it.

Climatic changes

Another problem is the effect the climate has on the dog. Although some dogs might be quite resilient we do hear of others who looked beautiful in this country but never regained their coats in other climatic conditions. Heat related problems can be very distressing for the dog, particularly in hot climates where there may be little veterinary expertise on these matters. This is one more factor which must be taken into consideration when export is considered.

Astona Boogie.
Photo: Diane Pearce.

3

Fox terrier
Breed standard

The British Breed Standards for the Fox Terrier (Wire) and Fox Terrier (Smooth) are quoted in full below, by kind permission of The Kennel Club. However, since it is sometimes difficult to describe a 'picture' in words, I have also given a summary of the points to look out for and some drawings to give some idea of the overall appearance.

The Breed Standard for the Fox Terrier (Wire)

General Appearance: Active and lively, bone and strength in small compass, never cloddy or coarse. Conformation to show perfect balance; in particular this applies to the relative proportions of skull and foreface, and similarly height at withers and length of body from shoulder point to buttocks appear approximately equal. Standing like a short-backed hunter covering a lot of ground.

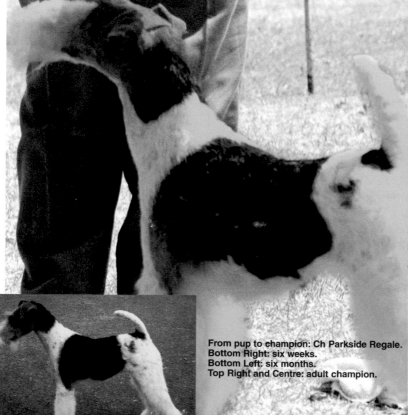

From pup to champion: Ch Parkside Regale.
Bottom Right: six weeks.
Bottom Left: six months.
Top Right and Centre: adult champion.

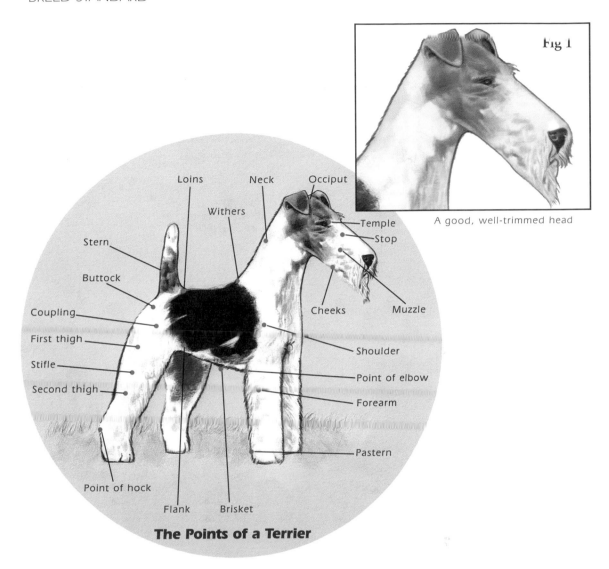

Fig 1

A good, well-trimmed head

The Points of a Terrier

Characteristics: Alert, quick of movement, keen of expression, on tiptoe of expectation at slightest provocation.

Temperament: Friendly, forthcoming and fearless.

Head and Skull: (see Fig 1) Topline of skull almost flat, sloping slightly and gradually decreasing in width towards eyes. Little difference in length between skull and foreface. If foreface is noticeably shorter head looks weak and unfinished. Foreface gradually tapering from eye to muzzle and dipping slightly at its juncture with forehead but not dished or falling away quickly below eyes where it should be full and well made up. Excessive bony or muscular development of jaws undesirable and unsightly. Full and rounded contour of cheeks undesirable. Nose black.

Eyes: Dark, full of fire and intelligence, moderately small and not prominent. As near circular in shape as possible. Not too far apart nor too high in skull nor too near ears. Light eyes highly undesirable.

Ears: Small, V-shaped, of moderate thickness, flaps neatly folded over and dropping forward close to cheeks. Top line of folded ears well above level of skull. Prick, tulip or rose ears highly undesirable.

Mouth: Jaws strong with perfect, regular and complete scissor bite, ie upper teeth closely overlapping lower teeth and set square to the jaws.

Neck: Clean, muscular, of fair length, free from throatiness, broadening to shoulders, presenting a graceful curve when viewed from side.

Fig 2: Conformation, front view

RIGHT: Stands straight in front. Legs parallel and the correct distance apart. Elbows flat against the ribs and directly under shoulder blades. Legs move straight like a pendulum.

WRONG: Legs too wide apart, shoulders too heavy and muscular.

WRONG: Chest too narrow, tied in at elbows, throws feet outwards when moving.

WRONG: Out at elbow, loose in shoulder, will weave when moving.

Forequarters: (see Fig 2) Seen from front, shoulders slope steeply down from junction with neck towards points which should be fine; viewed from side, long and well laid back and sloping obliquely backwards. Withers always clean-cut. Chest deep, not broad. Viewed from any direction, legs straight, bone strong right down to feet. Elbows perpendicular to body, working free of sides, carried straight when moving.

Body: Back short, level and strong without slackness, loin muscular, slightly arched. Brisket deep, front ribs moderately arched, rear ribs deep, well sprung. Very short coupled.

Fig 3: Conformation, side view

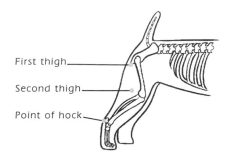

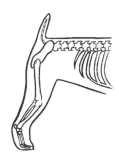

First thigh

Second thigh

Point of hock

RIGHT: Well bent stifle joining, with well muscled thighs. Hocks perpendicular and close to the ground.

WRONG: Straight stifle, narrow thigh, no muscle and nothing behind the tail. The hocks are not straight.

WRONG: Similar, but disguised by hair in the Wire Fox Terrier. These faults become apparent when the judge goes over the dog by feeling the bone structure.

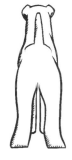

RIGHT: Tail set correct, on top of back. Well muscled thighs, hocks perpendicular, standing correctly (not too wide or too close).

WRONG: No muscle on thighs, short and straight stifle, feet in front of the hocks (out of perpendicular) thus making dog stand on its heels instead of its toes.

WRONG: Cow hocked (bent inwards). Low tail set, hocks to ground too long. Feet again in front of the hock (out of Perpendicular).

WRONG: Tail set correctly, better hocks, but bent inwards (toes outwards). Better length second stifle and more muscle on thighs. The flexing of the stifle joint and hocks develops the thigh muscles.

Fig 4: Conformation, rear view

Fig 5: Tails

Good set-on

Go-away

Low-set and straight stifle

Hindquarters: (see Fig 3 and 4) Strong, muscular and free from droop or crouch. Thighs long and powerful. Stifles well bent, turning neither in nor out. Hocks well let down, upright and parallel when viewed from the rear. Combination of short second thigh and straight stifle highly undesirable.

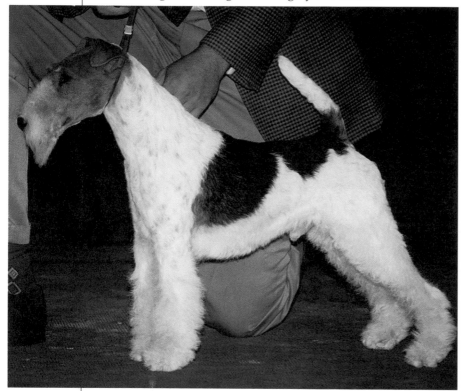

Ch Valken Downtown Boy. Good conformation: a Wire 'standing'. Note the deep chest, long, powerful thighs and well set-on tail.

Feet: Round, compact with small, tough and well cushioned pads, toes moderately arched. Turning neither in nor out.

Tail: (see Fig 5) Customarily docked. Set high, carried erect, not over back nor curled. Of good strength and fair length.

Gait/Movement: Fore- and hindlegs move straight forward and parallel. Elbows move perpendicular to body, working free of sides. Stifles turning neither in nor out. Good drive coming from well flexing hindquarters.

Coat: Dense, very wiry texture, 2cm (³⁄₄in) long on shoulder to 4cm (1¹⁄₂in) on withers, back, ribs and quarters with an undercoat of short, softer hair. Back and quarters harsher than sides. Hair on jaws crisp and of sufficient length to impart appearance of strength to foreface. Leg hair dense and crisp.

Colour: White predominates with black, black and tan or tan markings. Brindle, red, liver or slate blue marking undesirable.

Size: Height at withers not exceeding 39cm (15^1/$_2$in) in dogs, bitches slightly less. Ideal weight in show condition 8.25kg (18lb) for dogs, bitches slightly less.

Faults: Any departure from the foregoing points should be considered a fault and the seriousness with which the fault should be regarded should be in exact proportion to its degree.

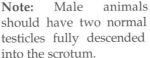

A well-conformed Smooth.
Photo: Anne Roslin-Williams.

Note: Male animals should have two normal testicles fully descended into the scrotum.

© The Kennel Club, March 1994

A good Smooth head.
Photo: Anne Roslin-Williams.

The Breed Standard for the Fox Terrier (Smooth)

General Appearance: Active and lively, bone and strength in small compass, never cloddy or coarse. Neither leggy nor too short in the leg, standing like a well-made, short-backed hunter, covering a lot of ground.

Characteristics: Alert, quick of movement, keen of expression, on tiptoe of expectation.

Fig 6: **Head Faults**

Dish-face

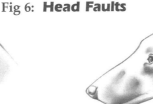

Overshot

Undershot

Roman nose

Fig 7: **Conformation, front view**

RIGHT: Shoulders fine, legs equal distance apart

WRONG: Broader shoulders, legs too close at the feet.

WRONG: Narrow shoulders, feet too wide apart.

Temperament: Friendly, forthcoming and fearless.

Head and Skull: (see Figs 6 and 8) Skull flat, moderately narrow, gradually decreasing in width to eyes. A little stop apparent, cheeks never full, jaws, upper and lower, strong and muscular, falling away only slightly below eyes. This portion of foreface moderately chiselled out, so as not to go down in a straight line like a wedge.

Eyes: Dark, small and rather deeply set, as near as possible circular in shape. Expression bright and intelligent.

Ears: Small, V-shaped and dropping forward close to cheeks, not hanging by side of head. Fold of ear above level of skull. Leather of moderate thickness.

Mouth: (See Fig 6) Jaws strong with a perfect, regular and complete scissor bite, ie upper teeth closely overlapping lower teeth and set square to the jaws.

Neck: Clean and muscular, without throatiness, of fair length and gradually widening to shoulders.

Good head and skull

Cheekiness

Fig 8: **Head and skull**

Gedstar Daisy Patch.
Photo: David Bull, *Dog World*.

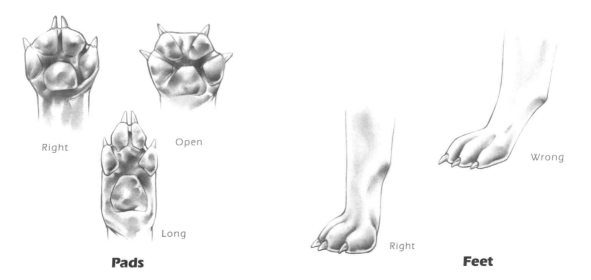

Right   Open

Long

Pads

Right

Wrong

Feet

Fig 9: **Feet**

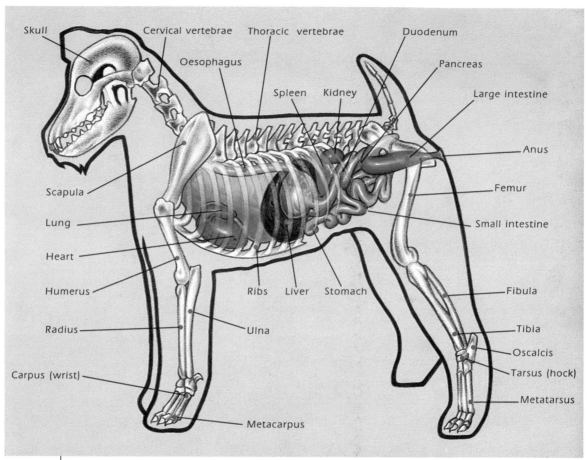

Skull

Cervical vertebrae

Thoracic vertebrae

Duodenum

Oesophagus

Pancreas

Spleen Kidney

Large intestine

Scapula

Anus

Lung

Femur

Heart

Small intestine

Humerus

Ribs Liver Stomach

Fibula

Radius

Ulna

Tibia

Oscalcis

Carpus (wrist)

Tarsus (hock)

Metatarsus

Metacarpus

More than skin deep: the inner organs of a Fox Terrier.

Fig 10: **Conformation, side view**

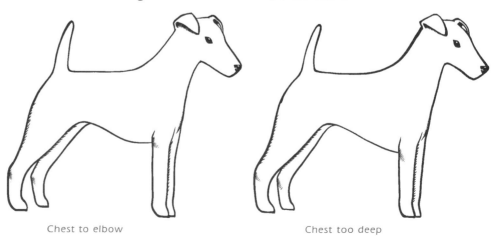

Chest to elbow

Chest too deep

Forequarters: Shoulders long and sloping, well laid back, fine at points, cleanly cut at withers. Legs from any angle must be straight showing little or no appearance of an ankle in front. They should be strong in bone throughout.

Body: (see Figs 10 and 11) Chest deep, not broad. Back short, level and strong without slackness. Loin powerful, very slightly arched. Foreribs moderately sprung, back ribs deep.

Hindquarters: Strong and muscular, quite free from droop or crouch; thighs long and powerful, hocks well let down, good turn of stifle.

Feet: (See Fig 9) Small, round and compact. Soles hard and tough, toes moderately arched, and turning neither in nor out.

Tail: Customarily docked. Set on rather high and carried gaily, but not over back, or curled. Of good strength.

Gait/Movement: Fore- and hindlegs carried straight forward and parallel. Elbows move perpendicular to body, working free of sides, stifles neither turning in nor out and hocks not close. Good drive coming from well flexing hindquarters.

Coat: Straight, flat, smooth, hard, dense and abundant. Belly and underside of thighs not bare.

Colour: White should predominate, all white, white with tan, black and tan or black markings. Brindle, red or liver markings highly undesirable.

Size: Weight: dogs: 7.3-8.2kg (16-18lb); bitches: 6.2-7.7kg (15-17lb).

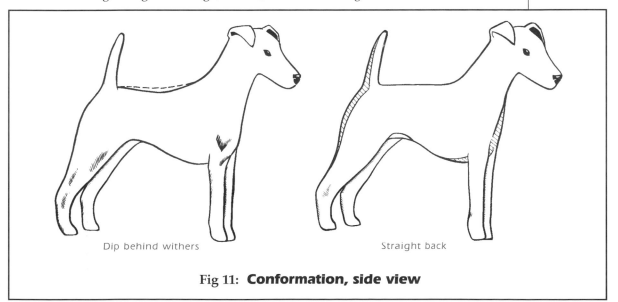

Dip behind withers   Straight back

Fig 11: Conformation, side view

Faults: Any departure from the foregoing points should be considered a fault and the seriousness with which the fault should be regarded should be in exact proportion to its degree.

Note: Male animals should have two normal testicles fully descended into the scrotum.

© The Kennel Club, March 1994

Explanation of the standards

As might be expected, the major difference between these two standards is in the description of the coat. Another difference exists in that the ideal size of a Smooth is given in weight only, not height.

When judges look at the dogs and assess the quality according to the Standard there will always be differences of opinion. For example the dogs with the longer and thinner heads will probably be taller and longer in the back than a dog with a smaller head. The judge has to decide which dog to choose, and he then looks at the overall balance of the dog.

General Appearance: The Fox Terrier is happy, lively and active. He has to have good bone and strength without being thick or coarse. He must look fit for his job: hunting the fox or rabbit and going to earth. If he is too big or thick he cannot go down the fox-hole.

General Characteristics: He should look bright, alert, able to move quickly and ready to react to the slightest provocation.

Temperament: He is a happy, friendly, forthcoming dog who fears nothing and knows his own mind.

Head and Skull: The main feature of the dog is the long lean head. The top of the skull is flat and moderately narrow, gradually decreasing in width to the eyes. The foreface is slightly longer than the skull and tapers gradually from the eye to the muzzle. There is not much stop (the dip at the juncture of the muzzle with the forehead). There should be a dip in the profile between the forehead and the top jaw which should not go down in a straight line like a wedge. It is important there is no falling away below the eyes, where it should be full and well made up. Bony or muscular jaws are ugly, and full and rounded cheeks are undesirable. The nose is black.

Eyes: Round, dark, bright and intelligent. They should be moderately small and not too prominent. A light coloured eye is a fault.

Ears: Prick, tulip or rose ears are faults.

Mouth: An undershot or overshot bite is a fault.

Neck: Should be long, clean, slightly arched (like a horse being schooled) strong and free from throatiness, gradually broadening to the shoulder.

Shoulders: From the front they should slope downwards from their juncture with the neck towards the points, which should be fine. Viewed from the side they should be long, and should slope back obliquely from the points to the withers, which should be cleanly cut.

Chest: Deep and neither too broad nor too narrow. Excessive depth of chest will impede a Terrier going to ground.

Body: Short and level with no dip in the middle. Loin strong and firm, slightly arched. Brisket deep but not broad. Ribs should be rounded rather than flat in front, rear ribs deep, well sprung. Very short coupled.

Hindquarters: A good bend of stifle is essential for good movement. When moving the legs must go absolutely straight, not turning inward or outward. The hocks should be near the ground, upright and parallel.

Feet: Small and round with thick hard pads close together.

Tail: Customarily docked level with the skull. It should spring from the top rather than the back of the body and is carried up straight, not over the back or curled. It should be strong and quite thick. A thin tail is undesirable.

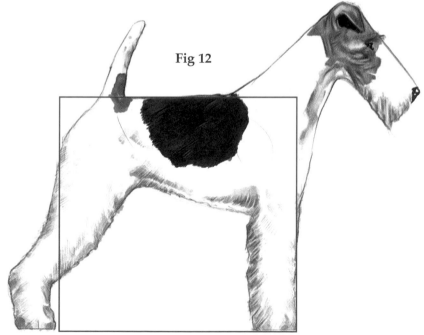

Fig 12

The Fox Terrier should fit into a square.

Legs: Should be straight, the bone of the fore-legs strong and thick right down to the feet. The elbows should be perpendicular to the body, working free from the sides. When moving the legs should be straight and not weaving.

Movement: The Terrier's legs should be carried straight forward while moving, the fore-legs changing perpendicular and swinging parallel with the sides. The principal propulsive power is from the hind legs. The best action is found when the Terrier has long thighs and muscular second thighs well curved at the stifles, giving a strong forward thrust or 'snatch' of the hocks. If the dog is out at shoulder the fore-feet cross, weave or dish. If the dog is tied at shoulder the feet move wider apart with a sort of paddling action. When hocks are turned in (cow hock) the stifles and feet are turned out, resulting in a loss of power. When the hocks are turned out the hind feet cross, resulting in an ungainly waddle.

Coat: The lengths quoted in the Standard for the Wires are intended as a guide to exhibitors rather than an infallible rule.

Colour: White should predominate for both breeds, brindle, red, liver or slate-blue being objectionable. Otherwise colour is of little or no importance.

Size: Height at withers approximately 39cm (15$\frac{1}{2}$in) in dogs, bitches slightly less. Ideal weight in show condition 8.25kg (18lb), bitches slightly less.

Disqualifying Points: Nose white, cherry or spotted. Ears prick, tulip or rose. Mouth greatly undershot or overshot.

Note: Male animals should have two normal testicles fully descended into the scrotum. Old scars or injuries, the result of work or accident, should not be allowed to interfere with its movement or with its utility for work or stud.

The American Wire and Smooth Standards
In 1984 The American Fox Terrier Club drew up two separate Standards to change the status of the Smooth and Wire from two varieties of the same breed to two separate breeds so that there could be two winners in 'Specials'. These new Standards were approved by the American Kennel Club on 11 December 1984 and became effective in June 1985.

The American Smooth Standard is similar to ours, but shortened in places and with a different lay-out. It states that weight is not the prime factor in deciding on the Terrier's fitness for the work. He must not be too leggy nor too short in the leg. Shape, size and contour are the criteria. The height is put as 15$\frac{1}{2}$in at withers, length of back to root of tail not more than 12in, head should be not more than 7$\frac{1}{2}$in or less than 7in. A dog of this size should weigh 18lb in show condition, a bitch 2lb less, with a margin of one pound either way. It also states that bitches may weigh 2lb less than a dog, with a margin of 1lb either way.

The ideal balance is when the proportions of skull/foreface and height/length of body are correct. The height/length of body should fit in a square (see Fig 12), height at withers being equal to length from shoulder-point to buttock.

The American Wire Standard makes reference to ear carriage as showing the character. (Ears go back when he is cross.) The skull should not exceed $3^1/2$in in diameter at its widest point. Wider than this is 'coarse' and a dog with a much narrower skull is 'bitchy'. The head is measured with callipers and should be from $7-7^1/2$in from the top of the head to the nostrils. Any longer measurement usually indicates an over-sized dog or one which is too long in the back. Little difference in length of skull and foreface. If the eyes are too high or too near the ears it is a fault as being 'foreign' in appearance. Slackness in the back is described as a dip behind the withers or to the flanks when there is too much space between the back ribs and the hip bone. A short space here is described as 'short-coupled' or 'well-ribbed up'. On coat it refers to 'crinkly' hair on some hard coats; a curly coat is incorrect. Optimum weights and sizes are similar to those for the Smooth.

The 'Disqualifying Points' for both are listed as Nose - white, cherry or spotted to a considerable extent with either of these colours. Ears - prick, tulip or rose Mouth - much undershot or much overshot.

The scale of points for the two breeds differs as follows:

	Wire	Smooth
Head and Ears	10	15
Neck	5	5
Shoulder and Chest	10	10
Back and Loins	10	10
Hind Quarters	10	15
Stern	5	5
Legs and Feet	10	15
Coat	10	15
Symmetry, Size and Character	15	10
Movement	15	
	100	100

4

Character & **Personality**

In 1899 *The Stable*, a weekly sporting paper, described the Fox Terrier thus:

> *No one will dispute the right of the Fox Terrier to figure first in the ranks of popular breeds. Attractive in appearance, cheerful in disposition, ever alert, and always displaying his powers, he is the beau ideal of a canine companion. Take him into the show ring, and the fire and energy of the breed at once become apparent, while in the family circle he is always the prime favourite, and leading artists constantly depict how popular the Fox Terrier has become.*

The anecdotes below will show how true this description still is today.

Long and healthy lives

As not many Fox Terriers are bred, over-breeding is not a problem, so they tend to be fit and well. Visits to the veterinary surgeon are rare and Fox Terriers generally live long, happy lives, often remaining very active at 10 years of age.

Beautiful and friendly

They are beautiful to look at and have lovely expressions as puppies which they keep throughout their lives. Cheerful and bright-eyed, they will protect you by chasing intruders away, but will be extremely welcoming and friendly towards friends, often kissing them or putting a paw gently on their hand.

There was one occasion on which my Mischief tried to carry friendliness a little too far. We were out walking together when we met ... a lion! Yes, this is perfectly true. It was in the days when regulations about keeping dangerous pets were less strict, and this lion was very tame, and regularly accompanied his owner on outings. He certainly looked peaceful enough, and Mischief was very keen to go and sniff noses with him. The lion's owner advised against it, however!

Fox Terriers retain their lovely expressions throughout their lives.
Photo: Isabelle Français.

THE FOX TERRIER

Good companions at home and at work

Fox Terriers are wonderful companions and adapt very well to changing situations. They are gregarious and like going out and about with their owner. Car rides are greatly enjoyed and, when they accompany their owners to work, to the pub, to visit friends or to have a picnic, they normally behave well. A farm is particularly suited to them. When I worked at a Probation Hostel, Mischief was a good companion and guard dog, and did not need any training for it.

Fox Terriers make wonderful companions.

He had another use too. On one particular occasion there was a large rat of which everyone was afraid. I confidently told my boss that Mischief would get it. At lunch time Mischief saw the rat by the bonfire, quickly grabbed it and then teased it, whereupon it bit his nose rather badly. Mischief let go momentarily but watched carefully and then, leaping right across the bonfire, pounced straight onto the rat, killing it instantly.

Fox Terriers often love to sleep inside the bedclothes. When they get too hot they have a rest on the floor before another session under the duvet This should not happen every night, or the dog will soon think he is the boss. Each dog needs to be treated as 'special' every now and again, however, and enjoys that bit of extra attention, whether it be bed, grooming, a dog show or something else.

The hunting instinct

These dogs still have a very strong hunting instinct. They will hunt fox, deer, rabbits, rats, mice, pigeons, squirrel, or anything else that looks fun to chase. It does happen sometimes that if they pick up a scent they can be off for half an hour or more. In a few minutes they can turn from a pet into a wild dog. The expression changes and they run and behave like a fox. Anyone attempting to get near the dog in these circumstances will probably not succeed. Once the chase is over they will respond to the owner. A whistle is the best means of calling them, and they can usually be found where you last saw them, or where you parked the car. Because of the Terrier's love of chasing anything that moves, if someone is throwing a ball for their dog I quickly put mine on the lead. If the other dog is running about too excitedly I ask the owner to try to keep it calm while I catch mine. On our walks

Other members of the household, human and animal alike, are accepted. They particularly enjoy the company of other Fox Terriers.
Photo: Isabelle Français.

through the woods it is usually the bitches who find something to chase first and lead the rest of the gang on. Terriers love to chase cats but it is seldom that a confrontation takes place, and every effort should be made to avoid it. However, the cat usually runs up a tree, whereupon the dog gives up the chase.

Other pets in the household

There is no problem about having other pets in the household. Obviously they need watching but they know who the members of the household are. However, it is important that other livestock is secure when the dog is not being supervised until it is obvious that it can be trusted.

Watersports: Fox Terriers enjoy chasing and tugs of war. For many, if water is involved, so much the better!
Photo: Ursy Burnand.

A Fox Terrier Fun Day.
Photo: M Bird.

Have fun

On being let off the lead out on the common the first thing my Fox Terriers do is to chase each other for fun. They also chase and tease each other in the garden and enjoy tugs of war.

Young dogs can have bursts of tearing round the house, jumping over every bit of furniture. Luckily this does not happen too often. They are energetic so when they get too boisterous they need a good walk to calm them down.

Adorable, a beauty, a darling

The Fox Terrier likes company, with plenty of love, attention and activity. He is so endearing that I feel the Alphabet song we used to hear describes the breed perfectly; it starts:

CHARACTER AND PERSONALITY

A you're Adorable
B you're so Beautiful
C you're a Cutie in my arms
D you're a Darling etc.

The Rev Dr Rosslyn Bruce also wrote one, which was published in *The Smooth Fox Terrier Association Year Book, Vol VII, 1946/47*, and thereafter revised:

A for my Action straight, spritely and sound,
B for my Bone which is ample and round;
C for my Coat, Smooth, abundant and hard,
D for Distemper, which I'm bred to discard;
E for my Ears and Eyes, lively and small,
F for my Feet, hardly showing at all;
G for my Gameness with fox or with vermin
H for my Head, which my parents determine;
I for In-breeding, if one's line is quite sound,
J for my Jaw for use underground;
K for my Kennelman, skilful and handy,
L for my Legs, neither knock-kneed nor bandy;
M for my Muscles on quarters and back,
N for my Nose, which is keen, and is black;
O for my Owner, who glories in winners,
P for the Prize cards, which comfort beginners;
Q for the Questions concerning our merits,
R for Replies from the rats and the ferrets;
S for my Shoulders, fine, sloping and long,
T for my Teeth, close fitting and strong;
U for the Use which I prove in all sport,
V for the Value "of such a good sort";
W for White, which must always predominate,
X precedes the dam that you nominate;
Y for my Youth which ever is manifest,
Z for your Zeal for me, British and Best.

The Fox Terrier is an ideal pet for a child: Jamie with Flyntwyre Flyntlock Simon, both aged five.

Playing with children

The Fox Terrier is an ideal pet for a child. Not too big, he is full of fun and loves to tease and be teased. He likes playing with children and will put up with a great deal and, although extremely active, he can be quiet when it is necessary.

Fox Terriers like to be entertained and play all kinds of games. Sometimes they have pretend fights, growling playfully with you and gently biting your hand. They love chasing the water hose or broom, and enjoy a tug of war with old tights, rag or newspaper. They also like chasing a ball, but they are not so keen on retrieving.

We had one Wire that escaped continually. At a stables some two miles away the owner telephoned the police about the dangerous dog in the yard. While on the phone he found his four-year-old child pulling the dog backwards with a rope attached to his hind leg. The 'dangerous dog' was thoroughly enjoying the attention he was getting from the youngster.

Photo: Anne Rosslin-Williams.

Children are clever at thinking up games and Fox Terriers are always ready and willing to join in. One day as I was walking with my dogs through a housing estate some children wanted to play with them. I said I would return that way. When I came back I found they had created an agility course for them. Each child took a dog and they went along happily with the children. Even when led out of my sight the dogs behaved and did not pull away to chase a cat, or even to find me. They were obviously having fun with their new young friends.

Some less desirable 'games'

The male dog has it all worked out. He sometimes advances towards a large dog and the moment that dog even looks at him he puts his legs up in the air and screams 'murder' before anything has happened. Everyone thinks that he is badly hurt, and he hopes that the other dog will be punished. There is another 'game' which he plays at dog shows. It can be quite crowded, and, despite being under tight control, he reaches out to nip a big dog. When it yelps he acts as if he cannot imagine why. This is mischief rather than aggression, and is not unusual Terrier behaviour, but it obviously has to be stopped. It is partly a protective reaction. If any dog is held tight on the lead it senses danger and promptly reacts defensively.

Intelligent

The Terrier is quick on the uptake and, if he wants to do something, he will do it. Escaping and stealing are two fine examples of his expertise. If he wants to learn, he only has to be shown once, and he remembers his lessons for the rest of his life. He will do almost anything for food, and loves showing off. He is a superb actor: when he is cross with you he will send the message loud and clear by pulling his ears back and looking furious.

Many people do not like to see dogs doing tricks, but some Terriers really enjoy performing them. I had a dog that did numerous ones, such as: 'sit up', 'dead dog', 'walk on hind legs', 'shut the door', 'roll over', 'ask', and 'shake hands'. He loved doing these and would not eat his meal unless he had done his full quota.

My elderly bitch learned a few tricks from Mischief. I very rarely ask her to perform, but if asked she remembers and performs them instantly, even after a five-year gap. On the rare occasions when she has been away from home she has used this expertise to endear herself to the new company.

Small puppies are quick to learn about 'spending' outside. The fact they may take a long time to do it is another matter. They have lots of other things to do first.

Dogs learn from each other, and the old ones will tell the younger ones off for bad behaviour. On the other hand, if I tell one dog off for something, the others will all put their tails down and go to their beds as if they too are guilty.

'Little Red Riding-hood.' Fox Terriers are great actors and love attention, so they do not mind being dressed up.

When it comes to road sense they have none. While walking on the lead they are aware that cars and lorries are dangerous, but if something worth chasing catches their eye when they are off the lead then that is the only thing on their minds. For this reason accidents can happen even when you think you are far away from a road.

The other danger area is getting into and out of cars. The dog is very excited on these occasions and, unless he is on a lead, he could easily use this opportunity to chase something, running across a busy road in the process.

The protector

Fox Terriers are superb house dogs, very protective towards owner and property. They know when to bark and whom to let in. They hate being stared at by passers-by, but are happy to have friends who stop to talk to them through the gate.

Once when some rough youths were playing in the car park Mischief thought they were up to no good. He approached them and made it clear they should behave in a normal manner. They swore at him but he bravely stood his ground until they had calmed down. The moment I called him he came, and the youths left quietly and did not return.

Another incident occurred on the common when a stranger came out from the bushes. The dogs scatter widely on walks, but Traffy spotted potential trouble and quickly came between me and the stranger, making it clear he was not to take one step nearer.

The favourite frolic

After a show, when they all look beautifully trimmed and white, there is nothing my Fox Terriers love more than to go for a walk in the woods, roll in some fox mess, and jump into the nearest dirty pool for a swim and a drink. When I am a little sensitive about them getting so dirty I try and choose a cleaner route. That does not worry them, however; they just find a new dirty ditch! Heart-breaking perhaps, but seeing their cheerful faces makes it seem more acceptable.

Jealous

Terriers are extremely jealous; if one gets attention, the others must also. They actually watch to see and note who is getting what. This may produce either a strong protest or a fit of the sulks.

The brightest and the best

These bright little dogs always keep you happy and are beautiful to behold. This is soothing and good for your well-being. I would never be without a Fox Terrier, and cherish to this day the memory of my first one, Grubby. I cuddled him on the stairs, fed titbits to him when I did not like my meals, took him for nice walks, and generally had super fun with him. He came to school Open Days and enjoyed playing with all the children. It was really upsetting when he did not recognise me dressed up as Bottom in *A Midsummer Night's Dream*; it must have been either because the acting was so good or because the clothes were so smelly. I think the latter is more likely.

CHARACTER AND PERSONALITY

Grubby became blind in due course, but his nose was so good he could go anywhere without running into anything. He loved to look into the log fire, and we often wondered whether that had affected his eye sight. We do not have that luxury now, but if a radiator or any other heat source is switched on, there the dogs will rest. The Fox Terrier is the ideal companion; when treated as an equal he behaves as one.

**Mummy, Daddy and Me: family likeness between three alert Smooth Fox Terriers.
Photo: Ursy Burnand.**

5

Buying a Puppy

Responsible dog ownership

Before thinking of buying a puppy, first consider whether you have the time and energy to cope with it. Puppies are fun. They are also time-consuming and demanding, requiring fresh air, exercise, good food, and a high degree of tolerance, and they will have to be trained.

Any first-time dog owner would be wise to go to weekly dog training classes as soon as the puppy has been inoculated. There are two alternatives: Obedience or Ringcraft classes. Even if you do not intend showing, Ringcraft is preferable, because the Terrier responds better to this type of training. Classes provide a good meeting point to discuss problems, and owner and dog train together. This can do a great deal to prevent problems later on, as the owner hopefully learns how to prevent the dog from becoming 'pack leader'.

One really important rule in dog ownership today is always to pick up any mess the dog deposits outside, put it in a plastic bag and leave it in a dog bin provided or take it home. It should also be picked up quickly in the garden because it is an unpleasant mess which the dog sometimes eats. In any case, someone may tread in it and deposit some on the carpets.

All puppies are delightful, but it is important to find out about the breed before you buy one. Photo: Lynn Bell.

Getting the right breed

To avoid making any mistakes when taking on a long term commitment of this sort, it is worth reading about the breeds you like and asking owners of these breeds about their dogs before making a final decision. When you have made your decision telephone a few breeders and seek their guidance and advice.

Outings

If you have decided that you would like a Fox Terrier the first consideration is: can you cope with it for 10-15 years or so? Can you stand being tied by a dog? It restricts what you can do and where you can go. For example it is not as easy as it used to be to take dogs to the pub, as most of them serve meals now. The warmer summers make it impossible to leave the dog in the car. Four minutes sitting in a car on a hot day can be too hot for humans sometimes.

Team bed-making: it is important to see your puppy with its dam and litter-mates before you make your selection. Photo: Lynn Bell.

There are now many restrictions on dogs at the seaside, parks and public gardens. Even if dogs on the lead are allowed in some of these places, they still need somewhere 'wild' where they can run freely and let off steam. Obviously there are many Fox Terriers that do not have this luxury, but the healthier their lives the better they will be. They do get bouts of surplus energy; if this can be released on a nice run in the woods they settle down quietly. Can you take your dog on visits to friends or relations? Does a dog fit into your lifestyle without being left alone too often?

Holidays

You need to have some idea about what you can do about annual holidays. Many hotels and 'Bed and Breakfast' establishments in this country will take pets, and guide books listing these are available.

If a trip abroad is planned and the dog needs to go to boarding kennels, it is worth finding out something about the local kennels. Ask your friends if they are satisfied with them. It can be difficult for a pet dog used to freedom suddenly to be kennelled.

Is your domestic situation settled?

The one thing we do not want is for the dog to land up at the RSPCA or the Rescue Centre because of domestic upheaval. Divorce, loss of job and small children are reasons often given for relinquishing the dog. Dogs make wonderful playmates for young children, but a puppy and a small baby can be too much for some mothers to handle. This can cause a great deal of sadness.

Expenses: can you afford a dog?

A good quality puppy from a show kennel costs £300-£400 to buy. Some may be more, others less. Sometimes puppies may be sold for considerably less; this may be because of domestic reasons and need for a quick sale, or there may be some less straightforward reason.

A Fox Terrier does not cost much to feed (about £2 per week) but other bills do mount up. Inoculations and veterinary bills are expensive, although the Fox Terrier seldom needs to see the vet unless he gets injured while hunting or has some other accident. Making the house and garden (or kennel and dog run) safe and puppy-proof areas may involve some expenditure, and there may also be some repair jobs. Puppies eat and chew everything, and special care is needed to ensure they cannot chew a live electric wire.

The garden must be made totally dog proof. Fox Terriers can be extremely clever at escaping and sometimes get stuck between fencing railings or into some other tight squeeze. They can jump, climb and dig to perfection; six-foot wire fencing is not always an obstacle to a stud dog or a bitch on heat. Despite this, although the unexpected can happen, usually it does not. Indeed, I had a dog that never went through the hedge no matter how great the provocation on the other side, and I know of other Wires similarly disposed. However we do have a public duty to make sure they do not get onto the roads and cause an accident. It is important to have third party insurance cover for pets, and this can be included under the household policy.

'Nelson' at 8½ weeks.

Puppy expenses

Before getting the puppy you will need to get a dog box with a door on the front that can be closed, and some comfortable bedding. This will be his bed and home for life. It is safer for travelling and he can be taken to friends in it without fear that he will damage their property. The box (or metal cage) is usually 38cm (15in) wide, 55cm (22in) long and 53cm (21in) high. To avoid carrying these out every time, I keep my dogs' boxes in the car, and additional 'beds' remain in the house.

Your puppy will also need food, treats (chocolate drops for example), dinner bowl and water bowl. He will need some toys and something hard and safe to chew and bite on, especially while he is teething; this is both soothing and necessary. Later on he will love squeaky toys which will be demolished in about two seconds.

Grooming equipment can be very expensive, but as a start have a comb, pin pad, stripping knife, nail clippers and a hard bristle brush. This will need building on as you discover more about grooming.

It is difficult to buy a collar of the right size before you have the puppy because its neck is so small, so it is best do so as soon as you have the puppy in your care.

Dog or bitch?

It is a good idea to try and decide whether you want a dog or a bitch, and whether you want a possible show dog or a pet. You should bear in mind that no-one can guarantee that a nice-looking puppy will turn into a show dog; you can only wait and see.

If the dog is wanted as a family pet I would choose a dog rather than a bitch. They are very devoted, love playing with children and will tolerate more than most breeds. They are protective and do not have moods.

Bitches are very sweet, but because of their cycle they have periods of being hunters and others periods of phantom pregnancy and nursing imaginary families. At these times they adopt toys or other objects as puppies, which could be a problem if it happened to be your child's favourite teddy bear. (See the sections on **Heat** and **False Pregnancies** in Chapter 6.)

A lively or a quiet puppy

What sort of temperament do you want: a fairly quiet puppy or one that is full of life? This must depend on your age and circumstances. The more space and garden you have the more energetic a dog you can keep but, no matter how large your garden, dogs do need to be taken out regularly. The best exercise is off the lead where possible, and it is even better if there are other dogs to play with and chase.

Where to find a puppy

It can be difficult to find a Fox Terrier puppy and it is not unusual to have to make a long journey to collect your puppy. The Kennel Club, in association with Healthcare Plan Puppy Insurance, now provides lists of people with puppies for sale. They can also give the names of Breed Club secretaries who often hear where there are litters.

Puppy Line have lists of current litters and they advertise in the weekly canine press. They work in association with Pet Plan insurance. These weekly papers come out on a Friday and are available in large news outlets or can be ordered from your local newsagent. Puppies are advertised in the back pages of these papers, but you rarely see Fox Terriers there.

It is strongly recommended that you buy a puppy direct from the breeder. Examine the rest of the litter and the breeder's other dogs to make sure you like their character and appearance before taking the big step of buying one.

Dogs or puppies reared in a private house will settle into new homes much more easily than those that have come from outside kennels. This is because they have been handled a lot more by people, they are used to the noises of domestic appliances and they have probably already had a certain amount of training and socialising.

Avoid buying a puppy from a dealer. (See the section in Chapter 8 on **Finding the Right Home.**) There are some unscrupulous dealers around who buy dogs from puppy farms purely for profit. In this case the young puppy may have been subjected to a long journey with complete strangers so could be badly traumatised. It may be in poor condition and not up to such treatment at this stage. The dealer will probably not be able to tell the new owners full details of the puppy's diet and they will not have access to the original breeder. This means that there is no one whom the new owners can approach for advice should the puppy refuse to eat, or become ill.

Such puppies are often sold too soon, sometimes at seven weeks or less, which does not give a puppy a good start in life.

Buying an older dog

If you want an older dog you may find one in the breed Rescue (get the name from a Breed Club secretary), the RSPCA or at kennels where they want to make room for younger show stock.

If you do this, get as much background information as you can about the dog, because it may take time, understanding and gentle training to get it used to its new circumstances. For example, kennel dogs may not be house trained, and they can be frightened by ordinary domestic noises. Calm, love, care, patience and understanding are needed and it may be months before the dog settles into the new system.

Show puppy

If you seriously want a puppy for show take advice from the breeder. Whilst no-one can say for certain how the young hopeful will turn out, the breeder is the best person to advise on its potential; he does not want a disaster to be seen in the ring.

It may be better to pay a little more and get an older puppy that is more mature. There can be no guarantee of success, even for the experts, but at least this may be a safer way to start. Consult the Breed Standard when looking at the puppy and try to make sure he has no blatant faults. Firstly he should have a good disposition and be friendly, forthcoming, alert and lively, with small, bright, round, dark eyes. His ears should be neatly folded on top of the head and not hanging down the

When making your selection, ask the breeder's advice, and look at the puppy's dam if possible. Photo: Diane Pearce.

side. His head should be long, lean, and flat on the top, with no signs of cheeks sticking out at the sides. Make sure that the puppy stands, shows and moves well.

For instance, the hocks should not turn in or out when he moves away from you, and the elbows should not turn out when he moves towards you. The legs should look absolutely straight and the feet small and round, and turning neither in nor out. He must have a good hard wire coat (furnishings on legs and face are better when the dog is older). A soft coat is incorrect, and harder to groom and keep clean. Look for a straight top line which has no dip in the back, tail set on top. Check the teeth are not overshot or undershot. Look for a good bend of stifle, a good length of

Above:
A Parkside litter at the dinner table.

Left:
'I know I left it somewhere!'
Photo: Lynn Bell.

neck which flows neatly into the back, good overall balance and a cheerful expression. It is difficult to find all these virtues in one dog so be prepared to make compromises. It is worth remembering too that the black on the head, and often on the legs too, gradually changes to tan over the next few months.

It has taken some breeders 40 years to get their first Challenge Certificate; these are not easily won. However if you start off with a good bitch, and take great care in the selection of the stud dog, you have a much better chance next time round when you show her daughter. (See Chapter 6: Breeding.)

As a general rule, dogs that have been reared for show are not treated as pets. They are often kept outside so that they are hardy and grow strong, thick coats. They need to be able to stand for hours on end, so sitting down for titbits is the last thing you want them to do; they have to stand and 'show' for their treats. They will not get petting and love in quite the same way as a pet dog; that 'pathetic' look will not win them any prizes if they decide to employ it in the ring. Therefore the show has to be their special treat, and preparation for the show is when they get their share of love and attention. They look at themselves in the mirror and bounce for joy when they are ready - and there is the show dog.

Make arrangement to see puppies

Having found one or two places where there are young puppies (or an older dog if you think that is more suitable) phone up and make arrangements to view. Do not go on the off chance, and if you are told there is no dog or puppy for sale do not be over-insistent.

On several occasions people have come to me, even on a Sunday, and demanded to take a dog away there and then. This is disturbing for the owner and disappointing for the client. Such clients should accept 'no' from the start. Admittedly when you see the dogs and the puppies it is hard to go away without one, but be realistic; the owner has the final say.

Show potential or the 'sweetheart'?

When choosing the puppy you could be faced with a dilemma. For example you might think you want one with some show potential (even if showing is unlikely to happen). Then one little puppy endears himself to you. What do you do? Do you take the one with possible show potential or do you take a nice-looking, happy and healthy puppy who appeals to you? I would go for the dog that chose me as he is going to live with me for the rest of his life.

Getting ready for the new arrival

So you have chosen a Fox Terrier puppy, having taken into consideration all the responsibilities that this will entail. The following is intended as a final list of points to consider before you pick up your puppy. Many of them have been mentioned elsewhere.

Dog-proofed garden and safe kennel area and run: Having made the garden dog-proof, for the safety of the puppy and because of the 'digging' period later on it is also advisable to make a little 'safe area' kennel and run.

Set behavioural boundaries: Before the puppy arrives have some idea of what you are prepared to let him do, what rooms he may go into, what special chair he may have (with an easily washable cover), which parts of the garden he may use, and where you hope he will relieve himself. Many of these ideas may change in due course. For example, you may vow 'he is not sleeping on my bed', then all of a sudden you cannot resist the temptation and he does. The problem with this is that the bed is every dog's idea of the best place to sleep. Once this becomes a habit the dog often becomes a 'dominant' dog and thereafter bosses the owner. For this reason, it is wise to keep your bed as a rare treat. (See Chapter 10: Training the young dog.)

The lawn may be another sensitive area if you get a bitch puppy because bitches' urine sometimes turns the grass brown. Although this can happen it need not be too devastating. If you want a really good lawn then this area may have to be out of bounds to the dog, but that would be a pity.

One major area of difficulty is when the dog comes back from a muddy walk. He does need to dry off in the utility room or kitchen before having access to the rest of the house. Most of the dirt drops off and can easily be brushed up, thus saving the carpets and furniture. Another way of dealing with this is to place a large piece of towelling or old curtain on the floor and when the dog is dry it can be shaken outside; in this way nothing is soiled. This is another case of thinking ahead rather than training the dog.

Dog box/cage: For his sake as well as yours, it really is essential to have an enclosed dog box or metal cage from the start. This is his bedroom where he feels secure. It is particularly useful to house train the young puppy and to keep him safe and avoid damage to your property when he is not being supervised. It further acts as an excellent means of obtaining obedience, because he loses his freedom to be with you.

Nursery: It is useful to have a 'safe' play area in the house: kitchen, utility room, or a play-pen.

Companionship: The young puppy needs companionship. In the wild he always has other dogs and puppies as playmates. If he has a canine companion so much the better; if not he will rely on you. Even before his inoculations are complete he can be amused by being taken out in a shopping bag, and he can also be taken for car rides to visit friends.

Toys: He needs plenty of toys to chew and chase so that he knows what he may and may not damage. Well knotted old tights or pieces of rag are good for tugs of war, and he will love to tear up paper. Marrow bones are good to chew, and you can get really hard chewing bones from the pet shop to keep him happy and amused. Companies such as Nylabone provide a range of toys designed to care for your dog's teeth as he plays.

Rubber bones, balls, garden plant pots, margarine tubs, rag dolls and cardboard rolls from toilet paper or kitchen towels all make good toys. Puppies are highly inventive when it comes to fun, too: they will have plenty more ideas about toys. For a start, they often like to pinch your slippers and underwear. Therefore, avoid trouble by giving them their own shoes or slippers and keeping the best ones for yourself!

Collecting your puppy

When you collect the puppy make sure you receive the signed Kennel Club Registration Certificate, a Diet Sheet and the Pedigree. Ask about inoculations and insurance cover. Get as much information as you can about rearing and training the puppy. Aim to do all the right things from the start so that you do not end up with a spoilt dog who will not cooperate with the vet or groomer and whom even you find hard to handle. Get some advice from the breeder on grooming and trimming and start as soon as you have the puppy.

Put the items listed under Puppy Expenses in a suitable place and take with you a box with a safe door on it and warm bedding to put the puppy in. (See also **Getting ready for the new arrival.**) As soon as you get home get in touch with the vet about completing the inoculations. In general it is a good idea to give the puppy time to settle into his new surroundings before being inoculated, but he should be looked over sooner if there is any doubt at all about his health. The puppy should not go out until fully inoculated. This really means he should not sniff dirty places, but could go to friends when supervised. (See also the section **Finding the right home** in Chapter 8.)

6

Breeding

Think first

Before allowing your bitch to have a litter think long and hard. If your motive is to sell some puppies and make a bit of money - dismiss the notion. It is a very expensive business requiring careful thought and education and the right environment. It also requires complete dedication as it is a full-time job. At the end of all the worry and work there will be little, if any, profit in it. The costs (in 1995) are listed below.

Expenses

Capital costs: For a start there is the capital expenditure of the 61cm (24in) square whelping bed, heat sources (radiator, heat lamp, infra-lamp, heat pad for under the bedding) as required, special bedding materials and items listed under **Preparation for the Birth** (see Chapter 7).

Stud fee: The stud fee can vary enormously. A young, promising dog in the show ring may command double the initial fee by the time he becomes a Champion. Here too the fee can vary greatly from about £40 to several hundred pounds. £80 is fairly usual for top stud dogs, but it depends on the dog and the location. In the South of England stud fees, like all other costs, tend to be higher. Places that are geographically hard to reach usually charge less because their expenses are less and they are up against competition from people located nearer the client. In any case, the size of the stud fee is no guarantee of the quality of the puppies.

Food costs: The bitch has to be fed on good quality minced beef or chicken during pregnancy to make strong healthy puppies, and afterwards to help her recover. The puppies from age four to eight weeks also consume a large quantity of good quality beef and chicken. Goat's milk is very good for the bitch and puppies. If you need Whelpi for hand-rearing a puppy this is a very expensive item.

Veterinary bills: Veterinary bills are high and not covered by insurance. You may want a blood test to ascertain whether the bitch is in whelp, or you may need an X-ray for some reason. When one of my bitches was two days late whelping (they usually whelp up to two days early) the veterinary bill for a consultation and X-ray was over £90.

Infection or Eclampsia (lack of calcium) can easily come after the birth and this is quickly remedied by an injection which again involves a veterinary bill. If the bitch growls, or all is not calm in the whelping box, it may be because an afterbirth remains in the bitch's vagina, and this too requires an injection. Panic also tends to make you call the vet, but it is always better to err on the side of caution.

Parkside Treasure.
Photo: Lynn Bell.

Heat and light: The electricity bill will go up substantially. There will be washing every day, heat lamps on all the time and a lot of cooking/warming food and milk.

The Kennel Club registration fee: It is necessary to register (and name) all pedigree puppies with The Kennel Club, which holds the pedigree and signed Registration Certificates of all pedigree dogs in the country. It represents a guarantee to the buyer that the puppy is genuine and his offspring can also be registered. The registration fee is currently £7 per puppy.

Names have to be agreed by The Kennel Club, but you cannot use a name that is already registered. To avoid duplication, the use of an affix is recommended. This is your own chosen name put in front of the dog's name, for example **'Highspring** Lotus Flower'. It costs £45 to register an affix, with an annual maintenance fee of £15. If you want a Three Generation Pedigree it costs £4 and a Five Generation costs £12.

The annual subscription for *The Kennel Gazette* is £25. This contains interesting articles and gives details of meetings and lists of dog shows and judges, and it keeps the reader in touch with the dog world.

Advertising costs: Another expense is advertising. Not many people today know what a Wire Fox Terrier looks like, and it can be difficult to find homes without considerable advertising. My advertisement in the local newspaper, to which I did not receive any replies, came out as 'Fox Terror puppies'. Advertising in local newspapers in country districts is more successful than urban areas. The Kennel Club now has a list of people who currently have puppies for sale, and will send it

An appealing Smooth Fox Terrier.
Photo: M Bird.

out to anyone making an enquiry. You can apply to go onto The Kennel Club's puppy register; this also includes a short term insurance cover. Puppy Line do a similar service and regularly advertise in the dog papers. In each case a registration fee of approximately £20 is required. Sometimes there can be a commission on each puppy sold, depending on the terms of the registration and with whom you register.

Our Dogs and *Dog World* are the best papers in which to advertise. Most litters are advertised on the back pages, but for specialist breeds like the Fox Terrier it may be better to advertise at the top of the Breed Column where it can be seen easily by people interested in the breed. Advertising in country magazines and national newspapers is very expensive with poor results.

Each dog paper also has an annual edition in which large colour and black-and-white advertisements can be placed. These cost from £50 for an eighth page to £340 for a full page colour advertisement.

Doing it on the cheap: It might be nice to think it can be done more cheaply but it is usually a case of 'you get what you pay for'. For instance, you could make your own whelping bed; it would do the job but might not look as good or be as efficient as a purpose-built, professionally designed one.

Heating bills cut down too much in the early stages could easily cause death to some of the puppies. However, some people do feel it is healthier for the young ones to be kept at a temperature nearer 21°C (70°F) than 24°C (75°F), which is very hot for the bitch. It is easy to see if the puppies are too cold as weight gain will be poor because the energy goes into keeping warm. Puppies need good quality fresh food, and each meal has to be freshly made and warmed.

Total costs for first litter: A sum of around £600 would probably cover most items. The first litter is by far the most expensive because you have the capital outlay in setting up a suitable place, making it safe, and buying the equipment on top of the running costs of food, heat and light.

Education

There is a lot to learn about looking after a bitch in whelp and how to cope with the actual whelping. There could be problems in looking after a weak puppy which also requires some knowledge. For example you may need to know how to put a puppy on a teat to teach it to suckle. If a puppy needs to be hand-reared you need to know how to feed it and what size hole to make in the teat. This requires some expertise as they can easily choke to death. It is worth finding out as much as possible about the whole breeding process so that you are aware of what to look out for and what to do.

The right environment

It is important to ensure that there is a suitable place for the bitch to have her litter and bring up puppies. It needs to be warm, sheltered from other distractions, easy to get at, and far removed from any possible germs that may come into the house. It is no good having workmen or extra visitors around, or contemplating moving house at this time. The designated area needs to be quiet and puppy-proof. It is quite amazing what they can crawl under, climb up or squeeze through. The washing machine needs to be in working order as the bed frequently needs changing. It is best to use Vetbed as the puppies strengthen their legs as they crawl about on it.

Dedication

Having a litter means you are virtually grounded for the next six months. Initially you cannot be away for more than, say, three hours, given that all are doing well. The bitch needs food and drink. Later the puppies need regular meals, each one freshly prepared. This is very time-consuming. The growing puppy also needs masses of attention as it is constantly looking out for something else to do.

Stress and workload

It is important to consider whether you can cope with the anxiety and work involved. People tend to think that the puppies are all really sweet, great fun and the bitch does all the work.

The first anxiety is watching for the heat and choosing the right day to mate her. The next worry is wondering if she really is in whelp. Then in about three or four weeks you see some clear mucus discharge and you wonder what is wrong. The nine weeks' wait seems endless. Then the bitch gets so fat you wonder if the puppies will come too early and fail to survive. (Luckily this very rarely happens.) You try to stop the bitch running upstairs or jumping on chairs and beds to prevent injury or damage to the puppies, while she takes very little notice of your endeavours and continues to do her own thing. The birth itself is exciting and draining, as it usually happens in the middle of the night or very early in the morning.

The workload is terrific, even though it is great fun. The major factor is the amount of bending. Constant attention to small puppies at ground floor level is very punishing to the back. Any signs of a weak back indicate the need for extra help.

If you need to hand-rear a puppy it means that it has to be fed every two hours, day and night. It can take half an hour or more for an inexperienced person to feed a weak puppy. Help for this is essential.

The bitch's milk glands can become red and hot and need attention, giving another cause for anxiety.

Kennel dogs often whelp better when left on their own because they are not so used to human attention. The bitch kept in the house needs careful observation and help when necessary. Too much interference is counter productive, however.

Is there a demand for puppies?

Unless you want a puppy for yourself and are confident that there is a demand for the others it is better not to have a litter. You could be left with the puppy you want plus an unsold one, a returned one, or at worst an unsaleable puppy. For these reasons you need to be sure that you have the time, space, energy and finance to cope with the situation should it arise.

Planning the first litter

If you can face all that hard work and anxiety and decide you want to have a litter, then you must find out as much as possible about what other people's experiences have been and read everything you can on the subject. No matter how well prepared you are there is always a surprise lurking round the corner, and you have to be quick-thinking to deal with it.

Mating a maiden bitch

A first mating should be neither before the bitch is two years old nor after she is five years old. Some people might let her have a litter on her second season, but she is too young then and it takes far too much out of her.

According to Kennel Club regulations, no bitch may have more than a total of six litters and she may not whelp after eight years of age. I would say not after seven years, as a large litter takes a lot out of the dam and she can take nearly a year to recover fully.

It is a useful exercise to watch the pattern of previous heats to identify when she is ready to be mated. Make a note of this and watch carefully next time round at about the same period of the cycle. Watch for the signs (especially between days 10 and 12): the swollen, open and more flabby vulva, the lighter discharge, and her behaviour, which is perhaps the biggest guide of all.

Puppies are very prone to get worms. It is therefore important to worm the bitch before mating and about three weeks afterwards.

A Wire Fox Terrier ready for action. Photo: Anne Roslin-Williams.

Choosing the right stud dog

There are not many Fox Terriers about and unfortunately many of the top winning dogs and bitches are exported. A journey of two or three hours by car to find the right match for your bitch may therefore be necessary.

A stud dog can be used from 10 months of age, but he needs the strictest supervision right from the beginning. It is best if his first bride is an experienced and well-behaved bitch who is ready to stand for him.

A stud dog that is a family pet may be a reluctant beginner. The owner should ensure the stud has not recently been exposed to a bitch on heat whom he has not been allowed to mate. If mating has been forbidden previously he may need some verbal encouragement and a calm approach from the owner. He may become more aggressive towards other male dogs in the future and consequently need more restraint on walks when other dogs are about.

It is necessary to make a study of available stud dogs. Progeny from the main stud dogs can be seen at the Championship shows. Their pedigrees can be studied either from the Fox Terrier Club's Year Books or from Kennel Club records.

The stud dog you choose should conform to the Breed Standard, be typical of the breed, of a type you like, and adequate or excelling in the particular qualities you need to improve in your bitch line. Make sure he has no bad faults and is of good character, strong and healthy. His parents should also be good examples of the breed to endorse the type.

This knowledge will give a guide as to what sort of puppies you might expect but does not tell you everything: every puppy is different and every mating (even with the same bitch) is different. The reason for this is that there are active and recessive genes and there is no guarantee where either of them might pop up.

People have strong ideas about what sort of line breeding or outcross should be undertaken in Fox Terrier circles. We have to use what information we have to make our decision, hoping that it will be the right one.

Genetics

There are dominant and recessive genes in each generation. Recessive genes can suddenly appear when the dominant genes fail to dominate. This can be seen when, in a family where everyone has dark hair, a red head suddenly appears.

From the above it can be seen that no amount of pedigree study gives all the answers unless you are acquainted with every dog in the background. Even then there are surprises as to how one gene will respond to another in any particular mating. There is therefore always an element of surprise and risk.

To conclude: the genes are what makes up the dog, so by inbreeding and line-breeding (see below) you are carrying on the character, size and type of the sort of dog you want to breed. As the genes will be homogeneous it also lessens the risk of surprise. A dog produced in this way reflects not only his own genes but what will be passed on, thus helping the breeder decide on a good breeding programme. Whilst the good points will be passed on it must be remembered that this will also endorse the faults (which can take generations to breed out), the fertility rate can diminish, and abnormalities and a less healthy dog may result.

Inbreeding

Inbreeding is having a litter from a pair with one or more ancestors in common. In dog and horse breeding this is accepted practice to some extent. In depends how close the relationship is. The real ban is on a mating between father and daughter or brother and sister. As has been noted in Chapter 1, close mating was used in the early days to establish the required breed type. If no undesirable traits are present it may be good and will establish the line, but it must be remembered that any bad recessive genes will also be carried on and magnified. These could include hair lip, cleft palate, blindness, deafness and deformities of various kinds and degrees. There is also a lethal recessive gene and this can produce a puppy with brain or heart defects so severe that it will not live. Other puppies in the litter could carry the recessive gene but live normal lives. Inbreeding should therefore be used with great caution.

Line-breeding

Line-breeding is a lesser degree of inbreeding. It has occurred when there is an ancestor who keeps popping up on both sides in the pedigree of the dog and the bitch. The appearance of a common affix on the pedigree of sire and dam is not necessarily evidence of line-breeding or inbreeding. Genetically speaking it would have to be the same dog(s) appearing on both sides in the pedigree.

Line-breeding can be between half-brother and half-sister, or to a cousin. This is often accepted, but it must be remembered that if the parents have also been closely bred the intensity of the inbreeding heightens and therefore the risk of passing on defects is also greater.

Outcross

An outcross is when two dogs are mated who have no common ancestors in recent generations. If the right dog is chosen this can produce good results.

Many Fox Terrier people are not big breeders but just keep a few dogs at home for their pleasure and the odd litter, and perhaps a little competition every now and again. This type of breeder is unlikely to have enough animals to choose from for a breeding programme, bearing in mind that he wants to endorse the good points and eradicate the bad ones. It follows therefore that an outcross that excels in a point upon which he wants to improve might be the answer. There is no perfect dog anywhere and, anyway, perfection is in the eyes of the beholder. It would seem that looking at the stud dogs, seeing their offspring, and studying their ancestors for quality (and character) rather than pedigree is the best way of improving the kennel stock. Many breeders prefer to follow a particular line of ancestors, however.

Crossbreeding

Crossbreeding is when two dogs of different breeds mate. This may be an accident or it may be planned. It is by this means that many of today's breeds have evolved.

Dogs may be crossbred to remove a fault, or to improve on a particular feature. This could be to change the colour, length or texture of the coat, to make the dog larger or smaller, or to bring about any other change desired by the breeder. Such a dog may not be registered with the Kennel Club as it is not a pure bred dog.

It will be seen that, despite much research, writing, learning, advice and trial, breeding the best is an elusive business. Perhaps that is why we go on doing it; it is so fascinating!

Arrangements with stud dog owner

Once you have selected a suitable stud dog, check with his owner before the bitch comes on heat to make sure arrangements can be made. As soon as she starts her heat advise the owner and agree a day.

Agree stud fee terms

The agreed stud fee is normally payable at the time of mating. Occasionally, in some breeds, payment is made only when the litter has arrived. In this case The Kennel Club's Green Registration Card is withheld until payment is received. Unless this card certifying that the mating took place has been signed, no puppies can be registered.

Occasionally the first mating for a potential stud dog is given free of charge to prove that he is capable of siring puppies. Another arrangement is for the stud dog owner to have pick of litter instead of the stud fee.

Two Gedstar Smooths.
Photo: Marc Henrie.

Normally the stud fee covers one mating but it would still remain the same even if there was a second mating two days later. If board was required that might be a separate arrangement. Fox Terriers usually mate successfully first time, but if the bitch is difficult to whelp, or there is some doubt about the success of the mating, the stud dog owner might suggest a second try to make sure. Nothing is usually said about what happens if there is no litter but it is generally understood that a free second mating is offered next time.

If the bitch has only one puppy and it is born dead, or dies within the first few days, there might be a problem unless a written agreement has been made in advance. This is not easily done as it brings in an element of tension and distrust. In this case the stud dog has produced a puppy, and therefore proved that he was fertile. The reasons for the puppy's death can be many and varied and difficult to prove. If it is a maiden bitch, she may not know what to do and unless someone is there to take it out of its sac it will suffocate. The puppy could be unable to suckle or it might get fading puppy syndrome; there are many possible reasons.

It might be tempting to rush at another mating free of charge, but this may not be the wisest move if, for example, it is felt the mating may not have been compatible with your bitch line. Before she next comes on heat it is worth considering the pedigree of another successful stud dog which might prove to be the better option.

The reproductive function of dog and bitch

Before going any further it is useful to have some idea of what is going on inside both the dog and the bitch.

The reproductive system of the bitch

The bitch has two ovaries which contain all the eggs (ova) which she will release during her life and some which will not be released. The ovaries are located behind the last pair of ribs, near the kidneys, and each one is encapsulated by one of the two fallopian tubes. Through these each ovary is connected to one of the two uterine horns, which join together to form the body of the uterus. This narrows down to form the cervix (neck of the uterus), which leads into the vagina. The uterus is connected to the vulva (the external female sex organ) by the vagina. The vulva can be seen just under the anus.

The heat: The bitch usually comes on heat for the first time at eight to ten months of age. The first sign of this is a small discharge from the vagina which will last up to 21 days. The next heat may be slightly unpredictable, but it settles down thereafter to a regular pattern, usually every nine or ten months and sometimes at longer intervals.

Some people are worried about the bitch dropping blood on the carpets or chairs. To this end traders do sell knickers and doggie sanitary belts for use with sanitary towels. This is not recommended; the bitch is very unhappy about being made to look so stupid and it is not as hygienic as when she can lick herself clean. It is very rare that there is any mess in unwanted places, and it is a simple matter to put a cotton cloth or towel over her favourite chair. The smell is sometimes more noticeable but there are various candles and sprays on the market that help to minimise offensive odours.

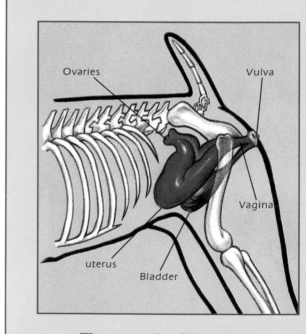

The reproductive system of the bitch

Before the onset of heat, some of the ova will have been surrounded by fluid-filled sacs called follicles. On average, and depending on the breed of the dog, six to eight of these grow towards the surface of the ovary. These follicles then burst and the mature ova are released into the fallopian tube and find their way to the top of the uterine horn. This process is called ovulation.

Ovulation: The actual time of ovulation (that is the most likely time that a mating will be successful) is hard to judge and can vary in different bitches, but is usually between days 10 to 15.

There are some physical signs to you help get it right. There is less discharge and it is paler in colour. The mammary glands (teats) swell slightly and become pinker. Sometimes they produce milk even though the bitch has not been mated. The vulva is normally closed, but prior to whelping and during ovulation it becomes swollen, quite open and soft and flabby.

Fertilising the egg: During mating, thousands of sperm cells make their way to the fallopian tubes and gather round attempting to penetrate the egg cell. Once one sperm has penetrated no more sperm can enter that egg. The fertilised egg now becomes attached to the wall of the uterus where it grows for the next two months.

The reproductive system of the dog

The foetus: Sometimes the foetus can be felt after three weeks; it feels like a small round ball. It is probably safer to leave this to a vet. There is always a danger of damage to the foetus, and it is quite likely that the bitch will cry out.

The reproductive system of the dog

The dog's reproductive organs are less complicated than those of the bitch.

The male dog has two testicles which descend into the scrotum at any time from about the age of six weeks. The scrotum is the pink skin bag which hangs between the inside back legs, or thighs. The testicles are connected to the penis by ducts.

As the dog becomes sexually excited he mounts the bitch, attempting to penetrate her. If the bitch is tense, or the time is not quite right, penetration can be very difficult, or even impossible. It has to be undertaken when she is 'ready', her vulva having become soft and flabby.

The penis becomes stiff and after penetration it swells and the bulbous bit at the end enlarges to the extent that it cannot be withdrawn. Hence the tie, lasting from 10 to 30 minutes, during which time the sperm-bearing semen is pumped into the vagina. It is only when the penis reduces in size that it can be withdrawn.

Once the sperm enters the bitch's vagina it only lives for 24 hours. As the ovum also has a short life, mating and ovulation have to be carefully synchronised.

The sperm is continually being produced by the dog, thus keeping him virile. If he is used too much the sperm count will reduce until he has had a rest; for example, he should not be used on successive days.

To be in good form the stud should be very fit and well. He needs good food, and plenty of fresh air and exercise.

Behaviour of dog and bitch

During heat the bitch urinates frequently to advise her suitors of her condition. She barks at the gate and generally makes her presence felt. She is playful with dogs and teases them.

As she approaches ovulation this behaviour becomes more blatant. She flaunts her backside at her suitors and will also mount other bitches and allow them to mount her. Sometimes they think this is great fun.

She also indicates that she is ready to mate by twitching her tail from side to side and standing fairly rigid, with a curious expression on her face, especially if you touch her either at the base of the tail or on the vulva.

Dogs do anything to get at a bitch on heat. They climb six foot wire mesh fences, they crawl, they dig, and as a last resort they mate through the wire mesh. I have known a dog who left his owners having a picnic to chase after a car which carried a bitch on heat. Dogs can also pick up the scent on clothing even if the bitch is not there. Occasionally they try mating the pillow, or worse, your arm or leg, or anything else they fancy. Usually a firm 'no' will stop it. If it is a serious problem a visit to the vet is the only answer.

Pet dogs usually behave themselves fairly well, but once a dog has mated a bitch he will always be looking out for another conquest. It is a good idea for the mating always to take place in the same place; that way the stud will realise what the visit is all about and know his job. My stud dog sometimes goes into his mating chamber to contemplate his conquests.

The dog also tends to urinate frequently, to mark his territory, sniffing the places where a bitch has been and licking both them and her vulva.

When visiting new places the dog sometimes urinates on chair and table legs, especially if other dogs have been in the area. This is marking territory and leaving his visiting card. He is not being naughty deliberately.

To protect the bitch from other dogs it is advisable to have at least two 'insurmountable' obstacles in the way. For example, she could be kept in a pen in the garden so that a visiting dog first has to find his way into the garden and then jump or climb into the pen. Inside the house, if the bitch is shut up in one room there should be at least one more closed door between her and any dog. Accidents can and do happen all too often!

Some people send the bitch to kennels during heat where she will be safely confined. I know of one case when the bitch actually took herself to the kennels when her time came. She knew the form and obviously accepted it quite happily.

There are tablets and sprays on the market which are said to create a smell that is offensive to dogs and will discourage any likely suitors. In fact they often smell rather like lemons and are unlikely to keep anything greater than a flea away - and there is some doubt even about that!

The mating

First of all, let the visiting bitch sniff around and urinate. The dog in his anticipation also urinates. Then let them meet, and see the reaction. The bitch may be rather nervous, so your manner should be calm. When they seem to be ready, take them to the mating chamber and put them on the table (it saves having to bend down for too long). It is rarely necessary to muzzle the bitch if the owner is there but, if she is aggressive, muzzling has a markedly calming effect on her and is not cruel.

The stud dog is always keen and knows immediately why a bitch has come to see him. His readiness to mount her may have to be restrained to prevent him from becoming 'burnt out' before she allows the mating.

Owners of Fox Terriers do not usually let a bitch run freely with a strange dog before mating. Both dogs are controlled by their respective owners throughout. This is because the bitch may not want to be mated (which quite often happens with an 'arranged marriage') and could seriously damage the dog. Equally, he may be too forceful towards the bitch and she may be injured. Even if they get on well he can quickly lose the ability to perform in his excitement and then your chance is gone for another nine months.

The owner of the bitch holds her head firmly, and the dog owner assists the dog at the rear end in the hope of getting a tie. The stud knows what he is about but often has surprising difficulty in finding the vulva with his penis. If he does not succeed at first, he dismounts and tries again, often panting. The handler can help by moving the bitch in the right direction. He may have several attempts before succeeding in getting a tie. The tie may last for anything from 10 minutes to half an hour or more, but it need not be that long to be successful, and it can work even without a tie. During attempts to penetrate, either stud or bitch may cry out.

Once the stud has penetrated, the bitch must stand still or she will seriously damage the stud. He now pumps for all he is worth as he ejects his semen. He rests for a while on the bitch's back and hugs her with his front legs, often licking her ears. By this time both are calm, but he may be panting from exertion. He then dismounts and they remain tied together, standing side by side or back to back. The stud often needs help to get his leg over the bitch's back. The handler gently lifts the nearest hind leg over her back and onto the ground the other side. The stud owner holds their tails together to make sure the bitch stays still. When the dog withdraws they quietly walk away from each other. Sometimes a considerable amount of fluid falls from the bitch at this time, but this is nothing to worry about. He has done his job.

After mating

Some people hold the bitch on her back to encourage the semen to flow in the right direction. It is best to put the bitch straight into her box where she will lick herself, and this will also prevent her from urinating for a couple of hours. It is essential to keep the bitch away from all other dogs after this.

It is now time to pay the stud fee. The stud owner should hand over the signed copy of the Kennel Club registration certificate giving the details of the stud dog, his stud number and the date and confirmation of mating. When the litter comes this form is used to register each puppy separately with the chosen name. It is essential that every detail requested in the form is completed, otherwise it is returned, causing extra work and unnecessary delay. You should also be given the pedigree of the stud dog to make up your own pedigree for the litter, or else acquire one from The Kennel Club.

Make a note of the date the litter is due to be born so that the arrangements can be made in good time. It is better for the bitch to become familiar with her nest at least two weeks before the arrival because at that time she looks all over the place to nest and her choice is never where you want it to be.

Some difficulties with the bitch

Unwilling: Sometimes the bitch will growl and snarl continually, making it impossible for the dog, and meanwhile he becomes more and more excited. This may be because she is reluctant, frightened, or it may not be the right time. Sometimes she is just being awkward and playing a game, and when the suitor of her choice comes along she happily lets him get on with the job. This was clearly demonstrated by one of my bitches. She was a most reluctant bride when I planned a litter but, next time she came on heat, when left to her own devices (and when I thought it was safe), she happily let the resident stud mate her on day 20. This happened in an unguarded moment when I had to apply a plaster to a cut finger. By the time I had finished they were already back to back.

If there is some reluctance on the part of the bitch, I sometimes leave them to play for a short time, watching through a window. Usually they are quite amenable provided the dog does not actually attempt to mount, but the bitch still provokes him. The dog signals when I should take them back to his mating chamber as he knows that is where he will be helped and protected.

No heat: If the bitch has extra long periods of heat or even no heat for over a year the vet can treat the condition. Some people increase daylight artificially and hope she will respond. Another method is for her to be with a bitch on heat, they often come on at the same time.

Owners present: Quite often pet bitches are difficult to mate when their owners are present. As soon as the owner leaves she relaxes and behaves. The same behaviour can occur with trimming.

Moving house: Moving house at any time can be traumatic for a bitch. During pregnancy it can even endanger the life of the bitch and the puppies.

Ovarian cyst: Sometimes a bitch has the misfortune to have an ovarian cyst just when she has a litter. This is regrettable and almost certainly means the whole litter will have to be hand-reared.

Two matings on same heat: If a bitch is mated twice in one season the puppies could have two fathers, both of which must be reported to The Kennel Club.

Some difficulties with the stud

Too eager: A stud may hurry so much that he ejaculates before penetrating the bitch. His penis is exposed and semen may still be ejected. In this event he should mount the bitch again immediately and, by continuing to pump, his penis should return to

A fnn Smooth: Ch/Am Ch Karnilo Chieftain.

Photo: Anne Roslin-Williams.

its normal position. If it does not, cold water should be applied. If the end of the penis has not returned because it is still too swollen, then gently rub on some petroleum jelly and pull the sheath forward until it is covered. If the problem continues call a vet at once.

Over-excited: Another cause for withdrawal could be because the stud is over-excited, in which case a calming voice is the best solution.

Vagina too tight: Sometimes, even when he has penetrated partially, the dog withdraws completely and the chances of a successful mating look unlikely. This could be because there is a stricture in the channel caused by tension or reluctance. The use of petroleum jelly as a lubricator helps. A lubricated finger put up the vagina will help loosen it.

Direction of the vagina: It may be the direction of the vagina that is awkward for the dog, and here the handler can assist by moving the rear of the bitch.
Infertility: A dog's fertility can be related to his living conditions. If he has a nice warm bed and good food, with plenty of daylight and exercise, he is much more likely to be healthy and fertile than if these criteria are not met.

An old stud: A good old stud dog can be successfully mated to a young bitch, but it is best not to mate an old dog to an old bitch. The best litters are usually the second and third.

Cryptorchid or monorchid: The testicles usually descend into the scrotum when the puppy is six weeks old but it can occasionally be as late as six months. It is not unusual for a dog to be chryptorchid, which is when both testicles are retained in the body and not descended into the scrotum. It is described as monorchid when only one testicle is descended. Normally it is recommended that these dogs are neutered in case they get cancer. Since this may be an inherited problem these dogs should not be used for stud.

Accidental mating

It can happen that the bitch is accidentally mated at any time from day one (I have known it happen even the day before heat started) to day 22. This could be a successful mating, but is likely to produce only a small litter, if any. A phantom pregnancy may result, or even resorption (also known as absorption or ingestion).

If the mating was undesirable (if, for example, the bitch was too old, the relationship too close, the dog of another breed, or home circumstances not right) a possible pregnancy can be terminated if an injection is given within 48 hours. There is some risk attached to such injections. For example, they prevent a further intentional mating on this heat and possibly the following one also.

Sometimes people ask for an injection to prevent or delay a heat. Whilst this can be done, it is not wise. The bitch's cycle is a delicate balance and is very sensitive to artificial hormonal changes. The effects of such injections can ruin the chances of pregnancy in the future and should not be undertaken lightly.

Is she pregnant?

The vet can do a smear test to ascertain ovulation and he can also do a blood test to see if the bitch is pregnant. This test is said to be 95% accurate. Despite this a positive reading can still leave the owner and bitch expecting a family right up to the very last day when the puppies should arrive, and then nothing happens. There are also pregnancy scan clinics, which are reliable. The current fee is £26.

Around the third or fourth week after mating she may be reluctant to eat, and at four weeks there could be a transparent substance coming from the vulva. These are two sure signs that she is in whelp. In the fourth to fifth week the teats may swell slightly and look pinkish. The abdomen also starts to get bigger.

Gestation period

Although the gestation period is worked out at 63 days from mating, sometimes there is a delay in fertilisation. This is because the life of the egg is usually only 48 hours, but can be up to three or five days, and not all the eggs are discharged at the same time.

The dog's sperm lives in the bitch's vagina for anything from 24 hours to three or four days. It is unlikely to fertilise an egg immediately upon its arrival or more than two days afterwards. Thus fertilisation may take place any time up to two days after mating. It therefore follows that puppies born apparently two or three days late may be arriving at the normal time for them. By the same token, puppies born early may be a day or two more premature than the date would suggest if they were conceived late. (See Appendix B: **Whelping Chart.**)

Make arrangements for docking

Once you know that she is pregnant it is time to think about arrangements for the puppies' tails to be docked. If you plan to have this done it is important to become a member of the Council for Docked Breeds. They will tell you the name of the nearest vet who is willing to dock. He should be contacted immediately so that if he is not available for the expected date of birth there is still time to ask another vet. (See section on **Docking** in Chapter 8 and Appendix A: **Useful Addresses** at the end of the book.)

False pregnancy

It is not uncommon for a bitch to have a false pregnancy, even when she has not been mated. The Fox Terrier bitch is very motherly and her maternal instincts will lead her to adopt furry toys or other objects as her phantom babies.

She will curl up and hide in dark places; she will look for nests in the garden; she will dig in her bed and tear up newspaper. She will also put on weight and refuse walks, and she can have milk in the teats. She even has the shivers and a drop in normal temperature when she thinks she is about to deliver. Then suddenly it is all over and she is back to the old routine again.

Absorption

In some unfortunate cases, some or all of the embryos may die at an early stage, and their fluids are absorbed back into the bitch's body. She may still appear to be pregnant but when the time comes there are no puppies. This is because her body has ingested or absorbed the tiny foetus. If the foetus has been growing for a couple of months and the bone has started to form then this part cannot be resorbed and is likely to arrive in the normal way at the predicted time of birth. It comes out as a messy strip of thick tissue or partially-formed bone.

Frozen Semen

Dr D R Morton at the Unit of Biomedical Services at the University of Leicester is a leading expert in storing semen for future use. Semen is collected from the male dog and stored, frozen, until such time as the bitch is ready to have the eggs fertilised by means of artificial insemination (AI).

This procedure cannot be used for dogs with defects but there are circumstances where it is appropriate. The most usual one arises when someone wants to use a stud dog from another country because of a limited choice in home bred dogs. If import regulations are strict and expensive, and there is a ban on docked dogs in the ring (as in Scandinavia), it is the only answer.

There are many benefits from AI. The provision of a wider choice of stud dog by this process helps to eliminate some genetic defects. It is also a means of keeping valuable blood lines stored for future generations, long after the good stud has died. It can limit the spread of canine venereal disease in countries where this is a problem, and, of course, it saves the bitch having to travel huge distances to meet the right stud dog. Frozen semen from dogs (and other animals) can also be used to assist in the search to eliminate some human diseases.

Since about 1987 it has also been possible to freeze the ova (eggs) of females.

This technique has been used in the attempt to preserve rare species, but has not yet been applied to dogs.

The dog should not have had booster injections immediately prior to donating semen for freezing. About two weeks before the due date he should have a blood test to ascertain he is not suffering from the diseases named on the importing country's health certificate. These may include *Leptospira canicula*, and *Brucella canis*.

Semen is usually collected in straws from the dog with a bitch present; after a long journey and in a new place he may be too busy to co-operate. Two ejaculations are collected and then tested for fertility and density. The semen is then diluted with a mixture of egg yolk and glycerol (this preserves the sperm during freezing and thawing processes), together with antibiotics and other chemicals. The straws are then frozen firstly in a refrigerator and secondly in liquid nitrogen at -196°C. They are stored in small containers weighing 10kg (22lb) which can be transported anywhere. After two or three weeks the liquid nitrogen needs to be replenished.

The success rate is usually above 60% under strict laboratory conditions. Since 1978 the average success rate for exported semen is about 30%. However, according to Brendan O'Loghlen of the Extreal affix, figures obtained from his veterinary surgeon, Ian Gunn, of The Yarroview Veterinary Clinic, Lilydale, Victoria, Australia suggest that a 60-70% pregnancy result can be obtained from semen of good quality, and Mrs Bergendahl of the Marsten kennel in Norway claims a 100% success rate. Sometimes the sperm of a particular animal will not respond to such treatment. Repeated insemination from a chosen dog gives a higher success rate, but litters are generally smaller.

The semen can be placed either in the uterus (usually surgically) or in the vagina; in either case detailed preliminary tests are necessary, together with a great deal of skill and expertise, for the correct timing and placing of the semen. Variation in the level of such expertise could account for the lower success rate in some exported sperm. The placing of semen in the vagina has been found to give a higher success rate.

This procedure has brought to light the lack of sufficient knowledge of the reproductive functions of both dog and bitch. Timing is worked out on the assumption that ovulation takes place within two days after the bitch will accept a dog (oestrus). The egg may not be mature at this stage (needing another two days) and even if the sperm penetrates it may not be effective unless the egg is mature. The sperm also has to be in the female tract for a period of time before it is capable of fertilising an egg. One way in which the veterinary surgeon can determine the exact time of ovulation with a greater degree of accuracy is by monitoring blood progesterone levels.

A fine example of a frozen semen pup: Swedish Ch Marstens Jackass Jan (Ch Killick of the Mess ex Norwegian Ch Marstens What A Chance). Breeder: G Bergendahl. Photo: A Konda Midtten.

Five pups from frozen semen (Ch Sylair Star Leader ex Int/Nor/Swe Ch Marstens Tricky Miss Smidth). Breeder: G Bergendahl.

These reach a peak 24 hours before ovulation. Maximum fertility is after the ova have been maturing in the reproductive tract for about 72 hours.

The straws in which the semen is collected must be labelled with date of collection, Kennel Club Registration Number, name and breed of dog and name of owner. Details of identifying marks on the dog are also required. Both the owner and the person collecting and freezing the semen sign the Certificate of Collection. The vet inseminating the bitch also certifies her identity with the owner, and records the markings on the straws.

Kennel clubs of numerous countries now accept the registration of puppies born from AI using frozen semen. In this country The Kennel Club agrees only after the reasons for using this method have been discussed in detail.

The first countries to use AI in this way were Scandinavia, other European countries, North America and Australia. Following these successes breeders in Asia, South America and Africa became interested.

Care of the pregnant bitch

As has already been stated, the gestation period is 63 days, although it may be two days early or one day late. For the first four weeks of this time, the bitch can live a normal life with the usual food and exercise.

Food: Most proprietary foods have been analysed carefully to give a balanced diet. Each manufacturer wants the owner to rely on his product, so it is when you mix various products that you change the balance. Fresh food and bits left over from the table make good additional nourishment and should provide an adequate diet.

The bitch has her normal diet for the first six weeks. After that the protein (meat, fish, eggs) level is increased weekly by about 10% so that by the time the puppies are born she is eating about one and a half times her normal intake. It is important that she does not eat too much as this can make the birth process more difficult. During lactation she could eat as much as two to three times the normal consumption. Eggs are best cooked, but raw egg yolks can be given. Fresh liver (vitamin B) can be given occasionally. The dogs love it, but do not give too much as it upsets their stomachs. Dog biscuits, dry food, raw carrots and Nylabone products help to keep the teeth clean. Bread is a good filler.

As the bitch gets larger there is less room in the abdomen to take the food. It is better to give two or three meals a day and a drink of milk in between. Goat's milk is excellent.

In the last week the appetite often goes and a little coaxing and special treats and cuddles help.

Vitamins: It is best not to give extra vitamins during pregnancy unless the bitch is in poor condition. They should be administered cautiously at any time. If necessary a teaspoon of cod liver oil (vitamin A and D) or Brewers Yeast/Vetzyme tablets (vitamin B) might be beneficial. A few drops of Abidec, which contains seven essential vitamins, will quickly put matters right if the bitch seems unwell.

To give calcium to the pregnant bitch is not recommended. This is because the correct balance of calcium and phosphorous (vitamin D2) is essential. If this balance is not achieved there can be serious consequences, including the birth of deformed puppies, not only in this litter but also in future ones.

After the birth of a large litter the bitch may get Eclampsia, a condition caused by a lack of calcium during suckling. In this case it is essential to give her some. The condition can start very quickly because of the sudden rush of milk flowing. She may show signs of fainting and weakness or she may seem really stressed and restless. In either case quick attention is necessary. Probably she will begin to recover as soon as she is given some 'Stress' or 'Calci-Care', a liquid calcium with vitamin D and Magnesium. Administer this according to the instructions on the containers. Call the vet if she has not settled fairly quickly; there could be other reasons for the discomfort, such as a retained afterbirth or an unborn puppy.

Exercise: Normal exercise is best to keep the bitch fit and well during the early stages. When she gets heavier walks will be slower and shorter. No walks for the last three weeks. No jumping on chairs and beds or running upstairs. She should avoid any over exertion and not go on long car rides.

Grooming: Bath and trim the bitch about the fourth to fifth week of pregnancy, then keep her clean and tidy by daily grooming. She needs to be well trimmed as she gets very hot at this time.

Shortly before the birth, wash her tummy with mild Dettol. Clear away all the hair from around the teats so that it does not choke the puppies when they go to feed. Cut the hair away from under the tail and inside the back legs, as this area becomes very dirty and is hard to clean up after the birth.

The bitch's coat gets into a very bad state after whelping and by the time the puppies leave she can be quite bald. The new coat starts to grow again in three to four weeks.

Prepare the whelping bed
About two weeks before the birth prepare a whelping box 61cm (24in) square and 35cm (14in) high. The bitch needs to be able to get out of the box easily and the puppies must be kept in or they will die of cold and lack of food. The top needs to be open so that if any assistance needs to be given you can do so easily. The front needs a piece of wood at least 10cm (4in) high to keep the pups in. For the first three

or four days they need a temperature of 21-27°C (70-80°F). Make sure that both dam and puppies are comfortable with the temperature.

Sometimes people put a guard rail all round the sides so that when the dam lies against the side she cannot squash a puppy. The Fox Terrier is normally a careful mother.

Heat sources: A heat pad (obtainable from pet shops) placed under the bedding will keep the puppies' tummies warm. However, although it has a very low voltage, there could be a remote chance of it over-heating. A hot-water bottle is safer.

An infra-red lamp can be placed over a corner of the bed to warm the puppies and allow the bitch a slightly cooler corner. The bitch is very hot after whelping, but the puppies need to be kept in a similar temperature to that to which they were accustomed prior to being whelped, (24-27°C or 75-80°F), or at any rate at a temperature at which they will not get cold and shivery.

One sort of heat lamp slots into the light switch. This provides a bright light as well as heat. The dam needs some darkness, so this form of heat should not be left on all the time.

A normal radiator or electric radiator is a good and safe heat source.

Bedding: Newspaper is probably best for whelping as it can be easily thrown away. Vetbed is more suitable once the puppies have arrived. It lets the urine through and keeps the puppies dry. It also strengthens their legs as they crawl around on it.

An old pillow case filled with pieces of clean rag or cotton sheets covered with a blanket makes a comfortable bed. Light soft pieces of blanket are useful to help the puppies get out of a draught. They love to go into these little warm tunnels and always find their way out at meal times.

A typical whelping box.

7

The birth

> Please note that the bitch and pup in the whelping diagrams are not intended to represent Fox Terriers.

It is prudent to tell the vet when you expect the family to arrive, just in case you need to make an emergency call.

Have ready:

- Vet's telephone number.
- Notebook and pen (record everything).
- Thermometer.
- Weighing scales.
- Soap.
- Disinfectant and a small hand basin.
- Cotton wool to clean puppies' noses and mouths.
- Small towels and a few pieces of cotton cloth.
- Cardboard box with blanket and a wrapped hot water bottle. (This is in case the bitch is inclined to trample on the puppies when subsequent new arrivals are coming. She usually copes without this assistance.)
- Plenty of newspaper.
- Tags (for identification).
- Catac feeding bottle (or similar) for hand feeding.
- Teats and bottle cleaner. Make a hole in each teat with a red-hot needle.
- Eye-dropper. (The easiest way to help a new-born puppy when only a few drops are required.)
- Infra-red lamp, heat pad or heat lamp (to fit into light socket).
- Vetbed.
- Cotton thread (in case the cord bleeds and the bitch does not seal it).
- Brandy/Rescue Remedy (for urgent recovery).
- Stress or liquid calcium in case of eclampsia.
- Goat's milk.
- Whelpi.
- Glucose powder.
- Bucket or sack to throw away dirty towel/afterbirth, etc.

Clean and quiet

It is essential to keep the new family away from other dogs and people. Germs are picked up very easily, the puppies have no immune system, and the bitch can be infected very easily with her vulva so exposed. Spray the 'nest' area twice a week with Formula H (one part Formula H to 12 parts water). Use sterilising tablets intended for cleaning baby feeding equipment to clean the puppy feeding equipment Alternatively, you can boil the eating utensils for 10 minutes. Do not spray the bitch or the puppies themselves with any antiseptics.

Quiet is also essential. Bear in mind that, if the bitch is interfered with too much, she will give up on the job and let you take over completely.

The first signs

The temperature drops: The bitch shivers and the temperature drops 24 hours before the onset of labour from 38.6°C (101.5°F) to 37.2°C (99°F). Take her temperature a week to 10 days prior to whelping to ascertain what the normal temperature is.

Lies stretched out: Instead of being curled up, her body tends to stretch out with the head between the front legs when she is resting. She looks sadly at the owner, almost as if she is ill, and makes you feel guilty you cannot help her.

Bed making: She is restless and uncomfortable for some days before the birth, looking in all kinds of corners to make her nest, outdoors and indoors. Block off places where she cannot be reached, like under the bed. Keep her as calm as possible and keep the environment calm. As the time approaches she will dig up her bed frantically and tear up the paper.

The puppy, in its sac, appears at the vulva.

Loss of appetite: There is also a loss of appetite. A drink of glucose and water (useful also for a weak puppy) is energy giving.

Panting: There is intermittent panting, which lasts for a considerable number of hours, even for a few days sometimes. This is not because the bitch is too hot, but part of the process when the vagina is dilating to let the puppies through. You will see it swollen and opening up. The bitch will look at the rear and lick it. There will be a clear, thick mucous discharge from the vulva several hours before delivery. This needs cleaning away as it is very sticky. Make sure she has some water.

Straining: She may strain for half an hour, but if it goes on for one to two hours before the first arrival get in touch with your veterinary surgeon. Normally Fox Terriers give birth very suddenly and quickly, without any difficulty at all. The next puppy can follow immediately, often after 20 minutes, but the last one can be hours later.

The first arrival

Leave the bitch to get on with the job but keep an eye open for the first arrival. A maiden bitch does not always know what to do when the first puppy arrives. Every puppy is born in a bag or sac. Make sure she opens the sac at once and licks the puppy's face to start it breathing. If the puppy is not out of the sac quickly it will die. Then she should sever the cord by biting it; if she slips it through her teeth afterwards it will seal. She will clean the puppy and soon it will find its way to a teat and start getting the colostrum (the first, extra-thick milk from the bitch which gives the puppy some immunisation).

Resuscitation

If the puppy does not appear to be breathing, rub it very vigorously with a warm towel. This method usually works.

A puppy looking blue, cold and dead may still be revived, even after a prolonged effort (up to an hour), without suffering any permanent brain or other damage. Open the mouth, pull out the tongue and blow into the mouth. Rub the puppy continually with a piece of towel. Blow again, rub and repeat as often as necessary. If this fails, any of the following methods, or a combination of them, may work:

- Hold the puppy with both hands, supporting its neck, and quickly swinging it downwards to clear the liquid from the air passage. Wipe the mouth and throat area with a dry cotton swab and rub the puppy (fairly vigorously if necessary) to stimulate breathing.
- Try putting your finger and thumb round the rib cage and press or pump continuously to start the heart beating.
- Rub the hair on the back of the neck vigorously backwards and forwards.
- Hold the puppy with the head down. This puts pressure on the lungs. Then turn the head up again to release the pressure. Continue with this 'up-and-down' motion about once every three minutes until it starts to breathe.
- One drop of brandy or Rescue Remedy might help.

Once the puppy chokes and splutters you know it is alive and has started breathing.

When to help

Help is sometimes needed when the puppies follow too quickly, and the bitch may not be able to reach round for the delivery of the next puppy. Sometimes the puppy does not drop readily and in this case too you can assist by cutting the cord and opening the sac. If the bitch has been straining for too long you can help the puppy by gripping it with a dry towel as she strains and gently rotating it from side to side,

THE BIRTH

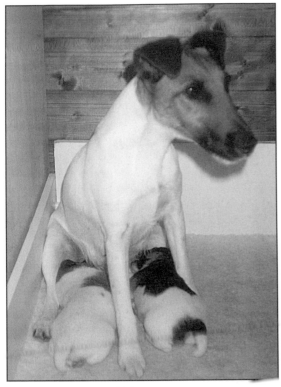

Photo: M Bird.

Proud mum: A Smooth with her pups.

pulling steadily downwards in the direction of the bitch's head, not straight or towards the tail. If the sac is not broken during the birth process, break it quickly near the puppy's nose to enable it to breathe. Hold the puppy's head down to let the fluid drain from its nostrils and throat. Wipe with a piece of clean towel.

Sometimes a bubble may appear and disappear before the puppy can be seen. This is the sac surrounding the puppy and is due to the straining pressure. Leave this alone until the actual puppy can be seen. If the sac breaks the puppy cannot breathe.

The placenta (afterbirth) does not always come out straight away, possibly arriving five to 15 minutes later or with the next birth. If it comes easily as you pull gently on the umbilical cord (not pulling on the puppy), so much the better. You can cut the cord before the placenta has arrived to get the puppy breathing and feeding. (If the puppy does seem to have stopped breathing, it can often be resuscitated if you are sufficiently prompt.) Cut the cord half an inch from the puppy and let the bitch take it through her teeth to seal. If she does not do this, tie the end with cotton to stop it bleeding, or paint it with tincture of iodine. The end piece quickly dries off and falls away.

The placenta is a disgusting greenish mess and should be thrown away if possible. The bitch will eat it if she can but too many upset her tummy afterwards.

After the first puppy has arrived the others follow quickly, at once or up to 20 minutes later. The last one may be an hour and a half later. The bitch licks away the fluids coming out with the puppy so whilst there is some mess it is not as bad as it might otherwise be.

If the bitch has strained fruitlessly for an hour or more and you cannot contact a vet, carefully slide a finger into the vagina, using a lubricated surgical glove. Feel around for the puppy's mouth. This may stimulate a contraction. If not, grasp what you can (possibly the head) of the puppy between your thumb and forefinger to get enough grip to deliver the puppy. The rest will follow normally. This has often been carried out successfully by following instructions given over the telephone.

Of course litters of puppies can be born during the night and early morning, and the breeder wakes up to find them all doing well. It is obviously better to be watchful, however, so that you are at hand to minimise losses if the bitch has problems.

As each puppy is born, use a cotton swab to clear the mouth, dry it off and put to teat. If a puppy is a bit weak, grip the teat between the thumb and forefinger of one hand, squeeze out a drop of milk, and hold the puppy with the other hand. Push the teat against its lower lip to make it open its mouth. Put quite a lot of the teat into the puppy's mouth above the tongue, squeeze the teat slightly and hold the puppy close to its mother. Sucking should start. Hold the puppy on the teat until it has had its fill. This will need repeating and watching.

Every pup is born in a bag, or sac, which must be opened at once.

Each teat has six or more openings. It sometimes seems as if a squirt of milk just comes out of the tip. This is not the case, however, so when a puppy feeds it needs to have quite a large amount of teat in its mouth. The rear teats have the most milk, the front ones needing encouragement from the hungry puppies, supplying according to demand.

The number of teats a bitch has varies but usually Fox Terriers have six or seven. Some larger varieties of dogs may have ten teats. If there are more puppies than teats this does not matter as they can feed in relays.

It is not unusual for a puppy to have difficulty sucking. Try putting a drop of honey on its tongue to get the action going. Noisy sucking with in-and-out movements of the tongue usually indicates that the puppy is not getting enough (if any) milk. As has already been stated, rear teats have more milk, so weaker puppies should be placed there before the stronger ones have had their fill. Getting milk is quite energetic work for the small puppies because they have to paddle with their feet as well as suckle. Make sure that the ambient temperature is at 21-27°C (70-80°F) for the first week. ID tags or indelible ink are sometimes used to identify puppies for keeping the records correct.

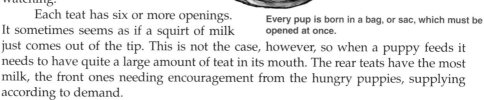

Cut or tear the umbilical cord half an inch from the puppy, and let the bitch take it through her teeth.

Call the vet

Your veterinary surgeon should be called under the following circumstances:

- If the bitch is exhausted before labour has finished she will need help quickly. Call the vet, but meanwhile start by inserting two fingers to get hold of the first puppy's head (as previously described). This will probably facilitate the first arrival and the others should follow.
- If there is still an unborn puppy.
- If straining finishes suddenly.
- If straining lasts for two to three hours and no puppy arrives.
- If the puppy jams in the vagina because it is in the wrong position.
- If the puppy seems odd in some way (for example, if it is deformed or not breathing correctly).
- If you suspect that a placenta is retained (It is extremely difficult to count them.) An injection will get it out and avoid infection. Many breeders ask for this injection as a routine precaution.

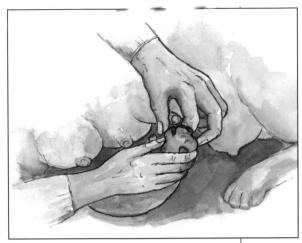

Put each puppy to the teat as soon as it is born so that it will get the essential colostrum.

Food

Provide the bitch with a light diet for the first three days, with plenty of milky products, goat's milk being particularly good. Too much food could upset her during this time. After that she will eat two or three times her normal intake of calories. She needs plenty of mince beef and chicken and warm milk to drink, and can have three meals a day until weaning. She may become tired of milk after a while. If so, give glucose in water for a change.

Aftercare

It is usually difficult to coax the dam out to relieve herself for the first couple of times. Give her a drink of water and spoil her, and leave her alone after cleaning the bed.

If she does not take it through her teeth, tie it with cotton to stop it bleeding.

The vaginal discharge can go on for two to three weeks or more. The bowel movement is very loose for the first few days. Powdered charcoal mixed with kaolin will help, but is not usually necessary. Avoid medication as far as possible as it gets into the milk.

The dam will want to go out about four times a day during the first week. She should have about 15 minutes break from the puppies so that she does not get fed up with them. Wipe her teats after each walk. Cover the puppies with a blanket while she is out.

The puppies should be kept in an environment heated to 24-26°C (75-80°F) for the first week only. As already stated, if they are warm enough at a slightly lower temperature, so much the better.

Try to avoid any visitors. If anyone does come only let them view from a distance.

Hand-rearing

If you are unfortunate enough to lose your bitch, or she is ill and has to be kept apart from her puppies, they should be kept warm and out of draughts. For the first week, maintain a temperature of 26-30°C (80-85°F). Keep a bowl of water nearby to humidify the air.

If it is at all possible the pups must get colostrum in the first few hours.

Emergency milk can be made by adding a beaten egg yolk to a pint of boiled milk. Tinned condensed milk is a good substitute for the first few days if need be. Add four teaspoons tinned milk to three teaspoons of boiled water.

If a puppy is really weak, two or three drops of milk and glucose can be sufficient to revive it.

Fill an eye dropper with the warm milk. Give just a drop at a time to avoid fluid getting into the lungs. Give enough to see the tummy firm and bulging, maybe half to even a full dropper. Small swabs of absorbent cotton can be used if a dropper is not available. Fill the swab with milk and squeeze onto the puppy's tongue.

A watercolour paint brush (No 6 or 8) is another useful substitute. It can be soaked in milk, then put in the mouth to stimulate sucking. Hypodermic syringes (no needles) are another alternative. I find this the best method, but be very careful applying the pressure: small puppies choke very easily, and they can get pneumonia if milk goes into the lungs.

Tube feeding, straight into the stomach, is a quick way to feed a litter. It is pretty drastic, however, and not recommended unless it is carried out by a trained expert when there seems no other alternative.

When they start eating more, bottle feeding is better and safer. (Catac bottles for cats are excellent.) Make a small opening in the nipple by using a red hot needle. The thumb rests on the top of the bottle to control the milk flow. Great care is needed here so that the puppy does not suck in air.

During the first week feed the puppies every two to three hours. It is difficult to state a quantity, but see that the tummy is well filled, firm and rounded, but not too tight. About 2.5ml a meal should be enough at first, but the amount each puppy takes varies greatly. It is worth making a record of the time and quantity of each meal and weighing the puppy at the same time each day to check on the progress. In the second week feed about 12ml every three hours.

If the puppy chokes, takes in air, or blows milk up and down the dropper, regulate the milk flow at once. It requires some skill to feed a small puppy without this happening. If some milk goes up the nostrils and the puppy splutters, support the neck and shake once downwards, starting in a horizontal position, then wipe the face with a towel.

After its meal, the puppy needs to have its back end lightly touched by a finger to stimulate bowel movement, which will follow instantly.

Puppies cry when they are hungry. If the skin on the back of the neck is slow going back into position the puppy is probably dehydrated and will need a drink. If it is well fed it will sleep between meals.

Feed according to what the puppy needs for its size. When it is full the sides should give a little when pressed. If it feels hard it ate too much, and if it looks rather flat it needs more food. The weight chart is the safest guide when unsure. The puppy must retain its weight. Normally it gains regularly, but there are times when it has a struggle to gain.

Foster-mother

If a foster-mother is needed it is best if she is the same size as the real mother.

If the bitch is happy with her litter and not too concerned about other things, give her one of her own puppies to lick, and then one orphan puppy. If she licks it straight away then probably it is accepted. If it is rejected or she growls, take it away at once.

Another trick to get the foster-mother to accept the new puppy is to put a couple of her puppies in a warm box with the new one so that it will pick up their smell. It is also worth rubbing their faeces over the new puppy.

You can also put butter on the backs of all the puppies so when the mother licks them on return to their nest they will all seem like her own puppies. Make sure they are all placed on a teat and feeding and all should be well.

Temperature/pulse rate

Puppy temperature is 37.8-38.9°C (100-102°F), pulse (or heart beat rate) 160 to 200 a minute, and breathing rate 20 to 30 a minute. It is the pulse rate that differs most from that of an adult, the adult rate being 100 to 130 beats a minute. A low pulse rate in a puppy is a bad sign. The pulse can be taken inside the thigh where the beat is felt in the artery. Otherwise, feel the heart beat on the left side of the chest above the level of the elbow.

Some surprises

These possibilities are listed here because they do happen occasionally. It is not always possible to get a vet to the scene on time, and obviously you want to save the bitch pain and save the puppy if possible. Each birth can bring a surprise and a swift calm reaction is needed.

Cord too short: Sometimes the cord is too short for the puppy to drop. Open the sac and cut the cord half an inch from the puppy and seal it. Check the puppy, dry it, weigh it and put it to teat.

Backwards: Coming out backwards does not matter at all. If the rump comes before the hind legs it is harder on the bitch but she can cope with it. It is preferable if the back legs come out first. Hold the feet gently but firmly to stop them going back inside the bitch again. If they do go back inside again, and the placenta is separated from the puppy, the puppy may suffocate because it no longer gets air from the blood supply, and if the sac breaks it will drown.

Although forwards is thought of as the 'usual' way, coming out backwards does not matter at all.

To get the puppy out, grasp what you can of it with one hand and do not let go. When more of the puppy is out, use the other hand if you can to get a better hold. Resuscitate if necessary. Normally this procedure it not necessary; the sac may break but the puppy is delivered within a minute and all is well.

Legs get stuck: Occasionally help is needed to get a leg out. It may just get stuck against the wall of the vagina. This is rather frightening because of the risk of damage to the tiny leg. Sometimes the leg position is wrong, in which case you may need to put a finger inside the vagina to correct the position.

If you see a leg sticking out, ease it forward to release one shoulder and then get the other leg out in the same way. Once the shoulders are out there is enough of the puppy to grasp with a towel and, with a gentle slightly rotating action, you can pull the rest out quickly.

Uterine inertia: This is when the water sac has broken, the bitch has shown all the other signs of imminent birth, and then she strains for hours without delivering a puppy. The other symptom is when she goes through the normal labour procedure but does not reach the final straining stage. This is a serious condition that can be treated. Keep in touch with the vet in either case.

Bitch stops straining during delivery: if the bitch stops straining during delivery, put your (greased) thumb and forefinger up the vagina and try to get hold of the puppy's head. Gently ease it forward, pulling downwards; this may be enough to

make the delivery and save the puppy. You may be able to get hold of the puppy with only one finger, greased with antiseptic cream, curling it round the neck of the puppy, then gently easing it out.

Large puppy blocking birth channel: an older bitch, even six years old, can sometimes have a large puppy in the uterus and this can make her pant for days and block the exit for the other puppies which could then die. Consult your vet if the birth process takes too long or if she seems distressed.

Slow birth: If the head is out but the rest is slow coming open the sac at once to let the puppy breathe. Hold the puppy round the neck and ease out, pulling the head down and forwards. If it is still tight, slightly rotate the head to release the shoulders.

Puppy arriving upside-down: Occasionally a puppy is delivered with its tummy up. This does not matter as a rule. You can attempt to turn it gently but will probably find it has arrived before you have time to do this.

Has the last puppy arrived/last placenta been expelled: It can be difficult to tell by feel if the last puppy has arrived. If the next birth does not follow quickly, the uterus contracts and feels hard as if it were a puppy. However, if she strains when she is taken out to relieve herself as if she is about to deliver again (and seems generally somewhat uncomfortable), another puppy or a placenta could be retained. Call the vet in either case for an injection. The injection gets the placenta out and clears up any infection very quickly.

Infection: If the bitch has a temperature she may well growl at the puppies until she feels better. Occasionally they may have to be removed and hand reared until the vet has been able to clear the infection and bring the temperature back to normal.

Metritis: A prolonged whelping or retained placenta can result in uterine infection. The symptoms are: a swollen vulva, with a discharge of dirty white pus or a bloody mess with white spots; a high pulse rate (normally 90-100 per minute); loss of appetite; and a change in posture (she sits differently, only half sitting up but resting on the elbows and hocks). The vet will give an antibiotic injection for this.

Absorption (or resorption) of foetus: As mentioned previously, foetuses can be absorbed into the blood stream at any time during pregnancy, and no-one will know anything about it. You seldom see an abortion, but occasionally an incompletely absorbed foetus is delivered with a large litter. This is when the bone structure has developed beyond the point at which it can be absorbed. Have a bin ready to throw it away quickly. (See section on **Absorption** in Chapter 6.)

Caesarean section: It is very rare that Fox Terriers need to have the puppies removed by surgery. The most likely reasons for the vet to do this are: a long and fruitless labour; a large puppy blocking the way for the whole litter; a badly presenting puppy; and inertia (inability to have contractions).

Gas is the safest anaesthetic. Some forms of anaesthetic can be damaging to the puppies, who will then require artificial respiration. They should not be returned to the bitch until she is fully alert. Watch carefully to make sure she accepts the puppies and they suckle properly.

Eclampsia: Eclampsia, or milk fever, quite often follows the birth of a large litter when a lot of milk is produced suddenly, so that a substantial amount of calcium is needed to redress the balance. Liquid calcium is excellent and will save the immediate situation. The problem can recur, however, and the bitch will have to be kept under observation to ensure that she gets the right amount of calcium. This is critical for the bitch and the puppies, as too much is also extremely harmful. Whilst this problem can arise at any time during the first three weeks of lactation it usually happens about the second day.

There are various symptoms: rapid breathing, extreme restlessness, panic, nervousness, and prolonged growling or crying. As the condition progresses, limbs may become stiff and the bitch may lie there unable to get up. The condition, caused by a malfunction of the pituitary gland, must be treated at once. Giving calcium before the puppies arrive is **not** the answer because it can result in deformed puppies. (See section on **Vitamins** in Chapter 6.)

Mastitis: This is when the mammary glands get hard because there is too much milk left. Keep an eye on the teats and, if they seem to be getting clogged, just press out a little milk; that should do the trick. If the teat has become red and hard, massage with olive oil first, or a warm cloth. Then release a little milk and put a puppy on to suckle.

Occasionally an abscess may result, necessitating surgery. In this case the puppies will need to be hand reared.

After whelping

When the family has arrived put the puppies in the box on a covered hot water bottle with a light blanket over the top of them to keep them warm and calm. Change the bed and clean the bitch (who can now be called the dam) thoroughly. Give her a drink of warm milk and honey or glucose and let the family settle down.

Leave water for the dam as she will be very hot. Make sure all the puppies are sucking. If one has difficulty, hold it to the teat; squeeze out a bit of milk with the thumb and forefinger, and hold the puppy there until it has had its fill, and has a nicely rounded tummy. When the puppies are getting milk they vigorously attack the teat and push with their paws also; it is almost like a tug of war.

If all is well, leave the family to rest without any outside disturbance at all.

Keep an eye on smaller puppies; put them on the back teats where there is more milk. Sometimes let them feed alone to get a good top up.

Keep a weight record

Weigh the puppies when possible and keep a daily record of weight and other useful information. There are times when not much gain is made, but actual weight loss needs urgent attention. A few drops of glucose and water or milk will often do the trick, and a drop or two of Rescue Remedy may save a life.

It is also useful to keep a record of length of head and body and of height at various stages, comparing these with the puppy's measurements at six months, to get some idea when they are young how they may turn out later on.

Spending a penny

The first few days the bitch is reluctant to leave the puppies to 'spend a penny', but she will go

She will have a greenish or blood-stained discharge for some days, even weeks. This becomes brown in due course. If it becomes smelly see the vet.

The eyes and ears

When the puppy is born the eyes are closed and do not open until between day 10-14. The ears are also closed but they can hear a little sooner.

Cut the toe nails

Cut claws weekly as they damage the tender skin around the dam's teats.

Regular worming

Worm the puppies at six, eight, ten and twelve weeks of age, and then monthly. Canovel palatable wormer, produced by Beecham, can be purchased at any pet shop and is cheaper than Endorid (also a Beecham product) which the vets sell. Although monthly worming is recommended after the first year, twice a year would probably suffice.

8

The new family

Watching the young puppies grow

At birth the puppies can weigh anything from 1.1kg to 2.3kg (4oz to 8oz). A 2kg (7oz) puppy is a nice, strong, healthy creature. By the end of the first week they should have doubled in weight. From the start, puppies are able to crawl around, find warm places to sleep (like the nice piece of blanket they can crawl under), and find their way back to the dam for a meal when they are hungry. They also make noises and cuddle up together in small groups. If they cry they need food. Take care that they are not cold.

Every puppy must get colostrum

Make sure every puppy gets some colostrum from the dam in the first 48 hours for its immune protection. Try to collect some from the teat if a weak puppy cannot feed itself.

Help the weak puppy at once

If a puppy is not doing well, try holding it onto the dam's teat having just squeezed out a drop of milk before embarking on hand-rearing (see Chapter 7). You need to put a fair amount of the teat into the puppy's mouth. While the puppy

From the start, the puppies are able to crawl around. Photo: Lynn Bell.

tries to suckle, squeeze the teat slightly with the thumb and forefinger of the other hand to help the milk flow. This might be enough to get it going. Another remedy for a weak puppy is a pinch of glucose in warm milk. Put the milk in a spoon and, with an eye dropper, suck it up and give to the puppy. Later this remedy can be slightly increased and given four times a day, the dosage being one saltspoon glucose in one tablespoon of warm water or milk. The problem about hand-rearing is not only that it is extremely exhausting mentally and physically; it is also that the puppy comes to rely on it entirely until it is weaned. There is no chance that the puppy will go back to the teat; it has had its food the easy way. Puppies have to work very hard to get their milk from the dam.

Weigh puppies every day

Puppies should feel firm, with round, hard tummies. If in doubt, weigh them. They visibly swell up after a meal.

First three days are critical

For the first three days the puppies need to be checked constantly. Whilst there can be some totally trouble free litters, accidents sometimes occur for no obvious reason. A litter that seems to be doing well one minute can be in a state of extreme distress half an hour later. There may be just one sick puppy or it could be the whole litter suddenly and inexplicably at risk. There is also fading puppy syndrome, when a puppy starts off well and suddenly seems to just give up. This takes a determined effort to keep going by hand-rearing. It is not unusual for a puppy to have inadequate sucking power but, so long as it has the will to live, it can probably be saved by hand-rearing. It will become a very devoted friend as an adult.

Care should be taken in giving medication to the dam; it could pass into the milk and then poison the puppies.

Hand feed initially with eye dropper/small syringe

It is hard to give guidelines about how much milk to give a puppy that needs hand-rearing. It depends on its size, weight and how well it is doing. At first a few drops of milk is enough to save a life and this can be given through an eye dropper. It is important to give the colostrum from the bitch for the first 24 to 48 hours to provide the antibodies for the puppy's immune protection. Then make sure it gets proper meals. With a small syringe, start by feeding about 2.5ml per meal, feeding every two hours. It will eat a lot more at some meals than at others. In seven days this could be more than doubled, and at three weeks it may consume a quarter of a pint per day. Weighing the puppy and feeling a round (but not tight) tummy is the guide. At some stages there may be no gain for several days, but do not let a loss of weight arise. (See section on **Hand-rearing** in Chapter 7.)

The biggest litter born to Newmaidley.

A good litter

Hopefully the above possibilities will not happen and the puppies will all do well with the dam for the first three weeks, so that it will be fun to watch their development and progress.

Let the dam out and for a rest

During the first two to three days the bitch should go out two or three times a day. Let her have a 15-minute break and a bit of attention. She will then be happy to resume her maternal duties. Fox Terrier dams do sometimes get fed up with the litter from time to time. They are good mothers, but everyone needs a break sometimes! Let her have one, or even a short walk, but clean her feet on return.

Feeding the dam

For the first two to three days give the bitch a light milky diet, little and often, with water always available. On the first day, give her warm milk (untreated goat's milk is much more tasty) with Farex, milk and honey or glucose. On days 2 and 3 add milky rice pudding, brown bread, egg, milk and cornflakes, and perhaps some steamed fish, rabbit, chicken, or cottage cheese. She could eat three to four times her normal intake of food while producing the milk. The amount of food she needs will depend on the number of puppies and their demands on the dam. Fresh good food is essential. Give three feeds a day while she is nursing, with drinks of warm milk in between, and a drink of milk and glucose last thing at night.

Pink noses

Noses are often pink at first, and they sometimes take longer to turn black on bitch puppies than on dog puppies. By eight weeks they are usually black. Mottled noses can take 18 months to change.

Ears

The ears lay flat at first and are closed for the first three to four weeks. When they do start to fold into the familiar place they are sometimes quite droopy, lifting higher later on. Ear and tail carriage is rather unpredictable even from eight weeks of age. During teething (four to eight months) the ears can 'fly'. This looks ugly, but they usually settle afterwards. Some people glue them down, or fix them in position with plaster. Most Fox Terriers do not need this help. The smaller the ear the more likely it is to fly. During teething it is better not to trim the hair on the ears as the prickling from pulling the hair tends to make them lift the ear upwards and thereby strengthens the muscles to do this.

Weaning

Lapping starts at three weeks. Begin with warm milk and a teaspoon of glucose. If you put this in a bowl on the floor they will walk in it, play in it and get covered in it. It is better to feed each one separately at first so that it gets the general idea of lapping. They learn very quickly, but some are more messy than others.

Then add Farex, baby rusks or brown breadcrumbs to the milk to make a slightly more solid meal. You could try Weetabix, but this is usually better when they are older. If they do not like this, try porridge, rice pudding or egg custard.

Liquidizers are excellent for making a mulched meal which they can easily digest. With this simple machine you can give them almost anything left over from the table. Keep the meals really sloppy.

Next add fresh chicken, minced beef, fish or egg to the menu with some nice gravy and carrots. Give alternate milk and meat meals. This way they get good quality fresh food, which is better than buying baby food from the chemist.

As soon as the puppies start eating meat meals the dam no longer cleans up their mess or licks their bottoms clean. Make sure you make them 'spend' after each meal by touching the rear end with a piece of flannel. If the rear gets caked with solid faeces, clean off with cotton wool soaked in olive oil.

Puppies are very fussy about what they eat. Each meal (four a day) must be freshly made or they will refuse it. They will literally starve themselves to death rather than give in. I have often given up to four different meals in the hope of finding one that was acceptable. This phase, needless to say, is not too long lived. The bitch will eat anything they leave.

While the puppies have their own meals they still go to the dam for a drink of milk whenever they can, but she gradually goes in there less and less until she just lets them have a quick drink and then dashes off again.

The Fox Terrier usually lets her puppies take the occasional feed from her for at least six weeks, often longer. Therefore it is important to ensure that she is dry (no milk left in the teats) before all the puppies go.

At four weeks they are crawling about all over the place and chatting away to each other. They look slightly less fat. They need five or six meals a day.

At five weeks, thicken milk with Farex twice a day and continue beef and chicken for two meals a day, increasing the amount. Feed the dam separately and return her one hour later. She might welcome going for a walk but do not go anywhere too dirty.

At six weeks puppies take four meals a day and are probably still pestering the bitch. She will kick them off when she is ready.

At six to eight weeks add puppy biscuit meal soaked in boiling (or boiled) water. Add liquidised meat and vegetable products to the biscuit meal or soaked breadcrumbs. Still give in a sloppy form. One egg per litter is good and sometimes a drop of cod liver oil.

At eight to twelve weeks they need feeding about every five hours during the day time, say 7.00 am, 12.00 noon, 5.00 pm and supper at 10.00 pm.

The puppies decide when they want fewer meals. Breakfast is usually the first meal they give up, opting for lunch too and supper. When this happens I usually bring forward the lunch; otherwise it is a long time since the last meal.

Depending on the dog, by five months it will probably be down to two meals a day and a biscuit and milky drink in bed at night. By the time he is a year old one meal a day is enough.

Too much food

Never let a puppy get too fat. It may store up trouble in later life.

In our anxiety to be kind to our pet it is all too easy to give it too much food and too many treats. It is not good for the dog. Dogs are always greedy and will look for food whenever possible. Keep an eye on the weight and appearance of the dog. Once it gets fat it is very hard to get it off again.

Feeding bowl

If the puppies all feed from one or two bowls, make sure they all take enough. There are always the greedy ones and the others that do not bother. Look at the thinner ones, weigh them and, if in doubt, feed each puppy separately.

If one puppy needs more attention than this try putting the food on the floor or in a different type of container. Some do not like plastic. They will usually eat out of your hand, but try to avoid spoiling if possible. Always have water available for the puppies to drink in a bowl that is not too deep.

A litter of Smooth Fox Terriers. Photo: Isabelle Français.

House training

They start 'spending' on their own at about three weeks. If it is not too cold or wet the puppies can go to relieve themselves outside from five weeks of age. They look delightful trotting out after each meal and all squatting down together. Usually there is one brave one that leads the whole gang.

Mine usually meet the milkman, the dustman and the postman at this time, and learn to accept them for life.

By the time they are eight weeks old they need to 'spend' every two hours, and more if they get excited playing games. The usual times are when they wake up, after a meal and soon after playing and enjoying themselves (say 10 minutes).

By eight weeks they last a bit longer, but the same rules apply.

Teething

The upper canines may start to show through at three to four weeks. These milk teeth are very sharp indeed. Sometimes the mouths gets very sore during teething and the food may have to be extra soft for a few days. The puppy may not eat much at this time and there may be no weight gain, but it is big enough to sustain this slight set-back now. In due course the roots of these teeth get absorbed into the system, loosening the milk teeth and making way for the permanent teeth to come through. This happens at about four to eight months.

It can happen that too many teeth come through at the same time at around five to eight months, making the mouth very sore indeed. Eating then becomes a problem for a few days. Avoid giving puppies extra calcium (unless essential) other than in a natural form like goat's milk or cottage cheese, as this could help cause this distressing condition. A teaspoon of milk of magnesia once a week during teething might help. However, the change of teeth usually passes quite unnoticed apart from the need for the puppy to bite anything available. Therefore, give it plenty of toys to chew. Terriers have a scissor bite, whereby the tips of the upper incisors (the front teeth) slightly overlap the lower ones. The long canine teeth sit close together when closed, the tips of the upper canine resting on the outside the lip, and the tip of the lower one resting outside the gum so that they do not damage the gums or lip.

When the dogs are young the teeth keep pretty clean. Marrow bones given occasionally clean the teeth but might cause tummy upsets. No other bone should be given as they splinter and could injure the dog.

Socialisation

From about five weeks of age it is important that the puppies meet people and generally start to socialise. It is good for them to be handled and played with and to get used to the human race. They can meet visitors to the house, but be careful about hygiene, especially that your guests have clean hands and remove footwear. It is essential that the pups become familiar with everyday things such as house noises, traffic, people and television.

Fresh air and outings

Puppies need fresh air and daylight to get strong. The more time spent outside the better, providing it is not too cold or damp. To get them used to the outside world, I often carry young puppies on a walk, either into town or in the woods. They learn very fast and the experience is no longer an anxiety the second time round. Car rides, visits to friends and other outings are all very beneficial to the young puppy before he leaves for his new home. They prepare him for the change and should enable him to settle quickly without distress.

With this experience behind him, when the young puppy leaves at eight weeks of age in a fit and healthy condition it is unlikely the new owners will have any problems at all. Many people have insurance cover for the first six weeks of new ownership. This is because some puppies can become seriously ill and distressed. It is most unlikely that this would happen to a Fox Terrier unless it was not being looked after properly; for instance, if the diet was wrong, or if he was traumatised by a long journey or had met with cruelty or neglect.

Finding the right home (See also Chapter 5: Buying a Puppy)
Take telephone number and address: Be sure to take the caller's name, telephone number and address. Try to get some information about whether they have kept dogs before, and especially if they know this breed.

Know the breed: When people enquire about buying a puppy it is advisable to ask if they are familiar with the breed and understand what is involved. It is also a good idea to make sure someone will be at home for the greater part of every day.

Match puppy to person/circumstances: It is worth trying to match the puppy to the circumstances and character and energy reserves of the new owner. Give the lively puppy to the family with children, and a quiet puppy perhaps to an older or frail person, or to someone whose space is limited.

Need for training and discipline: It is important for the buyer to understand there will be some accidents. There will be teething problems and the puppy will chew everything. However, if it is given suitable toys and training, things need not be too bad - indeed they are great fun.

A lovable scamp: 'Trafalgar' aged 8½ weeks.

Secure garden: The more space there is for the Fox Terrier the better it is for the dog. Tell the prospective buyer to make sure the garden is totally escape proof. Whilst some dogs are good about staying at home, others are not, and their road sense tends to be nil when other things attract their attention.

Beware of dealers: There are bogus buyers who are, in fact, dealers. They make a considerable amount of money by purchasing young puppies for export, which could be to anywhere in the world. They are often very plausible when questioned, saying that the puppy will go to a good, family home, and considerable detective skills are needed to verify this information. One giveaway is that they will often accept puppies without pedigree certificates, registration documents or inoculation certificates.

Another type of dealer buys puppies from 'puppy farms', where they are likely to have been intensively bred under dubious conditions, and sells them at a profit. In such cases the puppy has often been taken from its dam too early and has had a long, traumatic journey. The new owner has no access to a specialist to consult about diet and other problems and, with such a poor start, these could be many!

It follows from this that it is always best for the prospective buyer to visit the breeder and see the puppy with its dam and siblings, and for the breeder to find out as much as possible about the buyer before letting puppies go.

Best of friends: two young Wire Fox Terriers, ready for anything.
Photo: Isabelle Français.

Tail docking

Since January 1993 tail docking, by law, has to be carried out by a qualified vet, usually when the puppies are three days old.

There are mixed feelings about docking. Most Wire Fox Terrier breeders have joined the Council for Docked Breeds and they will give a member the name of the nearest vet who is willing to dock.

'Trafalgar': only 8½ weeks and already 'showing'.

Some vets are very reluctant to dock; others will do it but at the risk of being reported to the Veterinary College. Although it is lawful for vets to dock (and many were happy to do it before the issue was raised in Parliament) the College decided they were against it in principle. It therefore has to be done on the quiet.

When tails are undocked accidents can and do happen to terriers, resulting in severe pain to the dog and in veterinary bills. Terriers are working dogs, which is why they were docked in the first place, their tails often being used as 'handles' to pull them out of the fox holes. In France today a terrier still has to work to win in the show ring.

If you decide that you are going to have your puppies' tails docked, call a vet well before the litter arrives to ascertain whether he is willing to dock. As soon as the puppies are born, arrange for it to be done when they are three days old. The puppies do not feel it at all, and the tails very seldom bleed.

Vets are only just beginning to learn where to dock a terrier's tail, and they do tend to take off far too much. It is best to advise them that we only take the tip off, at most just a third of the tail. The aim is to make the tail the same height as the top of the head.

It should be cut so that the skin at the front of the tail is slightly longer than at the back. While the cut is being made the skin should be pulled down sharply, giving some surplus skin to cover the top to facilitate healing. A thick-set, cobby puppy with lots of bone and a thick tail requires less taken off than a racy type, lighter in bone and longer in back and tail (the two usually go together). It helps to pull the tails regularly at first to avoid 'gay' tails. After docking the tails are usually dipped in crushed permanganate of potash to prevent bleeding.

Happy family: a Wire Fox Terrier bitch with her pups. Try to see the whole family together when choosing your puppy.
Photo: Isabelle Français.

You can take off the dew-claws at home, but if the vet does the tail it is far better he does these too. Dew-claws are extra toes at the back of the front legs, which frequently get damaged if left on. If the joint is not completely removed they grow again, and it then becomes a major operation. The joint has to be cut back right close to the bone, which is best left to the expert. The puppies do feel these being removed momentarily.

The Council of Docked Breeds

The Council of Docked Breeds was set up to help owners and breeders of docked breeds and vets who were prepared to dock. Breeders and owners are all recommended to join the society for a subscription of £9.00, renewal: £6.50 (1995 prices). (See Appendix A: **Useful Addresses**.)

You will be given a receipt and membership number. When a litter is expected, write or call the secretary and she will send you the name of the nearest vet who will dock. Allow plenty of time for this because sometimes vets are away from their practice and their willingness to dock may change for some reason.

The Council is there to take up any ensuing legal action against the vet or the breeder. It is important to follow the law and to be discreet. Whole litters from customarily docked breeds have remained unsold because the vet refused to dock. This is regrettable. It is not always obvious whether or not a Fox Terrier has been docked, but always advise the owner/breeder of the position because some vets refuse to inoculate docked dogs, which is shattering for the new owner. I recommend legal docking; it is better for the dog and is what most people expect. At the time of writing no obviously undocked dogs have been seen in the ring in this country and, according to the Breed Standard, the tail is 'customarily docked'.

Photo: Isabelle Français.

9 *General* care

Healthy and fun

This chapter is essentially for the pet owner or for someone with just a few dogs for show, not for commercial kennels.

Fox Terriers are healthy animals, full of bounce and fun. They enjoy playing games and want attention, love and affection.

The main essentials are good food, with water always available, fresh air, exercise and, of course, a clean bed. This should be checked every day to make sure it is not dirty, and the bedding washed frequently to avoid flea infestation. In the house a dog box is recommended rather than a basket; it cannot be chewed, it is safer for the puppy and is helpful in training the puppy to be clean. It has the further advantage that a possible fight with a visiting dog can be avoided, each one having its own secure space and box. A towel put across the front at bed time usually stops any disturbances during the night.

A dog box rather than a basket is recommended because it cannot be chewed up and it gives the dog a secure place of his own.

If the dog is outside in cold weather he needs a warm kennel that is raised off the ground. Old carpets, newspapers and blankets will make it comfortable and warm. A converted tea chest can be used, or timber merchants can make a suitable kennel for you. Kennels can also be bought at Championship shows. (See also the end of this chapter.)

If there is a cat or another dog in the house they will work out who is boss in their own way. Not wanting to get hurt, they each push their luck, but soon reach a mutual understanding, and it is rare that any serious damage results.

In the summer my Fox Terriers enjoy basking in the sun, even to the point when they are panting from the heat. They then go and dip their feet and tummies into a baby bath I leave out for them as their swimming pool. I find this a useful item as their coats spoil very quickly when the weather is hot. I try to keep the bath full of rain water, this is good for their coats, and it saves me having to fill it up from the tap myself.

Travelling

For safety when travelling by car the dog should be in a metal cage, wooden dog box or dog harness. Even a well-behaved dog can be thrown off the seat if the car stops suddenly.

Food

Terriers often do not like tinned dog food and it makes some dogs sick. In some instances they cannot eat the biscuit meal either. It is therefore useful to try out various products and see which one your dog likes.

When travelling by car the dog should be in a metal cage, wooden dog box or dog harness.

Vary the menu as much as possible, using plenty of scraps from the table and as much fresh good food as possible. All the unwanted bits from a chicken are good (other than the bones), eggs (cooked mostly), vegetables, rice, brown bread and any other bits of meat. Proprietary brands of cereal are fine, including oat meal bran (not too much), and porridge. I also give my dogs a considerable quantity of vegetables, especially carrots, which help to keep their teeth clean. I am careful not to give much cabbage as this can cause diarrhoea.

Meat shops and pubs are often willing to let the pet owner take away some juicy scraps which are a special treat for the dog. In America it is common practice to take a Doggie Bag to the restaurant and fill it with left-overs from the meal for the dog. At first I thought it was rather naughty but now I always collect everything for which I have paid.

Never give the dog a bone from the table, no matter how suitable it looks. Remove the meat and throw the bone away. Unless it is a hard marrow bone it will splinter and harm the dog.

The pet owner does not need to rely on tinned foods, although they are carefully prepared to provide an adequate, balanced diet for pets. They are convenience foods and it is easy to get the idea that this is the only correct way to feed the dog. Humans would not be too happy to have every meal out of a tin, and I am sure the same goes for the dog. It is probably cheaper to feed fresh food, the dog prefers it, and there is no waste.

Once my dogs are beyond the puppy stage they are normally fed once a day in the afternoon. They have a few bits of biscuit at lunch time, queuing up for these treats. At night they have a hard dry biscuit of some kind to chew.

Photo: Isabelle Français.

Fox Terriers love to play, so it is a good idea to choose toys that are good for their health. This Smooth is carrying a Plaque Attacker® Dental Floss from the Nylabone® range, which is designed to reduce the build-up of tartar on his teeth.

Health

It is thought that the puppy's natural immunisation from the colostrum begins to wear off at six to eight weeks. Whilst it might be tempting to start inoculations at eight weeks it is recommended to wait a few weeks to let the puppy settle down first in the new environment. The stress of the new home and the vaccinations can be too much for a small puppy. The rabies vaccine is often not given until the puppy is four months old. Even a fully vaccinated adult dog can contract Kennel Cough (among other things) from the booster vaccinations. It is recommended that vaccinations be renewed each year, especially if the dog is likely to be left at kennels during the summer holidays.

Worming should be done at least twice a year, or as recommended on the packet. Beecham's Canovel tablets from the pet shop appear to be efficient and are not too expensive.

The Fox Terrier is normally very healthy and any minor injury or sickness will usually clear up in a couple of days.

In the summer dogs tend to pick up fleas or mites from the grass and itchy feet and skin irritation are not uncommon. Flea powder is essential, and the moment fleas are suspected the dog should be bathed using an insecticidal shampoo. Sometimes one bite can lead to an acute allergic reaction. Tetmolsol can be used to get rid of some irritation. Another help is goat's milk. It is worth bearing in mind that some dogs are allergic to wheat products.

Exercise

Regular exercise is an important feature of the dog's life. It keeps him fit, well and happy. It stimulates his brain, teaches him social skills, and through it he gets used to different noises and gains confidence.

The Fox Terrier is a hunting dog and his favourite exercise is doing just that. The woods and fields are where he gets his fun, nose to the ground in search of rabbits, squirrels, deer, foxes or even ducks on a pond. I was extremely embarrassed once when on a hot day I took my normally well-trained dog for a drink at the village pond when on an outing. He quickly jumped in and chased every duck present. He got a thrill seeing them take flight and no amount of calling would bring him back until the chase was over. No damage was done but he did not get a chance to repeat this activity.

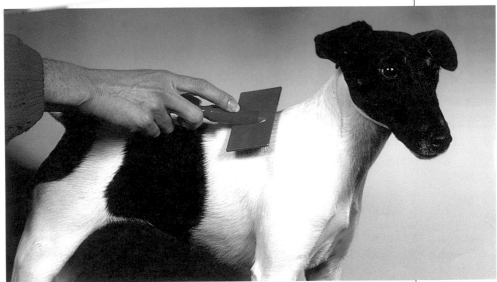

Even for the Smooth, regular grooming has advantages. It helps to keep the coat clean and parasite-free and can be a 'bonding' time for owner and dog. Photo: Isabelle Français.

Pavement walks on the lead, teaching him to wait before crossing the road, and 'leave' when passing other dogs is all part of his daily routine. If you have a garden it is probably sufficient to let the dog out morning and evening and give him a walk in the afternoon, or at any rate once during the day. Otherwise three outings a day are recommended; a short walk in the morning, a longer one in the afternoon and a short one at night. They always 'spend' when they go out, so it is important to pick up the mess in a plastic bag and put in the rubbish bin.

Where the owner has access to more exciting walks there are a few points worth remembering:

- The young puppy wants to do anything and everything, but exercise should be monitored in the growing stages. I once took a young dog for a three hour walk and he took more than three days to recover fully. At the time he enjoyed it and seemed perfectly fit and well, but afterwards it was clear it had been too much for him. This was a lesson learned by experience.
- In woods the young puppy can easily get stuck down a rabbit hole.
- When ascending a mountain the dog is under considerable stress, although he can come down quickly and easily. This activity should not be undertaken until the dog is about three years old.

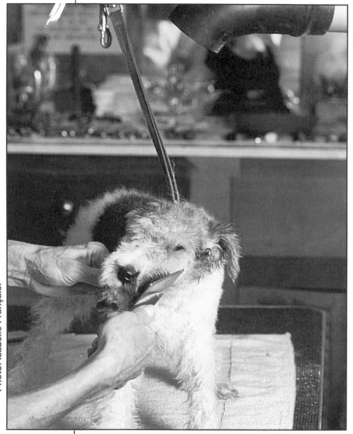

Photo: Isabelle Français.

Look at the dog every day on the grooming table.

In the hot summer months the dogs are usually happy to sun-bathe. Walks should be undertaken during the cooler hours of the day and can be shorter. On the other hand, dogs can become very lively in cooler weather, like bored children with plenty of energy to burn up. A trip to the nearest fields or woods is the answer, where an hour's good run will settle them for the rest of the day. I firmly believe that if they have sufficient exercise they are contented and not so likely to become aggressive.

Fox Terriers also love car rides. If the ride is linked to a specially nice walk, so much the better. When you are out on a walk, meeting other dogs that are rushing around chasing a ball or stick can upset the Fox Terrier, who will join in and try to take over. Since Terriers chase anything that moves, it is wise to put your dog on the lead quickly if this activity is going on.

Grooming

(The following paragraphs give a guide to everyday coat care. For full details of grooming and trimming, see Chapter 10.)

Look at the dog every day on the table, especially in the summer. Grooming every day is good for the coat, keeps it clean, prevents too many tangles in the longer hair, and gets rid of fleas quickly. Even when the dog is dirty after a wet walk, drying off and grooming is usually sufficient. White chalk helps to whiten the coat and gives a better grip when stripping or raking.

The daily grooming should consist of brushing the coat through with the pin pad or comb. Rake through the body with a rake or trimming knife; this will take out any dirty soft coat. Next use the trimming knife to take out the longer hairs that stick out, and then give the coat a final brush with a hard bristle brush or hound glove. The leg hair should be brushed up (the comb is more severe), and with the pin pad gently take out the matting. Comb into place carefully, trying not to take out too much precious leg hair. Bathing should only be done when absolutely necessary.

It is important to keep the toe nails clipped as they grow very fast and the dog cannot move properly when they are too long. Pavement walks help to keep them short, but the front toe nails often need cutting.

The feet need to be cleaned and any grass seed or matts between the toes removed. Muddy hair often get matted and can cause the feet to become very sore. Cut away any hair between the toes, just leaving a little, so that when the dog walks on grass his feet do not tickle too much.

Clean the ears, making sure there is no infestation or embedded grass seed

Homes and gardens

When a dog first comes to a house there are a lot of things to consider which are hard to imagine before its actual arrival.

You know about having the garden dog-proofed, but you do not know how good the puppy is at escaping. You know about having a dog box so that the puppy does not chew up everything, but you do not know about chewing the telephone cable and having a tug of war with the iron. You know about feeding the dog at meal times, but you do not know about picking up all kinds of disgusting things on walks, jumping on tables, leaping on chairs to get the chocolates, or unwrapping Christmas parcels. Do not despair: despite the odd thing that may be damaged, with care and good training you will have a healthy, well-behaved pet.

A utility room

A utility room is a great asset, particularly if it has a linoleum floor which is easy to clean. You can groom your dogs there, and if there is a large basin in which you can wash them, so much the better. They can sleep in there, and it is a place where they can run around safely when you are out. This room can double as a laundry room, a freezer room, and a repository for such items as muddy boots and umbrellas. It is also somewhere where you can dry off paws so that mud is not brought into the living room. Where there is no utility room, the kitchen is often used for this purpose without damage to health.

A special chair

The Fox Terrier is quite good at staying down when required to do so. He does, however, like the occasional cuddle on his owner's knee and his own chair. He will be most likely to sit either where you sit or on his special chair, preferably by a window so that he can bark at everything that goes by, especially other dogs. Cover these two chairs with towels and they will not get too dirty.

Stair gate

A baby-proof stair gate is useful to stop the dog going upstairs. They will always lie on your bed given a chance. When I am out I let them do this because that way they keep quiet. I simply put an extra sheet on the top, and it does not matter how dirty it gets.

Lunch time

The Fox Terrier can easily jump from the floor onto the dining room table and consume your meal. He does not want to get caught and will not usually do it if you are around. However, anything left on the table when you are out will certainly disappear. I put chairs into the bagging position, but that has never stopped them. All food has to be put somewhere totally out of reach, especially chocolates and biscuits. They will finish off the sugar, butter, cream cakes - anything.

Carpets

There is always anxiety about 'accidents' on the carpets. They will sometimes occur, but putting newspaper on an area of floor covered in linoleum may help to avoid too many disasters. Soda water is effective in cleaning up the mess.

Lawns

Sometimes it is found that when a bitch urinates a round, brown patch is left on the lawn. I find that with some stronger rye grass in the lawn it does not present a problem; the lawn can be cut really fine in summer without being damaged at all.

Flower borders

Although we used to train the dogs not to go onto the flower borders I do not bother any more. If you have a few dotted paving stones around, making little pathways (which you can use as stepping stones to do the weeding), they will use these and not damage the border plants at all. They tend to sniff around under the bushes and may even chase around, but still no damage occurs. They may urinate here too but this will help save the lawn.

Utility sheds

Get a nice wooden shed from a garden centre and put in a large cat-flap door. Put an old tea chest in there with some warm bedding for the dog during the day. Unless it is heated the dog should not be left out at night in the winter.

This shed can also be used for the garden tools which can hang on the wall, as a summer house, as a trimming room, or a place to rear young puppies in the summer.

I put an extra window in my shed, and took the electric power and lighting there too. I hung a mirror on two walls and set up my trimming table. My garden chairs are stored in there and it also serves as our stud room.

Dog runs

When planning dog runs in the garden make sure they are as large as possible, as these dogs need space. The wire needs to be 1.8m (6ft) high in a fine mesh. Concrete is easier to hose down and good for the dog's feet, but it can get too hot in summer. If possible have a grassy area also or some wooden boards for your dog to sit on. A large tree in the run would provide shade and something to run round.

You can also make a dual-purpose run reasonably attractive. Choose a suitable place for a patio. It can even have spaces for shrubs. Attractive paving stones can be used, and the area can be designed as part of the all-over scheme for the garden. One side could be a wall with a vine, another side could have attractive railings and wrought iron gates, and one or two sides wire mesh. A marvellous example of this can be found at Birdworld in Farnham. With the possibility of dogs being stolen this is quite a useful way of allowing the dog to be outside in a safely-padlocked enclosure.

Three types of dog bed: (from left to right) the vari-kennel, the box or cage made of wood and wire, and the traditional dog basket. The first two can be used as beds, for travelling and at dog shows and cannot be chewed so easily.

10

Training the young *Dog*

Understand the character

The Fox Terrier wants to please and to have fun, but will not stand being bossed around just for the sake of it. He knows what you want and may play you up a bit, but any attempt to be severe with him will make him totally defiant. He has to *want* to please you, and usually does. Therefore some means other than force or fear has to be found to train him.

The pack leader

Dogs are pack animals and the pack always has a leader. It is therefore important that in your household you maintain the position of pack leader; the dog will take over at the first opportunity!

To do this you retain the initiative, telling the dog when to go to bed, when he may have a meal, when he may have a car ride, and when he may run free in the house. This requires no formal training programme but should end with him looking to you to ask what you want next from him.

It is essential to maintain control because once the dog thinks he is the boss he will howl when you leave him and probably defecate in the house, possibly on your bed if he has the chance. Once he can boss the owner he will be hard to retrain and difficult for other people to handle, causing problems when you go on holiday or have to visit the veterinary surgeon or groomer.

Parkside Hero aged 8¹/₂ weeks. When you get home start training the young dog at once.

Be firm - say 'NO'

When you get the puppy home start the training at once. You have to tell him that 'no' means 'no' when he does something wrong. Treat him very gently, because all this is new to him and he does not know that what he is doing may not be acceptable. After that a low firm voice for 'no' and a higher voice for praise will help to make the dog a pleasant companion.

The more you are with him and control him with praise for good behaviour and 'no' for bad, the better it will be. Do not let any unacceptable behaviour go without a firm 'no'.

Rules

The young puppy needs to have restrictions on what he may do. By enforcing these limits you command his respect and lead him to accept you as the pack leader. An excellent method of teaching obedience involves the use of love and praise for good behaviour and of temporary loss of freedom (by putting him in his box for a while) for bad behaviour. He soon knows what will happen next time he does the same thing and hates to lose his freedom, as he likes to be with you. This effectively is removal of one of his 'perks', and he does not like it. It therefore serves to train him in a calm and effective manner. It seems to work rather like the system in prison: if a 'trusty' abuses his increased freedom then some of his perks are removed. The timescale in the case of the Fox Terrier is very short indeed, however.

From the start try to teach the puppy what is acceptable behaviour and what is not. The puppy is astonished at being told 'no' at first because he has always done what he likes. He quickly respects you for this and looks up to you for approval, which is really sweet.

Give love and praise when he is good and say a firm 'no' in a low voice when he is bad. It is best to have restrictions on the use of laps, chairs, beds and rooms from the beginning, although it is very difficult to do this because the puppy is so sweet and cuddly.

Limiting boundaries

Whilst it is nice for the puppy to have some freedom, initially this needs constant supervision because he explores everything and, during the teething stage, will chew anything available.

Limiting boundaries will keep him safe, especially in the case of temptingly chewable electric cables and telephone wires. It will also protect your belongings and will give you freedom from anxiety when you are visited by friends who either do not like dogs or bring their own with them.

The combination of having an enclosed dog box and an outside run is the most effective way of modifying bad behaviour. The better the dog behaves the more freedom he can have. When liberties are taken, such as begging at meal times, remove the freedom just for a short time, and next day he will behave. This is a simple and effective way of teaching him what he may or may not do. It works well; he may still let you down occasionally, but knows he will have to go to his bedroom for a while if he does.

The cage has a very calming effect on the dog; it is not a harsh punishment and the dog is quite happy about it. It is especially useful for a young puppy when he gets tired after playing. Let him relieve himself in the garden and then put him to bed to sleep. When you let him out again, immediately take him to the garden for another 'penny'.

Photo: Isabelle Français.

Limiting boundaries helps to keep your puppy safe.

The Fox Terrier likes nothing more than to be your constant companion. In general, the more time he can spend with you the more acceptable his behaviour is, but he must be reminded constantly that you are in charge. If he can go to work with you, or if he lives on a farm, he is a very happy dog. Even in these ideal circumstances he still needs to be used to other people so that he will not feel too lost when you do go away.

Avoid trouble by not letting it happen

It is often possible to avoid unacceptable behaviour by thinking ahead and preventing it; in other words, by outwitting the dog.

For example, if you do not want an 'accident' on your lounge carpet only let the dog into the lounge after he has been out. If there is any chance of an 'accident' when you are out, keep him in the utility room, kitchen or bathroom. If there is a possibility of a confrontation, then avoid that problem before it arises. If someone is afraid of dogs, put the dog in the box before opening the front door.

Dogs are liable to scratch doors when they ask to go out (or in). To avoid scratch marks, either keep the dog away from the door or put a protective cover in the appropriate place.

If you know your dog is going to bark at another dog who regularly passes your house, try to note the time of day it is likely to happen and ensure your dog is not in that part of the garden at the time. He may still be aware of the dog passing, but he will not annoy the whole neighbourhood.

These simple remedies save many upsets.

Do not tie a Fox Terrier to a long rope

Never tie a Fox Terrier to a long rope. They are very active dogs and, if their legs were caught up in the rope, could easily panic and break their legs, or even their necks. While out for a walk one day a young dog got trapped in the netting of the football posts. It became a desperate situation and, in the end, the dog had to be cut free.

Easy to train

The Fox Terrier is easy to train when he is treated correctly and understood. His outgoing personality is a delight and the list of dog problems below is there to help should any of them arise; it does not mean they are very likely to do so. It helps to have the basic understanding that a dog is an animal and not a human being, so he has his own code of behaviour which we do not always find acceptable.

Marking territory

Like other wild animals, dogs mark their territory and, if your well-trained pet dog goes to a new place, he, too, may mark the new ground, be it a new walk, a friend's garden, or even inside the house, especially at a kennel where bitches have been running around. It may never happen, but if it does it is best to deem it a 'one off' accident, and treat it with understanding and a gentle verbal reprimand.

Phone the breeder for advice

Get as much advice as you can from the breeder and if there are any problems discuss them over on the telephone. There is usually a simple remedy.

To avoid problems later on give thought, attention, training and discipline from the start. Even without any formal training the puppy will become a delightful pet so long as he is aware of the boundaries. These will be tested to the full (and any child would do the same) but he really wants to please. The main thing is do not spoil him and say 'no' firmly.

Use the lead

Sometimes more control is exercised if the dog is immediately put on the lead, and told 'no' firmly. This would help if he barked at someone, chased the pet rabbit, or if he did not come when called.

House training

A little has been said about house training at the end of Chapter 8. First be aware when the puppy needs to 'spend': after sleeping, after a meal, after about 20 minutes (or less) of exciting play. In any case take the puppy out every two hours, say 'spend' (or whatever word you choose), and wait until he has finished. This may require some patience, but wait; he will do it eventually. As a rule puppies are really good about this and an 'accident' really is an accident. Have an area in the garden where he gets used to 'spending'. Praise him and take him back inside again afterwards.

If you catch the puppy relieving himself on the carpet pick him up at once, saying 'no', and take him outside. Leave him there for a little while even if it is too late. Do not punish him. The old idea of hitting the dog, using rolled-up newspaper to make a noise, or rubbing his nose in the mess are counter-productive; he will get worse out of anxiety and confusion.

Use the utility room

When not supervised the puppy is best left either in his cage or in the kitchen/utility room where a few accidents do not matter. Last thing at night and first thing in the morning are important times to 'spend', as the puppy cannot last very long at this stage.

It sometimes happens that a Terrier is still bed-wetting at one or two years old. This needs to be treated sensitively if it is to be stopped. What would you do with a child? In my dormitory at school there was a child with this problem. All I remember now is that she certainly was not punished or scolded, and the problem went away.

The same thing happened with a bitch I owned. Even at two years old she was still bed-wetting. I kept her in an enclosure off the kitchen which was easy to clean. At night I took her out and waited until she had 'spent' before giving her a biscuit in bed. I fed her early (at about 4.00 pm) hoping that she would be able to finish 'spending' before bed-time.

She was never punished and every day I would have to clean the bedding and the floor. I was aware she always loved to have special attention and this problem could be related to that. The wetting stopped immediately she had had a litter; she then felt she was a **Top Dog** in the owner's eyes and received plenty of special attention and cuddles.

Continued bed-wetting can happen because newspaper has been put on the ground for the puppies when they are still with the dam. They were allowed to 'spend' indoors on the newspaper when they were growing up and, unless taught otherwise, they think they can go on using the newspaper and the carpets thereafter. Older dogs are particularly prone to use the carpets on nasty wet days when they do not want to go outside.

The older dog who has come from a kennel might be harder to train and he may take a couple or more months to settle in. With patience and kindness he will obey. Just take him on the lead to a regular tree or favourite 'penny' spot, give the command and praise him when he has done it. Do this every time he needs to go out.

Praise/reward

The Fox Terrier loves to be told he is a Good Boy and will wag his tail in great pleasure. Treats go a long way towards getting obedience, and mine always go to their own beds (not mine!) knowing they will get a biscuit there.

Out of sight, out of mind

In general, things that happen when the owner is out of the way are best left forgotten. Dogs hate being left alone, and any punishment given on return is probably useless because the dog does not know why he is being punished; it may even do harm. Taking steps to prevent him from repeating the crime is the best course of action.

Terriers do seem to be aware that 'what the eye does not see the heart does not grieve over' and jump on forbidden chairs, steal food or commit other 'crimes' when they think you are not looking. If they spot you looking they jump off quickly. I ignore these incidents because they are well aware of what they are doing.

Be tolerant and forgiving. Making the odd mess, stealing the Christmas chocolates, or chewing the chair leg is all part of being a dog.

The calm approach

I have always been impressed when visiting large kennels to see how well-behaved the dogs are. I am sure this is not from training (the owners and staff at these large kennels have far too much to do) but because the dogs know the routine; when it is their turn for attention they want to please the owner. They are treated very calmly at all times and respond dutifully when they are led to the run or trimming table. Dogs are very time-conscious and like a set routine so that they know exactly what to do.

Sitting still

If your dog is restless when you are sitting down and you want him to sit quietly next to you, he will probably get even more uptight if you command him to sit still. A firm voice saying 'sit', with hand firmly on his quarters, will make him sit for a moment, but he will probably get up again. Take no notice; he will soon relax with you. When he does, stroke him. He may then take that as the cue to move again. Remain still and when he settles just say 'Good dog'. A calm approach, subtlety, and the use of praise and reward is the best solution.

If the dog is taken out to a strange place and then required to sit quietly while the owner enjoys a meal, plays tennis, or whatever, the Fox Terrier will usually behave reasonably without any special training. If anyone goes to chat with him he will be friendly and give a good impression.

Jumping up

Jumping up at people should be stopped as soon as possible. Just stand back as he attempts to jump up and say 'no', Praise him quietly when he goes down. Any excitement will immediately make him want to jump up again.

The biggest problem here arises in public places when children raise their hands, possibly in fright. This makes the dog excited, causing him to jump up. The child must quickly be told to put his or her hands down and remain calm. Then call the dog to heel. Dog and child can then be introduced calmly.

He will not be put on the lead

Fox Terriers often like to have a game when it comes to having the lead put on. They desperately want to go for a walk and in their excitement they tease you. Just when you think you can catch him he escapes again, wagging his tail in pleasure. Do not worry, he will not want to miss out on his walk. He will come eventually. Always make him come to you; as soon as you start to chase him he will be off.

Other favourite 'sports'

Chasing feet to pull on the shoe laces, jumping on the sofa, and refusing to move from the comfortable chair or bed should all be dealt with promptly before the offence becomes too much of a habit.

Chewing

The biggest problem initially is the need for the puppy to chew things and do things. He therefore needs assistance here. Give him plenty of his own toys. Squeaky toys will be wrecked in seconds. Nylabone offer a good range of tough chews.

Another deterrent is to put something with an objectionable smell onto the objects the puppy likes to chew.

Postman/milkman/dustman

I have never had a problem with Fox Terriers and postmen, milkmen or dustmen. When the puppies first go outside at four to eight weeks old they see these people and get a pat. Although the dogs may bark, these regular callers can enter without fear of being bitten, despite several dogs running around together. When your dogs see you chatting to someone they accept that person as a friend.

Road training

Fox Terriers are stupid about roads and, if they are not on the lead, they will cross any busy thoroughfare to chase the object they are after.

Make the puppy stop every time you have to cross a road or drive. Sometimes you can make him look each way too. When it is safe to cross say 'over'.

Never frighten or hurt the puppy. They do not forget. I knew of a dog in South America that was sent away to be traffic trained. The result of this 'training' was that she was scared of everything outside the house and garden, so that being taken for a walk on the pavement became a nightmare for her. She improved, but she remained petrified every time a car came near. It was obvious that something heavy had been thrown at the dog to scare her off traffic once and for all.

Lead training

It is important to train puppies to walk to heel on the lead from the beginning. They can otherwise get used to taking you for a walk, and not the other way round.

When a puppy is first put on the lead it often jumps and prances around for a few minutes. When the prancing has stopped, gently take the puppy for a few steps round the garden. Give praise and finish the session. Next time the puppy will be more accepting.

To stop pulling, jerk the lead fairly strongly, saying a firm 'no' at the same time; the small puppy will usually respond.

If the problem continues you can buy a 'Halti'. Fox Terriers hate these contraptions, which resemble horse head-collars and restrain them from their noses. This requires far less effort on the part of the owner, but the disadvantage is probable loss of hair on the nose. If the dog is being shown you cannot really afford to do this.

The next trick is to swing a chain pendulum or stick in front of his nose so he cannot go faster than the stick. Lastly, you can stop walking every time he pulls and only move forward when he behaves. He wants to go for the walk and this is taking away his perks again.

Off the lead

I let my puppies off the lead the first time out. This may be risky and unwise but they quickly learn that, if they do not watch out for you, they may lose you altogether. You may miss your puppy for a short time, and it may get a scare, but hopefully you will not have that problem again. It is vital that the puppy is obedient and absolutely safe from traffic and other dangers and that freedom is only for a short time. A puppy may find a rabbit or deer to chase, but it is usually older dogs that do this, and they will probably go back to the place where they last saw you.

Another point about being off the lead is that puppies have to behave with other dogs because you are not there to protect them. Adult dogs are nearly always well-behaved towards a puppy.

Whistle call

To avoid yelling on the common I take a whistle with me (when I remember). My dogs needed no training at all for this, and they somehow know that I am doing the whistling and come promptly. This is easier than shouting and gets a much quicker response. I also call them in from the garden this way.

Photo: Isabelle Français.

He will not let me groom him

The Terrier is normally extremely good about being groomed, provided this is done regularly and he is well disciplined in other respects.

The spoiled dog however may mouth your hand, wriggle, or grab the grooming tool. He may persist in sitting instead of standing, twisting his legs violently when you try to groom them. In this case, he should be attached to the grooming hangar so he cannot run away, and you should have control. Use a firm voice to say 'no' when necessary. As you groom do not stay in any one place for too long. Move around the body and be gentle. As soon as he gets sensitive again groom somewhere else.

If he is very distressed use a soft scarf to act as a muzzle. The dog immediately calms down and you will not need it next time. I have never had to do this myself. The dogs, rather than the bitches, may growl or cry out occasionally, even when you are not touching them. This is just a try on. Be sympathetic, quiet, gentle and firm.

They always feel good afterwards. Give him a treat and take him into the garden for a 'spend' and a game as a reward.

Your puppy will need toys to play with. This Smooth is carrying a Gumabone® Frisbee® produced by Nylabone®. This soft, flexible flying disc will provide entertainment and exercise for dog and owner alike.

Begging

If a dog gets naughty about begging at table I shut him up in his box. Next day the culprit will behave like an angel. After that a little reminder, using the word 'no', is sufficient.

Noisy

If the dog is noisy in the garden you can distract it by calling and offering a titbit. Even without a treat they get used to coming in when called.

Alternatively, you can get a device called The Silencer which the dog wears as a collar; when he makes a noise it makes a high pitched sound in the dog's ear. This sound stops the barking because it is painful to his ear, but so high that the human ear cannot hear it. It still permits the dog to bark enough to protect your home.

You can also put the dog to bed when he is noisy. He will soon get to know this routine, always keeping quiet in his bed unless there is something particularly wrong.

Chasing

The desire to chase anything that moves, including children and bicycles, is strong and the puppy will have to be taught not to do so. This training can only be done on the lead. Jerk the lead and say 'no' very firmly when he attempts to pull and run off. He will calm down in time. You can even say 'no' when it is clear he is thinking about chasing, which is better still. He must be kept under control. If by chance he starts to chase a child or cyclist it is essential to tell them to stand still immediately; the dog will calm down immediately. Once he has started on a chase it is hard to stop him unless the object disappears or stops moving. He will easily become over-excited, and it is important to regain control of him before this happens.

If there is a particular object he likes to chase, it would help if he can see this object moving from a safe place (on the lead or in a car) so that he gets used to it without being able to give chase. Ringcraft classes are particularly useful here when the big dogs run round in circles while yours has to sit and watch. If he has his own ball or stick that he may chase he does not lose out on his fun.

Eating faeces

Whilst this is disgusting, I am afraid dogs do it sometimes. The main objective is to stop it. It is obviously important to remove any faeces as soon as the dog has defecated. If you put a little pineapple in the dog's food for a week or so it makes the faeces smell so awful he totally loses interest.

Not eating

Young puppies can be fussy sometimes and it is not uncommon to try four different meals before getting one that is acceptable. Then, just when you think you are winning, they change their minds and decide they want to try something else. This phase will go but a more serious problem can come later.

For no apparent reason sometimes a dog refuses to eat anything for up to two weeks. This is extremely distressing, and no matter what little treats you try she just turns her nose up at everything.

The first method of tempting her is to have another dog nearby who she knows will eat her meal if she does not.

The next step is to give her special food by hand, with love and affection. Try all sorts of different things like fresh chicken, minced beef, fish, ham, cottage cheese, or even a biscuit or a piece of cake. You can try various prepared pet foods, especially the ones that smell really tasty. A tiny bit might be taken with great reluctance.

Another possibility is to liquidise the food and spoon feed the dog with soup. She will get something, but not much.

I tried all these things once and then went to the vet, who thought she did not look too bad despite the lack of food for over a week. After 10 days I was desperate and thought there was only one path left. When she again refused to eat I scolded her, shook her and put her to bed, not trying to give her any more food. At her next meal time she ate normally and never again reverted to that behaviour.

We humans sometimes need slightly firmer treatment to get us out of a certain mental state, and this could apply to dogs too. I only took this action as a last resort.

Jealousy

The Fox Terrier is inclined to be jealous, especially of other dogs. It is important to give the animals equal attention, or, in their eyes, slightly more than equal. They are very aware of who gets what and watch carefully what is going on.

Mine all get the same titbits and a cup of tea, and they will await their turn patiently. If one dog has a night on my bed the others know it and sometimes demand their turn next time. So long as they each get some special attention they are happy.

Never over-spoil the terrier. The moment a problem starts, nip it in the bud. If the dog does something undesirable, try to stop it at once before it becomes a habit. If he demands attention, try not to give in. The attention must be given when you decide to give it. Of course it is another matter if the dog wants to be let out or have a drink of water.

Good training makes the dog acceptable wherever he goes.

Digging

Most puppies do a little digging in the garden and think they are copying you. You plant out your expensive pansies and they quickly 'replant' them for you. They may try eating a few plants, and they like making holes in the lawn. Luckily this phase usually passes before it starts to present a problem.

Getting out of the car

When you let your dog out of the car make sure he is on the lead and under your control. It happens all too easily that the dog rushes across the road into the path of an on coming car.

In the car

As I have already mentioned, it is best for the dog to be in a cage when travelling in the car; otherwise, use a dog harness with the seat belt.

If it is a cool day and you have to leave your dog in the car for a short time, give him enough air, but do not leave the window too wide open. I once had a dog who had fallen into a well at a friend's house; by the time I found him he was in a very bad way and was partially paralysed. To take care of him I took him with me everywhere. During that winter I had to go to a funeral and so I left him in the car with the window partially open and went into the Crematorium. It was not long before he crept in and joined me at the service. It was appropriate that he came to the service as he knew the person concerned very well. Luckily the whole incident seemed to pass without being noticed, but to me it was something of a miracle that it happened at all.

Obedience classes

Mixing with other dogs and humans is an essential part of the young dog's development. Dog training classes are useful for this purpose.

There are two types of classes: the Obedience Class (not the Fox Terrier's first choice) and the Ringcraft Show Training Class. The latter class may be more suitable even if you are not showing, as the dog sees all the other different breeds relaxing at the side of the ring while others do show training in the centre. Watching the large dogs running round the ring is excellent training to stop chasing, and close proximity to other dogs soon teaches him that they are generally friendly and there is no threat. He enjoys the outing and improves quickly. The problem about Obedience classes is that the instructor is often someone used to training large dogs, who react very differently to the Terrier. The Terrier gets too excited and is sometimes hard to control. If he does not respond well he can be expelled through no real fault of his own.

Ringcraft classes

Owners and dogs relax sitting at the ringside. The puppies are then asked to stand in line down one side of the ring. The instructor goes over to each dog gently, giving him a pat. Table size dogs, which includes Fox Terriers, are put on a table in turn for the judge to 'go over' them, which includes looking at the teeth as the judge would in the show ring. A final look at the conformation, and the puppy is required to walk in a triangle. He may have to do this two or three times - walking to heel, head up, alert and moving with drive. He may also be asked to walk straight up and down a few times. At the end of this he must stand and pose for a final look by the judge.

Sometimes the dogs are asked to move round in a circle and to stand and pose without being stood by the handler. This is an excellent exercise to make the dog 'show' on his own. This exercise is sometimes done going in the opposite direction, in which case the handler must change sides to make sure the instructor sees the dog and not the handler.

To teach the dogs to tolerate each other they are asked to move in tandem across the ring, stopping in the middle next to each other for a few seconds, and then continuing to the other side. They also have to weave in and out between the dogs placed in a circle, and there are other useful exercises so that they know to 'leave' the other dogs. They behave themselves and respond very well in this relaxed atmosphere, without giving any hassle to the owners.

Broaden the dog's experience

The dog that has a daily walk (no matter how big the garden is) and is well-trained is a happy and acceptable dog. This can be taken one step further. Take the dog into every kind of environmental situation possible: the fields, the woods, the parks, the shopping centre, the railway station (useful if you ever need to take the dog in a train), the bus stop, the local shops (especially the pet shop), the fete, the garden centre, or the seaside. All this is extremely good to train the dog to accept every situation calmly and sensibly. Keep him under proper control, making sure you pick up any faeces left in public places, and dogs and dog owners will be accepted more readily.

In strange places

Treat every new experience as normal with the dog on a relatively relaxed lead. A tight lead makes the Fox Terrier turn protective. If you meet another dog and you shorten the lead the Terrier will nearly always show aggression because this is a signal that you and he sense danger. The dog must however be controlled.

Parkside Thunderbolt. It is helpful to teach the future show dog to 'show' rather than 'sit' for treats.

Let the dog meet children

It is good for the dogs to meet children when they are out. Many children are afraid of dogs and this is a pity. However the more the dogs are introduced to other people the better for all.

Out shopping

It is sometimes a good experience for the dog to take him shopping. The place must be chosen carefully because so many premises cannot accept dogs now. If he is tied outside for a moment you need to be confident the village is 'safe' from dog thieves. I would not risk a town centre unless you just walk through the market place with the dog on a lead.

My wonderful pet dog Mischief would always wait for me outside a shop without being tied up and without any formal training. He would even wait outside the pet shop. If only he could be seen today, he would boost the reputation of dogs generally, and the Fox Terrier especially. This is no longer possible as dogs in public places have to be under control with collar and lead.

Training the show dog

The show dog is the dog on view to the public at Dog Shows, representing the breed in character and conformation. He must therefore have a superb temperament and be well presented. Added to this he must have seen quite a bit of the world from the age of eight weeks so that he is not afraid of all the noise and crowds around at shows. Dogs normally hate being glared at, and they have to get used to this too. There are a few people with show dogs who keep them in kennels all the time (sometimes very small ones), and their only outing is to the dog show. The owners think that the dogs will 'show' better because the dog show is **their** outing, **their** special treat. In my opinion it is very unfair to give a dog this kind of restricted life.

Photo: Isabelle Français.

An alert, happy Fox Terrier, groomed and ready.

Additionally, despite all the successes they might have in the show ring, show dogs are sometimes not even allowed in the house. Whatever they do to please the owner they are often deprived of any affection. So much for dog lovers! The owners might consider how they would feel if they were treated like this. In some countries there are lectures to professional handlers which include reference to the need for the dogs to have a good life.

Fox Terriers will always show if they have the true Fox Terrier temperament and live happy and free lives as well as being show dogs. Indeed the dog that is free will be happier, healthier, more friendly and a better all-round character. He will have more bone and substance and better muscle, and will move well.

From six months

In Great Britain we can show puppies from six months of age; it is only three months in Australia. Sometimes Fox Terrier puppies are not taken into the ring until they are ten months old, because the younger puppies do not stand so much chance of winning until they have grown on a bit; they tend to lack body and furnishings.

Matches

We can take them to Matches (see Chapter 14) once they are inoculated, and some young puppies respond really well and look very cute 'being good'.

Exemption Shows

Exemption Shows (see Chapter 14) are good places for a puppy to get used to dog shows, even if he is not actually entered. There are many people there and there is a considerable amount of noise, which the young puppy quickly learns to accept.

Lead training

I lead train my puppies in an empty car park. I walk them up and down the lines, aiming for a loose lead but keeping the dog looking bright, alert and with his head up, by talking to it all the time. If the puppy goes a bit wide I say 'heel', and at the end I say 'stand', placing the dog with the command 'show' and presenting a titbit. The training session is very short and repeated for the next few days. The dogs respond very readily indeed.

'Show' for treat - not 'sit'

It is helpful to teach the dog to 'show' for a titbit rather than to jump up or sit down. This is essential in the show ring. Otherwise you have to use other devices to interest the dog to get the best expression.

Posing

When 'standing' the Wire, minimise the handling. Lift the front and let the fore-legs drop straight down. If the legs are too far apart, use the lead to unbalance the dog slightly and he will put his feet together. Lift the rear to place the hind legs and let them drop gently to the ground. They should fall in place. If not, repeat once more. Have one or both knees on the ground, hold the head high to give reach of neck and interest the dog if possible.

It is often necessary for a dog to be in the ring for an hour or more in Stakes classes. Because of all the grooming there is no problem about posing the Wire for a long time, these dogs are used to doing it every day.

The Smooth species is placed by turning it in a circle; it will position itself again and wag its tail. The handler normally stands when showing.

The triangle

To teach a Fox Terrier to walk in a triangle may sound easy but it is often done incorrectly.

Maximise the ring area. Walk from the judge to the far end, turn left across the top of the ring, turn left again and walk in a straight line towards the judge, keeping the dog directly in line with the judge. The judge can then see the dog from behind, from the side and from the front. Stop well before reaching the judge so that he or she does not have to step back to have a final look as you stand the dog.

Watch where the judge is

For the 'up' and 'down', watch where the judge is standing and make sure you are not standing between him or her and your dog. Turn neatly with a flowing movement at the top and walk back with drive and purpose. (See Chapter 14 for further advice on handling.)

Commands

Give commands firmly with a voice and tone suitable to the command but do not shout. (For example, say 'Down' with a low voice, 'Stand' with a higher voice.) Use your acting ability to tell the dog what you want. Talk to the dog: he listens and respects you, and he likes what he is doing. If the dog starts to go too fast say 'Walk' or 'Steady' slowly and quietly to calm him, give a quick unobtrusive jerk on the lead, then walk normally. Walking quickly excites the dog and he may jump about a bit, so try to get the dog's natural pace moving with drive, but not too fast.

Expression

It is worth trying various methods to get the right expression when the dog is on the table. This requires not only good trimming but also getting the head held in the most advantageous position and finding what makes the dog look his best and most interested: a squeaky toy, a special word, a piece of liver or whatever. Having decided the best method of achieving this, work on it to get the required result, give praise, and leave it. If it is done too often the novelty will wear off.

11

Stripping & **Trimming**

Stripping and trimming a Fox Terrier is a repetitive exercise. Much of the description that follows may therefore seem unnecessary, but it is important to give a full and detailed guide, or something important may be left out. This guide will help anyone to keep a Fox Terrier looking reasonably smart, clean and tidy. The following tools and equipment will help greatly, and the expense is not too great when you consider you will have the dog for 10 to 15 years.

With careful attention to detail there is sufficient guidance here to take the dog

Ch Parkside Regale
Before: A Champion ready for the show ring ...

to an Open show, but it must be remembered that show trimming is for the experts and cannot be learned quickly. Show trimming requires a thorough understanding of the Breed Standard and an ability to transform the dog to look as near that standard as possible. It takes hard work, dedication, skill ability and a knowledge of how fast the coat grows so that it is the exact required length on the day of the show.

The expertise, even with a natural ability, takes a few years to achieve. Even then when you think you have done a good job it will be hard to get those top prizes at Championship shows.

Size

Much is said about the size of a dog for show. Big dogs can win; so can smaller ones. On average the smaller bitches will stand a better chance, but if a dog is too small he may have more difficulty. On the other hand, many of the dogs are quite large, but they do not necessarily sire large offspring.

After: ... and the same Champion after a walk in the country!

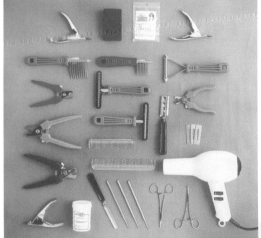

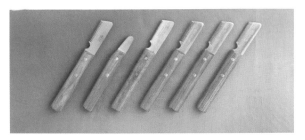

A selection of stripping knives.

Above: a wide selection of grooming accessories is available.

Opposite (clockwise, from the left): Hound glove, flea comb, slicker brush, stripping stone, bristle brush, coarse and medium comb, nail clippers, pin pad.

Photographs of grooming tools on this page and of the grooming table on the following page are reproduced by kind permission of Allbrooks Products Ltd (Animal Grooming Products).

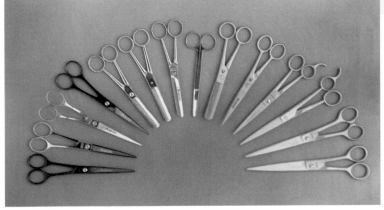

A selection of scissors and stripping shears.

It is also very difficult to get the right body weight for the show dog. He needs to be fit and well, neither too fat nor too thin. The dog needs to have some shape to look pretty. If the outline is correct you should be able to see the spring of ribs and loin while looking over the top of the back.

Setting up the grooming room

The ideal place for grooming is a large, well-lit room with linoleum on the floor for ease of cleaning. If there is a basin there for washing, so much the better. Heating and cooling systems are also needed in our climate.

Grooming table

Grooming the terrier is best done on a table, using a 'control post' which has an adjustable arm on it. On the arm are two rings onto which is attached a strap. The dogs head goes through the strap. The head is held high, you can see the shape of the dog and he is calm (once he gets used to the process) and under control. You can buy these grooming posts with arms and straps from Championship shows for around £20. You can make your own by putting a bracket on the top of a tall pole from which you can hang a chain, or you can hang the chain (or lead) from a metal ring screwed into the ceiling. Tap the ceiling first to make sure you find a piece of timber to screw into. You also need to be able to adjust the height - an 'S' bend in a wide link chain will to do this. The dogs do not mind being 'hung' at all. They keep calm and very patiently let you get on with the job.

This is a purpose-made grooming table but, with a little ingenuity, you can make your own. Never leave your dog unattended on the grooming table.

Mirror on the wall

Large mirrors on the wall are a 'must', so that you can see the outline that the judge sees in the ring. It is easy to take off too much when standing over the dog and not seeing the overall picture. If a mirror can be placed both at the side and front of the dog, so much the better.

Grooming tools

Grooming tools are expensive but essential. Many unsuitable tools can be purchased before you find the ones that work for you. The dog's coat varies in texture, condition and length, creating a need for different trimming knives, ranging from fine to medium, to be able to get the final good finish.

The main grooming tools will include:

- A 19cm (7\fin) metal comb with teeth 3cm (1in) in length. This comb is divided into two halves, with teeth 0.3cm (^{1}/$_8$in) apart and 0.16cm (^{1}/$_{16}$in) apart, described as coarse and medium respectively.
- A fine flea comb, useful for keeping a short coat flat and for combing out any fleas.
- A pin pad to smooth the top coat, remove tangles in the 'furnishings' (face, leg and belly hair) and to pat the furnishings into place.
- A hound glove made of horsehair, for polishing the coat and keeping it flat. It also gives the skin a good massage.
- A hard bristle brush for daily grooming, keeping the top coat flat, and massaging the skin to help promote good hair growth.
- A strip stone removes the loose dead hair quickly from the top coat and improves the appearance of the dog.
- A set of trimming knives. You need several trimming knives, preferably about five. This is less damaging to the hands, and different lengths and textures of coat require different knives. Use a fine one for the neck, head and shoulders, and wider ones for the body. These knives can also be used to scrape out some of the thick undercoat, making the dog look clean and allowing the hard top coat to grow. It also makes the top coat much brighter and glossier. Some suitable knives include the Mars stripping knives Nos 328, 330 and 326, the Hauptner Nos 68513 and 68510 and the American Macknyfe blue and yellow. There is also a Mikki stripping knife (fine and coarse) from MDC Products which is sharp, (too sharp for showing) effective, and cheap.
- Scissors, one pair of ordinary ones for tidying up the coat round the back end, the head, the leg furnishings and underneath, and one pair of small, curved, blunt-ended scissors for cutting out the hair between the pads of the feet. As already noted, this needs to be done regularly.
- Guillotine nail clippers. Nails need clipping regularly.
- A nail file, to fine down and shape the nail after clipping.
- Thinning shears are occasionally needed to even the coat. They do not always work very well and seem to be blunt.
- A slicker brush is useful for going over the dog and ensuring that every hair is in place for a perfect finish. The comb and pin pad can also do this.

The following grooming materials are also needed:

- Shampoo is best bought in bulk and will last a long time. An insecticidal type is ideal because it kills fleas and mites. I find Vetzyme shampoo the most effective.
- White Powder whitens and cleans the coat between baths, which should not be too frequent. Raking is more effective; it is easier to grip the hair when stripping if you dip your fingers into it. This product may not be used at dog shows, but may be used at home provided it is washed or brushed out before leaving for a show.
- Block white chalk does a similar job but makes less mess. It is more suitable for using in a confined area.

Electric Clippers

Among the many makes on the market are:

- Aesculap Favorita 11 Clipper costs around £230. Blades cost between £37 and £68 each. The No 1 blade is used for feet. The No 10 is used for tummy.
- Andis AG with a No 10 blade costs about £100 and may be the most suitable.
- Oster A5 Clipper £110. The 4F blade (£25)

NB: All prices approximate for 1995.

Oster and Andis blades are interchangeable and cost about £30 each. Blade No 4 for the back costs £25; No 30 or 15 is used for feet and No 10 or 15 for the body. For Wires No 7 or 10 is used.

Electric clippers are used in dog grooming salons and by some breeders, for speed, when trimming pet dogs. The dogs will look presentable after being trimmed, but the texture and colour changes, especially in the Wire. Electric clippers are sometimes used on the Smooth Fox Terriers for show but they cannot be used on the Wire.

I am not detailing stripping by this means as it is not the purpose of this book. The blades suggested are those that some people find useful in salons but you may find another size better.

It should be noted that a Wire Fox Terrier that has been stripped in a general dog grooming salon will not look the same as one that has been groomed by an expert who is familiar with all the finer points of the Breed Standard. He will still look nice and neat, but it would not be cost effective for the salon to take the time necessary to groom him to show standard.

Presenting the Smooth Fox Terrier

The Smooth Fox Terrier has a short coat that does not require stripping, but he does need regular brushing with a hard bristle brush and a comb through with the flea comb. You can also rake through the coat with a trimming knife to take the dead hair out. Make sure his back end is clean and tidy. His eyes sometimes need a wipe with a damp flannel, and the feet and ears need to be cleaned out and toe nails clipped.

The outline of the Smooth for show is similar to that described for the Wire, but the coat is not stripped out; it is tailored by the skillful use of scissors or electric clippers. The aim is to make the coat look completely natural without any hard cutting lines. It is best to start doing this about two weeks before the show.

For this variety the only grooming tools required would be a brush, comb, curved scissors, straight pointed scissors, thinning scissors, nail clippers and file.

The hair does grow thick and lumpy in places and trimming is needed to make the dog look neat and tidy. Details of this are described for the Wire. The main essentials are to look at the Breed Standard and try to make the dog look as near that standard as possible. This is done by leaving the coat on where needed and thinning it down in other areas. For example you may need to fine down the ears, cheeks, throat, neck and shoulders. The back end will need tidying up and make a nice shape to the back legs. The feet and nails are done as described.

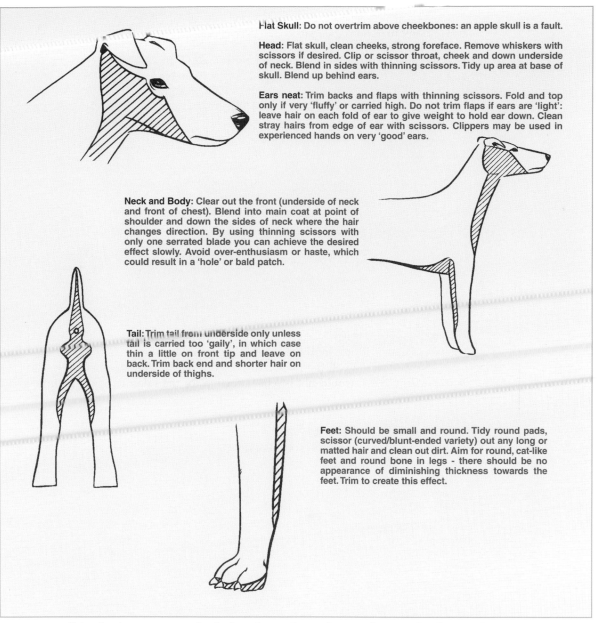

Flat Skull: Do not overtrim above cheekbones: an apple skull is a fault.

Head: Flat skull, clean cheeks, strong foreface. Remove whiskers with scissors if desired. Clip or scissor throat, cheek and down underside of neck. Blend in sides with thinning scissors. Tidy up area at base of skull. Blend up behind ears.

Ears neat: Trim backs and flaps with thinning scissors. Fold and top only if very 'fluffy' or carried high. Do not trim flaps if ears are 'light': leave hair on each fold of ear to give weight to hold ear down. Clean stray hairs from edge of ear with scissors. Clippers may be used in experienced hands on very 'good' ears.

Neck and Body: Clear out the front (underside of neck and front of chest). Blend into main coat at point of shoulder and down the sides of neck where the hair changes direction. By using thinning scissors with only one serrated blade you can achieve the desired effect slowly. Avoid over-enthusiasm or haste, which could result in a 'hole' or bald patch.

Tail: Trim tail from underside only unless tail is carried too 'gaily', in which case thin a little on front tip and leave on back. Trim back end and shorter hair on underside of thighs.

Feet: Should be small and round. Tidy round pads, scissor (curved/blunt-ended variety) out any long or matted hair and clean out dirt. Aim for round, cat-like feet and round bone in legs - there should be no appearance of diminishing thickness towards the feet. Trim to create this effect.

It is also important to check that the teeth are clean and to get the dog used to this process, because that is what the judge does. The dog quite often hates this being done, so it creates less of a problem if he is used to it.

The Wire coat

The Wire Fox Terrier, as already described, has a coat that constantly grows. For his health and comfort he does need to be regularly stripped, as it becomes very long and thick. His top coat should feel harsh and he has a soft undercoat to keep him warm. If his coat is kept short and close he is better protected against cold weather than when it is allowed to grow long and the wind can blow through it.

The coat gets particularly long under the armpits, inside the back legs and around the tummy. It can get very matted and should be kept tidy and clean.

Bathing

Although bathing is rarely necessary, it does help if the dog is very dirty or if the presence of fleas is suspected. Putting a rubber mat on the bottom of the bath and using a power shower is the easiest method for the domestic dog. He can be towel-dried and, as you tidy his coat up on the trimming table, he will dry off completely. Trimming is easier when the coat is wet. Care is needed when the dog is about to be shown; it could result in some unsightly bare patches because too much hair has come off.

Getting the coat into top condition

Olive oil or Solvitax in the meal helps the coat condition. If the skin becomes raw Benzyl Benzoate quickly puts it right. Rain water helps to strengthen the leg hair when the edges become brittle and fragile.

When your dog is being shown it is best to keep him away from heather and brambles on walks to preserve the leg hair. I find difficult to achieve this as it spoils their fun.

After the coat has been 'topped' for some months it becomes tired and dull and has to be stripped right out so that a new coat can grow. The time for stripping is obvious; either the coat is too thick and long or, if it has been well kept, it gets dull and straggly and does not lie flat. It also comes out very easily. The bitch always goes out of coat after a heat and can be stripped about two or three weeks afterwards.

Taking all the old coat out leaves the dog pretty naked, especially in a hot summer, when there may be little or no undercoat. The new coat may take three weeks to start to come through, but soon he will have a lovely new jacket, as though he has been to an expensive tailor or dressmaker. Allow 8-10 weeks (sometimes 12 weeks) to have the dog's coat in show condition. In some Terrier breeds it is thought the dog is at its best when the third coat comes through.

Get the right height

There are hydraulic trimming tables which enable you to adjust the height, but these are expensive. It is fairly comfortable to strip the back of the dog on a table while standing, but the head, throat, chest, rear and underneath are more difficult without bending into uncomfortable positions. If a hydraulic table is too expensive, use two stools of varying height, and sit on whichever is more comfortable for the job you are doing.

There are extra 'stands' you can make or buy to put on the table to raise the dog. Whilst it sounds like a good idea, they can topple over very easily. The dog tends to be remarkably cooperative and the head is easier to do when it is not in the sling.

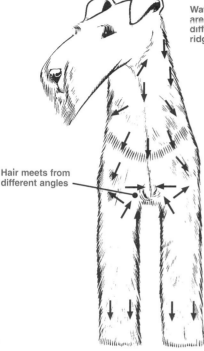

Watch the direction of the hair growth carefully. There are some harder areas where the hair meets from different angles. Special attention should be paid to the ridge down the side of the neck and the chest area.

Hair meets from different angles

Study a picture of the show dog's coat and shape

Look at exhibits in the show ring and pictures of the breed to see what a well-groomed Fox Terrier should look like. Get an idea of the shape to be aimed for when trimming is completed. Like any hair-do, you can make or break the good looks by not paying sufficient attention to detail.

Pull the hair in the direction in which it grows

You will see that there are three main areas where upward-growing and downward-growing hair meet, making a kind of ridge. These are on the chest in the front, from the top of the head down the side of the neck, and at the back end down the sides of the quarters.

These are sensitive areas and should be carefully stripped, taking a few hairs out at a time. As soon as the dog gets restless, move to another area and go back later on.

The secret is to take out just a few hairs at a time, pulling the hair in the direction in which it grows and holding the skin tight as you pull. The trimming knife is held at an angle of about 45 degrees, and this becomes a repetitive, rhythmic action. Do not dig too deeply, but 'top' the coat, using a quick sharp movement and pulling in the direction in which the hair grows. Sometimes it is only necessary to use the point of the knife.

As you strip, use the knife to scrape the unwanted surface undercoat to make the top coat lay flat. Then take off any surplus coat to make the outline. If this is not done, too much top coat may be removed. It will also help promote top coat growth.

Trimming correctly is lighter work, easier on the dog and produces the best results. Never be afraid to ask anyone how experts do it. The more different descriptions you get, the easier it is to find what suits you.

To 'top' the coat you just take off the long bits of hair that do not sit close to the rest of the coat. Scraping removes the dirty undercoat and leaves the thick harsh top coat.

Also look at the length of coat in different parts of the body. Specifically it will be seen that the coat on the head (except the 'furnishings'), cheeks, throat, neck and back end is very short.

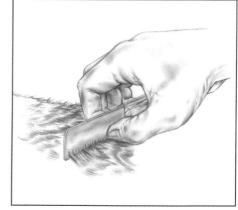

The correct way to hold the trimming knife, smooth side of knife facing towards you.

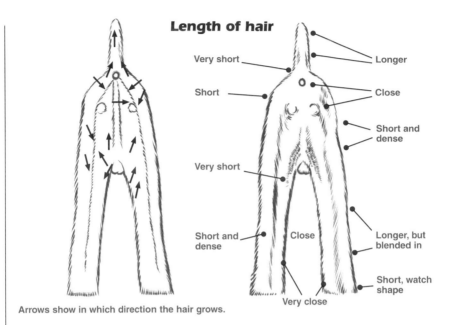

Length of hair

Very short

Short

Very short

Short and dense

Close

Very short

Longer

Close

Short and dense

Longer, but blended in

Short, watch shape

Very close

Arrows show in which direction the hair grows.

Move around the dog

Although trimming can be hard work and takes time and patience, if you are careful it does not hurt the dog too much. It helps to move around the dog a bit so that you do not pull hair for too long in any one place. They can stand for three hours without minding, in fact they like the attention and it makes them feel happy and frisky afterwards. They even look at themselves in the mirror and you can see they are pleased with their appearance. Terriers like to look good and, after being groomed, they go to show off to other dogs and humans with great delight. The other dogs watch the grooming from a safe distance, hoping they are unseen. Sometimes if a dog feels it has been neglected for too long it will queue up to be groomed next.

Some points to note in the Wire Fox Terrier

Head and expression: Create a straight line, leaving plenty of furnishing under the eye. A line from the corner of the eye to the corner of the mouth backwards is stripped off clean. Leave some hair over the eyes to form the eyebrows and brush forward. The top of the muzzle is straight from the eyes to the nose. Leave the whiskers as long as possible to give the long lean head effect. Brush forward to get an even outline. Take any hairs off bit by bit; they take months to grow once removed.

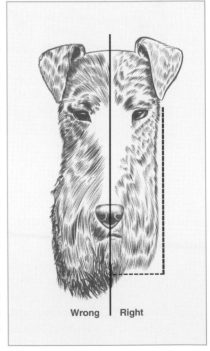

Wrong | Right

  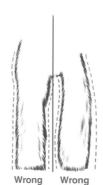

Wrong   Wrong   Right   Wrong   Wrong   Wrong

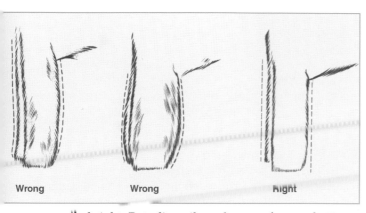

Wrong   Wrong   Right

Ears: Trim the ears very close, especially the edges. Clean the inside of the ears carefully. I usually use fingers for the long hairs in the ears and the small American blue knife for the edges. Care is needed where the inside of the ear meets the head. This needs to be cleaned right off, pulling in the direction of hair growth, with the skin pulled tight. Put olive oil on the ear afterwards to prevent soreness. Do not strip a puppy's ears until later because it may affect his ear carriage. I sometimes trim the edges with scissors until the ears have settled.

Neck: The hair is short at the top (and well scraped through) and gradually gets longer. The length can vary due to the need to obtain a perfect straight top line into the back. Take care not to remove too much hair around the withers; the required outline must be obtained, showing the long neck and short back to advantage, with a good overall topline. Use of the mirror is essential to achieve this line. The hair is blended and gently tapered from the neck down to the crown, which is the ridge where the downward growing hair meets the upward growing hair from the chest.

Chest: The neck and chest are difficult to reach and need to be stripped clean. Hold the head up with one hand and strip the throat down to the chest. When you reach the crown, pull the hair upwards.

Sides: Longer and softer hair, tapered gently to flow down to the bottom. Care is needed to leave enough coat here because it is softer and comes out more easily.

Bottom line: This is straight, giving depth at the front, and short at the rear. It can be achieved hair by hair, looking in the mirror, with a final touch, using the point of the scissors.

Top line: This is a very important part of the overall picture. Blend the neckline from behind the withers into the back and create a straight top line to the root of the tail. This usually means the coat is slightly shorter at the very end.

Tail: Tubular in shape, not too thin, and with good coat. The hair is longer at the top than the bottom.

Front legs: Cylindrical in shape, the hair crisp, and the feet should be 'lost'. The leg hair does not have to be long, but dense and of good quality. Care is needed to have plenty of hair at the bottom of the legs to cover the feet. It helps to brush the leg hair upwards to check that it is even. Use the pin pad to get the tangles out and then the wide end of the comb, working upwards first, then down the front and backwards from the sides. Take out any long hairs that spoil the outline by finger and thumb.

Back legs: The hair at the top of the back legs should be gently blended from the back into the quarters. It forms a curve from the 'tuck up' to the back end under the tail (point of buttocks). From this curve downwards the hair gradually becomes longer. The furnishing at the front of the back legs (which should be of sufficient length and crisp in quality) are shaped into a gentle curve down to the pastern just by pulling out a few longer hairs. Some of the 'rubbish' can be eased out, but leave sufficient for the outline, especially from the hocks down, which should be tubular. The back of the hind legs is short and tapered to make the required curved shape.

Trimming the back legs correctly

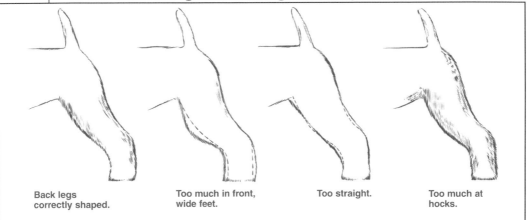

Back legs correctly shaped.

Too much in front, wide feet.

Too straight.

Too much at hocks.

Feet: Toe nails should be cut very short. Use the clippers first and finish off with a file. The dog often objects to this and it is better to do a little and often to avoid a confrontation. Trim underneath the feet in between the pads with scissors. Trim the outsides of the feet carefully to make them round using the stripping knife and finishing off with scissors to blend into the hair above.

Tail: The tail is trimmed short and the hair pulled upwards from the front, back and sides.

Hindquarters: There is another crown here, so pull only in the direction of hair growth and this area is kept short. Remove the long hair downwards from the back of the quarters to where it meets the crown, looking in the mirror to get the right shape. Then you can trim the rear more easily by putting the dog's front feet on the ground and rear feet on your legs. It is easier to do and once the dog knows what you are doing he is happy to let you get on with the job. You just have to be careful about the 'shape' because you could take too much off, spoiling a nice round contour.

Furnishings: The leg and face hair can take several months to grow, so great care is needed not to remove too much. You need good crisp and dense hair. The finger and thumb method is safe, careful and especially useful for shaping the fore-face and the sides of the dog.

Daily Grooming

Daily grooming involves combing through the coat first and then raking through with a suitable trimming knife to remove any unwanted undercoat. Use the pin pad to remove any tangles in the longer furnishings. This is done by slightly rotating the pin pad in the hair, lifting it out and doing the next bit. It can then be combed upwards and any extra long bits pulled out. Top off any long loose hairs on the body of the dog and finish off with the hound glove.

Whilst it is recommended to groom the dog every day, a 'topping' once a week would keep the dog looking pretty tidy, and twice a week even better. Constant attention is easier, quicker and gives a better end result. (See the section on **Grooming** in Chapter 9.)

GROOMING FOR A SHOW

If you buy a young hopeful at eight weeks old, his coat will soon start to grow and he will look like a fluffy ball. You can start pulling the long bits out as soon as they

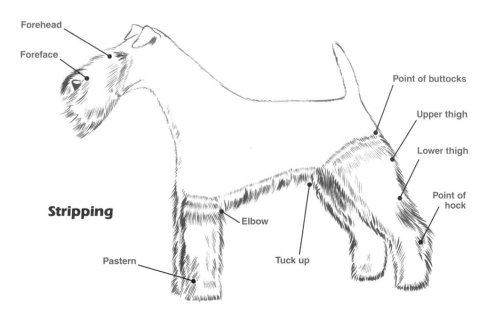

Forehead

Foreface

Point of buttocks

Upper thigh

Lower thigh

Point of hock

Stripping

Elbow

Pastern

Tuck up

begin to look untidy to keep him looking smart. Just do a little at a time until he gets used to it, using either finger and thumb or the trimming knife.

Stripping

Start to get the dog ready about 12 weeks before the show. Put him on the table (in front of the mirror), with his head in the sling attached to the grooming arm so that you have control and can see the outline you need to build up. If the phone goes do not leave the dog on the table because he may try to jump off.

Use the pin pad and comb to brush out all mats. Rake through the coat. Pull out all the long, dead hair with your finger and thumb or a stripping knife. Keep the skin taut with one hand and pull the hair in the direction in which it grows with the other.

Using the stripping knife, take all the long hair off from the neck, down the back to the base of the tail. Trim it and carefully tidy up the rear end and inside the back legs. Strip the head bare in a line from the corner of the eye to the corner of the mouth, leaving the hair in front of the face to shape later. Strip the ears, cheeks, throat, neck and chest very short.

Form the eyebrows (not very easy) by taking the hair out bit by bit between the eyes and continuing the flat line of the forehead. Only a few hairs are needed and scissors can help to make the shape without losing too much hair. Tidy under the eyes but leave plenty of hair to the front to make it 'full'.

Strip really short the side of the neck from just behind the ear (the occiput) down over the shoulders to the elbow, to give the layback of shoulders described in the Breed Standard. The outside of the elbow is also fine, blending into the leg hair.

On the quarters, strip the body to a curved (or arched) line as described under Back Legs in Chapter 11. The hair below this point gets longer and is blended in. You will see some exhibits that look as if they are wearing trousers!

Trim the sides of the dog (rib cage) and behind the elbows, taking care not to remove too much hair.

Leave the hair on the belly longer in front and shorter towards the back, where it might be really short. Use the mirror to guide the length you need to obtain a straight and even line. Pull just a hair or two at a time. Avoid holes in the outline by finishing off with scissors.

The hair at the bottom of the chest in front should be even with the front legs so that nothing sticks out.

Scissors are sometimes used around the rectum, the tender places on the inside of the back legs, the tummy and for straightening the chest hair. Use the scissors carefully to avoid any 'cutting' lines, guiding the points to give a smooth natural outline.

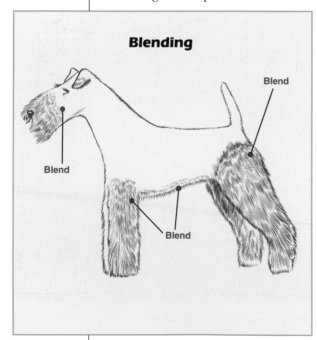

Blending

Blend

Blend

Blend

For the next four weeks, while the coat grows, just go over the dog regularly with the hound glove to make him feel good and promote the new coat. Take off any unwanted fuzzy hair.

Blending

The whole coat should have the appearance of 'blending' (tapering from long coat to short coat), fore-face, elbows, neck, top of hind legs (upper thigh) and the line of the lower chest to the belly.

Blend the hair over the rib cage into the longer chest hair. Take care not to remove too much. The effect should be a depth of chest, not a dog wearing a skirt. A good maxim is 'what you leave on is important, not what you take out'.

Shaping

Shaping is putting the finishing touches to the furnishings (leg hair and whiskers) having done the normal stripping. It also involves getting the correct outline.

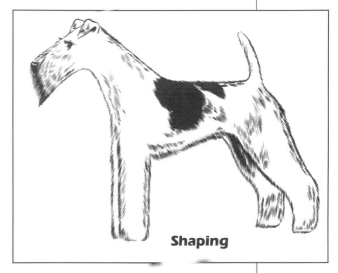

Shaping

Whiskers: Brush the whiskers forward and shape into a rectangle by gently finger picking a few hairs at a time. Leave plenty under the eye. The hair on the nose should be short and dense, and level with the forehead. There is a slight dip at this juncture (the stop) which should be filled in, making a continuous straight line. Even up the edges of the eyebrows and tidy the thick hair along the lips with scissors.

Front Legs: Comb up the hair on the front legs. Pull out a few long hairs from the top where you stopped stripping the body coat. Pat into place with the pin pad and look at the leg from all angles to achieve a smooth cylindrical shape. Brush up again, take out a few more hairs further down, comb into place and look at the result. Continue this process downwards, leaving enough hair to make a straight, cylindrical shape from the shoulder to the ground.

The finished product: a well-trimmed Wire.

Brush up the hair on the feet and aim to hide them altogether. See how the dog stands and whether his toes turn out. Adjust the trimming to hide the fault.

Walk the dog up and down to make sure his movement looks correct. This is most important. If he turns his toes either in or out, again make the necessary adjustments by trimming to correct the fault. Go over the legs again and try to make sure the lines are straight.

The length of coat on the legs will depend on whether the dog has a broad or narrow chest, and on how well the coat grows. If the dog is a bit 'wide', perhaps leave a little extra on the inside leg, and vice versa.

Use the scissors to clean and shape the feet.

Back legs: Blend the arch over the upper thigh at the top of the back legs. Starting at the top, brush up the leg hair and take out a few of the longer hairs and comb into place and see if it lies flat. Brush up again, and repeat as necessary. Use the mirror and only take out a few hairs at a time.

You need to be particularly careful about shaping the back of the hind legs to give a gentle curve from the upper and lower thighs to the pastern.

As before, look in the mirror from all angles to get the shape right. Work from the side and the rear as you go along. Blend the tuck-up into the inside of the leg. Tidy the front edges either from facing the front or from inside the hind legs where you look for a straight line.

Make sure there is sufficient hair to give a full outline from the hocks down. The shape here is cylindrical and the feet should be almost lost, but looking as if the dog is on the tips of his toes. At this point you also trim to hide faults. If a toe is turning out (cow-hocked), trim close on the outside and leave a little more hair on the inside. If the legs are too wide apart, leave the hair on the inside a bit longer. If the legs are slightly bowed, achieve a straight line to hide the fault.

Try to get a straight line down the back of the legs when viewed from behind. Seen from the side, the front of the back legs should gently curve to the point of the hocks, which should look well let down (short). Again looking from the side, the back of the hind legs from the top of the leg to the hocks should curve gently, showing a good bend of stifle and strength for movement.

Carefully shape the inside back legs from the top to the ground. The rear should look straight from the upper thigh to the ground. Brush up the hair on the pastern, keep short, trim and perpendicular to the ground.

Cut the toe nails short. Use scissors to shape the round feet and clean out between the pads.

Walk the dog up and down to check that the movement and trimming are correct. If the dog appears not to walk straight, or if he walks wide or too close, adjust the trimming to improve the movement. It took me years to realise that with one of my dogs the problem was not him but my bad trimming and shaping.

General maintenance

The head, cheeks, throat, neck, ears and rear grow fast and need to be kept short by constant attention, say twice a week.

As the new coat comes through it should be brushed and combed every day (or every other day) to promote a healthy new one. It is useful to use the pin pad to see that the coat lies flat. As the coat grows it should be topped. This means taking off the hairs that stick out, thus keeping a tight close-fitting jacket on the show dog. This is not stripping, just keeping a tidy coat. Keep working on the pattern of raking, brushing and topping every second day and the coat should look superb.

Before the show

Do plenty of lead walking on pavements to strengthen the pasterns and accustom the dog to walking at heel. By this means he also gets used to other people, dogs and noises.

Three weeks before the show make sure the usual places are stripped right down: head, ears, cheeks, throat, neck, shoulders, back end and tail. Go over the legs, whiskers, eyebrows and 'skirt' again. Also shape the top of the hind legs and the bend of stifle. Make sure the inside of the hind legs look straight when the dog moves. Use just the point of the scissors at times to avoid hard straight lines. Keep scraping and brushing the longer top of neck and body coat, topping as necessary, and keeping an eye on the overall shape daily until the show.

Ten days before the show, see that the cheeks, neck, throat and shoulder are fined right down and make sure again that the stifle and back end are right.

Five days before the show, bath the dog.

Three days before the show, double check on the above points. Brush up the leg hair and shape these as previously described. Check the movement looks right, in both directions. Any slight turn of toe or elbow can be somewhat disguised at this stage by careful detail to trimming. Sometimes just the point of the trimming knife is sufficient to get the required result. Make sure the inside of the ears are clean and no wax or infestations are present. Check that the feet are clean and the movement not impaired. The nails should be cut really short.

The night before the show, wash the legs and face, and chalk the white areas. Blow drying makes the leg hair more fluffy.

12

Preparation at the show

What to take

Before leaving for the show you need to go through a check list to make sure you have everything:

- petrol in the car.
- money.
- show entry card and car park pass.
- map of route.
- grooming kit .
- pin holder for Ring Card.
- water and bowl for the dog.
- treats.
- grooming table (with grooming arm).
- chair to sit on.
- picnic (though most shows have plenty of refreshments for sale).
- coffee.
- show lead (always white and as thin as possible).
- towel (to put on table or to cool dog if he is hot).
- overall (to protect your smart show outfit).
- ordinary lead to walk dog.
- bags for collecting any mess the dog may make.
- **TAKE THE DOG!**

On one occasion I was taking several dogs to a show. After bathing the best dog I put her in her kennel. The next dog, duly bathed, went into his box in the car, and so did the young dog. Having loaded everything, I set off. On reaching the show, I suddenly realised that my best dog was still at home! I wondered if I could make a dash back to collect her, but it was foggy and I did not have enough time. Frantic cries for help were not on either. In the event the young dog won Best in Show.

If the weather is wet, take a bowl and shampoo in case you have to wash the dog's feet. The advantage of last minute washing is that the dogs are cleaner.

If the furnishings are not washed the night before the show they can be done either in the morning of the show or when you get there, which is what the professionals do.

Blow drying, which you cannot do at the show, makes the leg hair more fluffy and dense. However, it also tends to make it brittle if done frequently, so some conditioning is needed.

The professional handlers arrive at the shows very early in the morning. They usually have special parking facilities nearer the benches as they have so many dogs to carry. The dogs are carried in Terrier boxes 60cm deep, 35cm wide and 55cm high (23in by 14in by 21in) made of wood, or the plastic Airline type. The handler often needs two grooming tables, and (like everyone else) such equipment as grooming tools, chairs, food, washing bowl, overall.

Start early

An early start helps you avoid any traffic congestion, makes for a faster journey and enables you to park nearer the main entrance. It also gives you and the dog plenty of time to settle before going into the ring. The dogs can be let out, washed, and the last minute preparation done without haste. They can then rest in their boxes until near the actual showing time.

If you do ever arrive at the last minute and have no time to prepare your dog, I can assure you that you will make sure it never happens again. You cannot do your dog or yourself justice and, after so many weeks of daily attention to detail, you do not want to throw all that effort away by being late for the big event. You get a lot of knocks along the way, but let the knocks come when people see your dog looking lovely.

Above: Helen Frizell, professional handler, preparing Baxee Bosuns Mate for the Blackpool Show.

Below: Breeds like the Wire Fox Terrier that are trimmed have special places allocated where grooming tables can be set up.

Find your bench

At Championship shows (and some Open Shows) the dogs are benched and your bench number is written on the entry card. The tent for the Terriers will be clearly displayed. The catalogue will give the judging order and ring numbers. This will also be displayed on a large board. The dogs are all checked in and checked out to make sure none are stolen.

Breeds that are trimmed, like the Wire Fox Terrier, have special places allocated to them for grooming and putting up the grooming tables. This is usually at each end of the tent. However,

sometimes people find there is enough space by the benching, down the side aisle or, if it is a fine day, outside. There are Kennel Club rules about not blocking gangways, and so grooming in these areas is dependent upon the amount of space available.

Get your grooming area sorted out and then find out where your ring is. Let the dog out and then make yourself comfortable.

The final check

Put the dog on the table, stand back and look at him with a really critical eye. Check you have done all you can to present him well. Wash and dry him now if this has not already been done. Tidy up anything that requires attention, and look at him from all angles. When you are satisfied, put him in the box to rest. At this stage do not spend too much time on the dog or he will get fed up.

Dog shows have traders selling interesting and useful things for show dogs, professional groomers and pets. Now is a good time to go round and have a look.

About 15 minutes before going into the ring put the dog on the table for a final going over. Timing this last preparation is difficult, and should not be rushed. By standing the dog in show stance on the table you are rehearsing him for the performance in the ring.

With the pin pad (or slicker brush) go over the whole body of the dog, brushing the hair in the direction in which it grows. Brush the coat straight along from the top of the neck to the tail. The sides go slanting downwards. Make sure you groom the hindquarters to advantage.

Use the hound glove to smooth the coat over, to give the close appearance. Then make sure no hairs are sticking out anywhere. Look at the top line and especially maximise the neck line. Make sure the sides and bottom line are neat and tidy. Finish off the bottom line with the point of the scissors.

Fluff up the front leg hair with the pin pad and then lightly pat it into place. Look from all angles to make sure you have the tubular shape. Trim where necessary.

Brush up the back leg hair and pat into place. Try to create a curved line from the top of the back leg to the hock. From the hock down it is cylindrical in shape and the toes should be hidden.

Photo: M Bird.

Judging at the Fox Terrier Fun Day.

Make sure the inside leg is completely straight, scissoring where necessary. Make sure the back of the hind legs is nicely angled by careful trimming and not leaving too much hair there. When standing, the dog should look as if he is on the tips of his toes.

The face hair should be brushed forward and put in place. Make sure you have achieved the expression you want. It may only need a hair or two removed to make all the difference.

When it is very windy it is a good idea to stand the dog so that the wind blows his whiskers and leg hair forward, otherwise you spoil the outline.

Throughout showing, the furnishings need constant attention to keep them in place. The outline is of paramount importance.

Final check at the Fox Terrier Fun Day.

Photo: M Bird.

Hopefully you will have a nice-looking dog to take into the ring. The dog is usually carried so that he does not get dirty.

It is amazing sometimes how the professional handler can change a rather dull and uninteresting exhibit into a spectacular winning Champion. Two things come in here: firstly, excellent grooming, and secondly, good handling and motivation.

Many people today take nice-looking dogs into the ring, but to get the final professional touch and finish is an expert job. It takes time, effort, skill and experience to get there. It is only by trying and trying again that you can achieve the best results.

In the past people have used all kinds of aids to improve the quality of the coat, hasten the growth or improve the colour. This is strictly prohibited by The Kennel Club show rules. There is no reason why your dog should not have an excellent coat if he has a good diet, plenty of fresh air and exercise and lives a happy contented life. Watch out for fleas in the summer and generally take notice of anything going wrong. Particularly see that toe nails are cut and that there is no matting between the toes and there are no parasites in the ears.

The dog's feet

It is not unusual to see dogs in some distress either walking in long grass or on an indoor slippery surface. To avoid the grass tickling the feet it is best to leave some hair between the toes but make sure it is not too thick and there is no matting. To prevent slipping you can apply Tacky Paw to their toes to enable them to walk properly.

Be ready

Before leaving your bench for the ring make sure you are ready; that you are not smoking (dangerous in tents), and do not need to use the toilet or blow your nose. (It is impossible to move your dog and blow your nose at the same time.) Have your clothing in order, with no flapping scarves, and remember the pin holder for the ring card.

Make sure that the dog is ready too; he may also need to use the toilet, and all too often it is done in the ring.

Hopefully, with attention paid to every detail, the dog and handler will look good and will be admired by all around the ringside.

13

Handling
in the ring

You now have some idea what it takes to prepare the dog for show, but some degree of expertise and experience is also necessary to handle the dog so that he makes the most of himself on the day. If you are lucky the dog will do the showing for you, but that is the exception rather than the rule.

The owners of some breeds employ professional handlers to handle their dogs in the ring. Terriers benefit particularly from professional help as the dogs require so much expertise in preparation and handling.

One eminent handler, Jo Cartledge, worked at Mr Barlow's Crackley kennels, learning his trade there and from his uncle, Arthur Cartledge. He became a professional handler and was highly regarded as such, possibly only being surpassed by Mr Ernest Sharpe. After winning with an Airedale at Crufts in 1961 he stopped handling and ran his own business. During this time he was in demand as a judge until he died from cancer. Other notable handlers include Albert Langley, Frank Kellett and Andrew Hunt.

Show pose

Try taking a photo of your dog in show stance. It is extremely difficult to get the right pose the moment you want it for the camera. If you assume the judge is the camera, you can see how important (and difficult) it is to get the timing right.

Work at getting the right expression.

Put the dog on the table and try various things in front of the mirror to see when the dog makes the best expression. Bait your dog with different objects, such as treats, toys, crackling paper, make funny faces or noises (quietly), or pretend to eat a nice sweet, to see what makes the best expression. Also see how his head looks and decide how you want him to hold it. You can move your arm around to get him to react while holding the bait. It is best if it is like a horse being ridden 'in hand', with the head slightly down and well under control.

It is surprising how what you think looks right on the ground looks quite different when you see it in the mirror. Let the mirror be your judge.

Ch Parkside Vanity Fair 'showing'.

Show lead training

It is a good idea to start show lead training the puppy as soon as possible, even at eight weeks old. They always kick up at first but the kicking is shorter if you begin early and show you intend to go on with it. When he is happy about walking on the lead without pulling too much, start show training.

After grooming the puppy, look at his teeth so that he gets used to the idea. Give him a treat and praise him, and then he will be in a good mood.

Get the show lead and take him outside for lead training. First stand him in show pose and praise him if he does it well. Then walk him up and down in a straight line, giving a command as you turn. This is how it will be done in the show ring. At the end of each 'up and down', ask him to show, and give him a treat for good behaviour. Make it fun. Teach him to pose, and give a reward, but not if he sits or jumps up for it.

To pose he should look alert: head up, front feet together, back feet further apart and on the tips of his toes, ears pricked and looking interested, tail up and generally looking bright and 'showing'.

He must behave well with other dogs and not bark or misbehave. He must be happy to let the judge go over him, without being afraid.

Some dogs are car sick, but those that travel from a young age rarely have this problem. Car sickness pills can be given to the dog, but while these may resolve the sickness, they can also dull the 'showmanship'. It is better to accustom the puppy to travel.

The young puppy usually does try, even if it does not go as well as you might wish. Do not worry if the puppy is a bit full of himself; he will settle in time.

Reluctant puppies will take longer to come to terms with lead training and showing. It can be done with bribes and pampering but it may be hard work.

I had one dog who did not like showing and always looked miserable. One day a Junior Handler took him in the ring and he won. Ever since then he has really enjoyed it. Before this his sister always beat him; I cannot help thinking they are fully aware of how they look and how well they do in the class.

Puppies are inclined to be very bad movers at first, probably because they are interested in everything around them and think about going off hither and thither. They also have some growing and muscle building to do.

As I have already mentioned in Chapter 10, it is helpful to go to Ringcraft Classes. Here the dogs get used to meeting a variety of other breeds and learn to move and show as required, and the handler can get a lot of useful tips too. Often it is quite noisy and, being indoors, the dogs get very close to one another. If they can cope with this they can manage a show without fear.

At these classes the instructor goes over the dog and looks at its teeth, to prepare him for what the judge will do. The dog sometimes objects to his teeth being examined so it is worth preparing him for this yourself. The various exercises and experiences gained at these sessions form a vital part in fostering the young dog's good behaviour and ability to cope with the show scene.

In the early days only train for very short periods at a time. Puppies soon get fed up, so make it a 'fun' thing to do; you want them to enjoy it to bring out the best. Treats and praise play a big part in this early training. If you have difficulty there is nothing like letting your dog see you train another dog. Next time round he wants to be the 'top dog'.

Having (hopefully!) perfected the lead training, and fostered a nice flowing movement for the turn round at the top of the 'up and down', you then need to check for the show stance and expression you hope to achieve at the end of your walk out. If the dog does not look bright enough when left alone, handlers often drop a pin pad, treat or keys in front of the dog to make him look alert. If he will 'use' his ears it is a good thing.

Once you have some idea of how you want to show your dog you need to bring this into practice in the ring. He cannot be in top show stance and expression for half an hour or more, and Stakes classes for puppies often last over an hour. Therefore be vigilant, and see that the dog is always interested in something so that he looks good most of the time and extra good when you really need it. Talk to him and let him enjoy himself in his own way. Pretend to eat something, or do something so that he looks to see what he might have to do next.

Before entering the ring make sure your dog is 'ready' so that as you go in your dog is seen to be a contender and not an 'also ran' specimen.

In the ring you may all be asked to walk round in a circle first. Do not give loud commands to your dog at this time, or use squeaky toys, as this is very upsetting to the other dogs. Then each dog is examined individually.

The judge is checking the bone structure, teeth, layback of shoulder, muscle and overall balance and expression according to the Breed Standard. When the dog has been seen on the table the exhibitor is asked to lead him in a triangle, and then straight up and down.

HANDLING IN THE RING

Linda Beak with one of her Newmaidleys. Get the expression right just as the judge turns to look at your dog.

While the dog in front of you is walking up and down, place your dog on the mat on the table and do a last minute pin pad job on the whiskers and legs. Stand your dog, checking that the front legs are parallel and not too far apart, the back legs are correctly placed with the hocks coming straight down, and he looks as though he is on 'tip toes'. Get the expression right just as the judge turns to look at your dog. Do not put the hind legs too far back; the dog should look square.

Movement is crucial and many people think that if the dog moves correctly then it is correctly built. When moving the dog make sure that you are not between the dog and the judge, obstructing his view. Watch other exhibitors to see how they use the ring for the triangle and how to make a good turn on the 'up and down'. It helps to keep the lead well up under the dog's throat, right behind the jaws, to keep his head up on the walk out. If in doubt about his willingness to go, lift his chin up with your hand before starting to move with a command to make him look alert and pay attention.

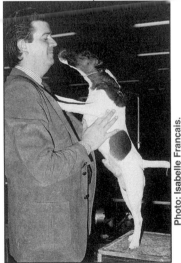

Remember to thank your dog afterwards!

Photo: Isabelle Français.

Another point to watch is how tightly to hold the lead. The dog must neither be pulled off the ground nor allowed to pull away from you. He must hold his head up, look smart, and move with drive. This requires alertness at the time to 'bond' with the dog. If it goes well there is a very good feel about it. Keep the dog moving all the time.

On the return of the 'up and down' you show the dog in front of the judge. Give him or her a chance to stand back and look at the dog; do not walk up too close. The dog should stand in show pose and look alert. This is usually achieved by showing him a treat or dropping keys or pin pad on the ground to make him use his ears, and is worked at during training, using the word 'stand' or 'show'. If the dog is not really standing square (he should fit into a square) then adjust the front legs by upsetting his balance with the lead to correct the front legs, or just lifting the back to place the hind legs correctly (they usually drop into position automatically). Again, alertness is needed, as any correction must be done quickly but without any appearance of rush. The judge is not going to wait hours for you to stand your dog.

If the dog does not walk to heel willingly, it sometimes helps to let him walk wide (so that he does not lean) as you go away from the judge and to hold the lead tight on the return to give a good front movement.

Handling the Smooth Fox Terrier is different in that they show more naturally and do not need to be stacked. If the position is not correct they can be turned round and should automatically stand correctly. They are also more inclined to wag their tails and look happy. The handler therefore seldom needs to bend down or kneel.

WHAT TO WEAR IN THE RING

Whilst many people look quite sloppy when handling their dogs in the ring, it will be observed that professional handlers do not. For training and showing it is best to wear close-fitting clothes which feel comfortable.

Shoes need to be comfortable and well-fitting so that they do not drop at the heels when you are walking. Sandals are bad as sometimes the toe gets caught or the heels drop down so that they come off altogether. Avoid high heels and any shoes with metal tips as they make distracting noises indoors. The dog's movement is extremely important and he can only move well if the handler can move well too, so he or she must not be impeded by bad shoes or clothes that get in the way.

Trousers or skirt

Whilst some people recommend that women should wear a skirt for smartness, it is important that it is not so wide as to obscure the dog from the judge; this does sometimes happen. A smart, plain-coloured suit brings out the colour contrasts in the dog and shows him to his best advantage. Well cut trousers with a smart jacket look very neat and do not inhibit walking.

Whether you decide to wear skirt or trousers, make sure that they are neither too long nor too loose or bell-shaped at the bottom, to minimise the risk of tripping up. This also applies to the length of the raincoat if it is a wet day.

Because handling the Wire often requires squatting or kneeling on one or both knees, be very careful that your foot cannot get caught in your trousers or the hem of your coat as you get up, causing you to fall. It does sometimes happen.

If it is cold, wet and windy your legs can easily get caught in the flaps of your raincoat. This can also upset the dog's movement: he might either get under the coat or walk very wide, thus spoiling his straight line. It is worth trying the clothing out before you leave to ensure you will not encounter these problems.

Wet weather clothing

We can usually shelter in the tents when it rains really hard. However there are occasions when the weather is so bad that there is virtually no way of keeping dry. If possible it is best to wear a nice pair of trousers or slacks. We may, however, have to wear a raincoat or other more bulky clothing. Nylon waterproof over-trousers are sometimes worn, but these look rather baggy and are inclined to rustle, which could distract the dog.

The right colour

This may sounds a bit far-fetched, but the Fox Terrier is such a beautiful dog that it is worth looking at yourself and your dog in the mirror to see which colour suits the two of you best. Some colours make the dog stand out much more than others.

Jewellery and keys

It helps not to wear any noisy jewellery (bangles for example) as this could distract the dog from what he is doing and distract the other dogs also. Keys jangling in the pocket can also be a problem.

The final line-up, with Ch Gedstar Sun Boy in the centre.

Long hair

Hair should also be tidy, not flopping around the shoulders and neck, as this again can get in the way of good handling. Also avoid a flapping scarf, tie, or any other piece of clothing that might blow about in the wind and obstruct the judge's view of the dog.

14

Dog shows

Background

There are over 1,500 different breed clubs and canine societies in this country. At the dog shows organised by these groups are many people selling an enormous variety of pet products, including food, grooming equipment, cages, kennels, toys, protective clothing and food. Pet equipment has become very big business.

Once embarked on dog showing one inevitably gets involved in buying the latest equipment, and it amounts to a great deal of money. Add to this the cost of entry to shows, travel, some expert help in trimming and probably some professional handling and it will cost about £3000 to make up your first Champion. A survey recently quoted a similar figure to make up champions in other breeds. A few exhibitors will manage to do it for less, but the competition is great and normally you have to attend all the shows 'campaigning' your dog before you can get the top honours. This compares with a price of £700 in around 1976. Why we show when it is so expensive, and there is no prize money on offer, is hard to understand. It is an ego trip which becomes addictive, and we always hope to do better next time.

The first three years are the hardest. It takes time to become known and to learn the trade. After five years in the ring more success will be achieved, especially at the Breed Club shows. Many enthusiasts come to dog shows without exhibiting. They are there for a day out, to enjoy watching the judging and probably to do some canine shopping. This is a worthwhile exercise in that it is much more relaxing than exhibiting, there is a better chance of talking to other enthusiasts, and you see the dog showing business from a broader perspective.

The earliest form of dog show was held among farmers, who showed off their hunting and sheep dogs. This in turn led to the Field Trials, as the farmers were looking for the dog that did a good job on the farm.

It is believed the first real dog show was in Belgium in 1690 where there was a lot of competition among Schipperke owners, whose dogs wore elaborate collars. There were also various exhibitions where dogs and other livestock were displayed and sold. The first organised dog show with a judge was at Newcastle in 1859, but it was limited to Pointers and Setters. There was an entry of 60 dogs, with three judges for each class. The Birmingham Dog Show Society held its first Exhibition for all breeds the following year giving one Open class for each breed.

A show was held at Crystal Palace in 1872 and, after a second in 1873, The Kennel Club was formed to tidy up the show scene. They introduced rules for dog showing, registration of names and a Stud Book. The rule book started with 10 rules. today there are over 200 pages of rules and the book is revised every year.

Charles Cruft was first asked to organise a Canine Exhibition in Paris. This made a lot of money and was such a success that he repeated the exercise at the Agricultural Hall in Islington. He died in 1938 and it was in 1942 that this show was taken over by the Kennel Club. The first show, delayed by the Second World War, was held at Olympia in 1948.

Crufts 1988: Terrier Group. (Gedstar Sun Boy in the foreground.)

Photo: Marc Henrie.

The Kennel Club

The Kennel Club is the governing body for all canine affairs in this country. They have their own Gazette, they register all puppies, they approve and license all dog shows and training classes and they will answer any queries from the public. They also list the show winners, send out Challenge Certificates (CCs), and have a complete list of pedigrees. Anyone can buy a copy of this for a small fee. They also have a complaints procedure. There is a rule that if exhibitors show registered dogs at unlicensed shows they will be banned from entering any future licensed show, and may be banned from registering any further progeny. The Kennel Club will also supply names and addresses of Breed Club Secretaries, and a list of people with puppies for sale.

The six groups

Dog breeds are split into groups: Hounds, Terriers, Gundogs, Working, Utility and Toys.

There are classes for most breeds at the big shows, usually under five grades for both Dog and Bitch: Puppy, Junior, Postgraduate, Limit and Open. A winner is taken from each grade, and the Best of Breed (BOB) is taken from the best winning dog against the best winning bitch. This dog or bitch then goes on to compete for Best In Group (BIG). The winner of the Group then goes on to compete for Best in Show (BIS). At Open shows where the Group system is not in operation the winner of the Breed classes goes on to compete in Best in Show, provided it remains unbeaten. A winning dog from a breed class may be withdrawn from further competition to remain unbeaten if the exhibitor wishes to compete for the BIS.

Breeds for which there is no specific class can compete in a class for Any Variety Not Separately Classified. The winner here may also go to the appropriate Group for further competition if it remains unbeaten. Winners of Any Variety classes do not enter further competition towards Best in Show but can enter Stakes classes and other special classes.

The Fédération Cynologique Internationale (FCI)

The Fédération Cynologique Internationale (FCI) is the European system which divides the dogs into small groups. Sometimes the mixture looks curious to our eyes as the groupings appear more like an Exemption Show. Every dog on the continent is supplied with a written assessment for the owner to take home. The dogs are given graded coloured cards (see end of this Chapter).

I saw one such show in Chile. It was held at Vina in the grounds of what used to be a private house. There were raised stands on which to sit, and the dogs were shown in the arena below. The atmosphere was relaxed and there was a continuous commentary about what was going on. There were relatively few exhibitors of any particular breed, and it was easy to move around and find a good seat. The show was run by an English person and lasted two days.

The beginner

Beginners who have nice little dogs they would like to show are advised to go to small local shows first to see what goes on. Look at the classification of classes, the appearance and grooming of the dogs, the handling and the way the judge goes over the dog. Watch how the dogs are required to pose in show stance and how exhibitors try to demonstrate their dogs' movement to best advantage. Do not be afraid to ask questions. There are a lot of surprises in store so it is as well to be prepared.

Above: Smooths and Wires at a Fox Terrier Fun Day.
Below: Best Pet Wire at the
Fox Terrier Fun Day.

My first mistake was to go to a Championship show in the Open class thinking I could not be disqualified from that. Having a busy full-time job I did not have time to study the schedule and I had no-one to ask what it was all about. I washed my dog and proudly went along to the show. I was amazed at the benching, the chalk being used (not allowed now) to whiten the dogs' coats, and all the general fuss and preparation that was going on. I also could not understand why my brown leather collar and lead were out of place. Why do they use a thin white lead for a tough working dog like a Terrier?

Advertisements for dog shows

Dog shows are all advertised in the two main dog papers, *Our Dogs* and *Dog World*. The shows are listed at the back of the paper, together with the name, address and telephone number of the secretary. It gives the show time and place, and the closing date for entries.

Exemption shows are often also advertised at veterinary hospitals, pet shops and in the local newspaper. Because there are not many classes scheduled specifically for the Fox Terrier it is often necessary to enter Any Variety Terrier Not Separately Classified.

Breed Club shows

When breed clubs put on a show it is most important to support them. Some of these shows offer CCs; others do not. The Breed Club Open shows are small and friendly,

Photos: M Bird.

Fancy dress: Flyntwyre Fairytail as 'a little devil'.

and they often offer delicious home-made refreshments! They provide a good environment in which to learn the trade and to meet fellow exhibitors, who will often be willing to help the beginner. Remember, however, that they need time to prepare their own dogs for show. Success can be achieved by continually looking, watching, asking and trying. Showing is a skill which takes time to perfect and some will do so quicker than others.

There are seven different types of shows which can be approved by The Kennel Club:

Exemption shows

These are small, fun shows held in the community to raise money for charity. They do not have to be approved by The Kennel Club, but there are a few rules they are required to observe and they pay a licence fee. They give the winners rosettes, and quite often dog treats as well when these have been donated. They usually start around 1.00 pm and accept the entries from one hour earlier.

Exemption shows generally have at least three (a maximum of four) pedigree classes: a Puppy class (six to 12 months), Any Variety Sporting, Any Variety Non-Sporting, Any Variety Open. There may also be a Veteran class for dogs over seven years old (open to pedigrees and mongrels). The classes for non-pedigree dogs include such classes as The Dog The Judge Would Most Like To Take Home, The Dog With The Prettiest Eyes, The Dog With A Waggly Tail, The Dog That Looks Most Like Its Owner, The Best Six Legs, or The Best Fancy Dress.

These shows are often held at fêtes and flower shows where there is plenty to see and do. The entry is only £1 and the dog does not have to be registered with The Kennel Club. Some successful exhibitors go round all these small local shows thoroughly enjoying themselves. It is a very good starting point for both dog and handler. The show only lasts about three hours which is not too long for a young puppy. CC winners may not enter.

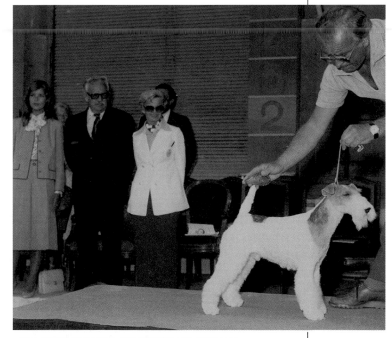

The Monte Carlo Show 1979: Whittingford Weapon (Ch Seedfield Meritor Superflash ex Whittingford Wagtail), with handler Mr M Marshall, winning BIS, watched by Prince Rainier and his family.
(Owners: Mr Marshall and Mme Bastié.)

Match

A Match is a competition where the dogs are judged one against one in an elimination process. Matches are often held at registered Ringcraft Society classes, either within the Society itself or against another similar society. The Society can hold up to 12 Matches a year and a Kennel Club Licence must be obtained first. There is a limit of 64 entries. Normally CC and Reserve Challenge Certificate (RCC) winners are not allowed to enter.

The dogs are placed on two lists as they are entered with the Secretary. Two numbers, one from each list, are drawn out of a hat and the dogs are judged, the winner going forward to the next round until there is only one dog left - The Winner!

These Matches are usually held in small village halls where dogs get used to being close to each other. The general atmosphere is relaxed and it is a very good training ground for the Fox Terrier.

Sanction shows

These shows, like the larger ones, come under Kennel Club rules, and a schedule of Rules, Classes and Judges has to be published and sent to The Kennel Club. Entries are received in advance, and a catalogue is printed giving the names of the dogs entered in each class with names of owner, breeder and parents of each dog. These are usually evening shows confined to members of the society holding the show. CC winners are not allowed to compete.

Primary shows

These shows often start after 5.00 pm, except on Saturdays, Sundays and Bank Holidays, when they start at 2.00 pm. Entry is confined to members of the Society holding the show. Schedules and catalogues are not required.

There can be up to eight classes, the highest one being Maiden. No dog which has won a First Prize at any show (except Puppy classes) or a CC or RCC may compete.

Limited shows

These are small shows confined to members of the Club. There may be a Specialist Judge for one or two breeds, and another judge for Variety classes. Again, no CC winners may enter.

Open shows

The Kennel Club approves the facilities offered and dogs entered must be Kennel Club registered. Entry fees range from £3 to £5 for the first class, and 75p for a second class with the same dog.

When these are run at an Agricultural show (where there may be over 200 classes) they are usually benched. If they are held at Leisure Centres or similar locations, exemption from benching is obtained from The Kennel Club. They can range in size from 10 to over 1,000 different classes.

Benching is like cattle stalls, comprising rows of wooden partitions with a number on for each dog. Usually there are two cards bearing the number, one for the bench and one for the ring. When there is no benching, the ring card number is given to the exhibitor in the ring before judging commences.

To sum up...

These are the main shows to enter before embarking on the Championship shows at which the top awards, the CCs, are given. Three CCs are required from three different judges to make a dog a Champion. Whilst CC winners are not banned from entering Open shows they seldom do so. This may be because they are being used for breeding, they may have been sold on or retired, it may be seen as giving someone else a fair chance, or it may be because the owner does not want a Champion to be beaten by a lesser dog.

Wire Fox Terriers at The Windsor Dog Show.

There are some really fine dogs at these shows, and many experts will bring along their young stock for training and familiarisation. It is a pleasant atmosphere and a good place to learn the trade from some of the more experienced exhibitors. There are some excellent Junior Handlers here too.

Judging usually starts at 10.00 am, occasionally earlier. Exhibitors may leave after completion of their classes.

It is worth taking a folding chair with you until you get to know which shows supply enough seating. The dog box is something to sit on, but is not sufficiently comfortable for a long day out.

Championship shows

These are big shows, often lasting three or four days, where the dogs are benched. Entries usually have to be in at least two months prior to the show date. Entry fees are around £13.

Entry forms must be completed in full and the dog registered with The Kennel Club under the name of the person completing the entry form. Every detail must be correct. There are strict regulations about preparing dogs for exhibition and agreement to these conditions is signed on the entry form.

Competition is very strong indeed and all the experts are there, not only those showing their own dogs but others all around the ringside observing what is going on. Many overseas enthusiasts are also present to look at the dogs and their pedigrees, often making arrangements to take one home. These fellow exhibitors come from Argentina, Australia, Belgium, Brazil, Canada, Denmark, Eire, Finland, France, Germany, Holland, Italy, Japan, Luxemburg, New Zealand, Norway, Singapore, Sweden, Spain, and the USA.

Breed Club Championship shows: Apart from the 14 Championship Shows that offer CCs to the breed there are four Breed Clubs that do: The Wire Fox Terrier Association and The Smooth Fox Terrier Association, The Fox Terrier Club, The Fox Terrier Club of Scotland and The Birmingham and District Fox Terrier Club.

The Breed Club Championship Shows have a dinner/dance on the night before, where exhibitors can meet and chat. They book accommodation at a hotel where a special price has been agreed.

Championship Shows that do not offer CCs to the breed often still hold breed classes and these results count as Open Show results.

Classes at Open/Championship shows - definition (summary)

The definition of classes at any show is detailed in the show schedule. The higher the class the more winning the entrants will have done.

Note: (1) applies to Championship and Open Shows only.
(2) applies to Limited, Sanction and Primary Shows only.

Minor Puppy: For dogs of six and not more than nine calendar months of age on the first day of the Show.

Puppy: For dogs of six and not exceeding twelve calendar months of age on the first day of the Show.

Junior: For dogs of six and not exceeding eighteen calendar months of age on the first day of the Show.

Beginners: (1) For owner, handler or exhibit not having won a first prize at a Championship or Open Show.
(2) For owner, handler or exhibit not having won a First Prize at any Show.

Maiden: (1) For dogs which have not won a CC or a First Prize at an Open or Championship Show.
(2) For dogs which have not won a First Prize.

Novice: (1) For dogs which have not won a CC or three or more First Prizes at Open and Championship Shows.
(2) For dogs which have not won three or more First Prizes at any Show.

Tyro: (1) For dogs which have not won a CC or five or more First Prizes at Open and Championship Shows.
(2) For dogs which have not won five or more First Prizes at any Show.

Debutant: (1) For dogs which have not won a CC or a First Prize at a Championship Show.
(2) For dogs which have not won a First Prize at an Open or Championship Show.

DOG SHOWS

Under graduate:	(1) For dogs which have not won a CC or three or more First Prizes at Championship Shows.
	(2) For dogs which have not won three or more First Prizes at Open or Championship Shows.
Graduate:	(1) For dogs which have not won a CC or four or more First Prizes at Championship Shows in Graduate, Post Graduate, Minor Limit, Mid Limit, Limit and Open classes, whether restricted or not.
	(2) For dogs which have not won four or more First Prizes at Open or Championship Shows in Graduate, Post Graduate, Minor Limit, Mid Limit, Limit and Open classes, whether restricted or not.
Postgraduate:	(1) For dogs which have not won a CC or five or more First Prizes at Championship Shows in Post Graduate, Minor Limit, Mid Limit, Limit and Open classes, whether restricted or not.
	(2) For dogs which have not won five or more First Prizes at Championship and Open Shows in Post Graduate, Minor Limit, Mid Limit, Limit and Open classes, whether restricted or not.
Minor Limit:	(1) For dogs which have not won two CCs or three or more First Prizes in all at Championship Shows in Minor Limit, Mid Limit, Limit and Open classes, confined to the breed, whether restricted or not at Shows where Challenge Certificates were offered for the breed.
	(2) For dogs which have not won three or more First Prizes in all at Open and Championship Shows in Minor Limit, Mid Limit, Limit and Open classes, confined to the breed, whether restricted or not.
Mid Limit:	(1) For dogs which have not won three CCs or five or more First Prizes in all at Championship Shows in Mid Limit, Limit and Open classes, confined to the breed, whether restricted or not, at Shows where Challenge Certificates were offered for the breed.
	(2) For dogs which have not won five or more First Prizes in all at Open and Championship Shows in Mid Limit, Limit and Open classes, confined to the breed.
Limit:	(1) For dogs which have not won three CCs under three different judges or seven or more First Prizes in all, at Championship Shows in Limit and Open classes, confined to the breed, whether restricted or not, at Shows where Challenge Certificates were offered for the breed.
	(2) For dogs which have not won seven or more First Prizes in all at Open and Championship Shows in Limit and Open classes, confined to the breed, whether restricted or not.
Open:	For all dogs of the breeds for which the class is provided and eligible for entry at the Show.
Veteran:	For dogs of not less than seven years of age on the first day of the Show.
Stud Dog:	For stud dogs and at least two progeny of which only the progeny must be entered and exhibited in a breed class at the Show.

Brood Bitch:	For brood bitches and at least two progeny of which only the progeny must be entered and exhibited in a breed class at the Show.
Progeny:	For a dog or bitch, accompanied by at least three of its registered progeny. The dog or bitch need not necessarily have been entered in another class, but all progeny must have been entered and exhibited in another class. The dog or bitch and the progeny need not be registered in the same ownership.
Brace:	For two exhibits (either sex or mixed) of one breed belonging to the same exhibitor, each exhibit having been entered in some class other than Brace or Team.
Team:	For three or more exhibits (either sex or mixed) of one breed entered in some class other than Brace or Team.

Prizes

Most shows select the first five dogs from each class. These will receive the appropriate card or rosette, red being first prize and blue second.

Although prize money at Championship Shows used to be about double the entry fee for a First Prize (entry £1.00 prize £2.00) prize money is seldom given today at Championship Shows in the breed classes. Puppy Stakes may win £20 but mostly the prizes are vouchers to purchase dog food. A BIS might get £100 worth of dog food, RBIS £75 and the Group Winners £50 worth of vouchers. BOB winners usually get six large cans of food and mixer and a choice of carrier bag/towel to take home. Puppy winners get a similar prize. Some BIS winners may get a silver trophy, a goblet or a small shield.

The Winner of the Grand Final of Pedigree Chum Special Champion Stakes can win £400 product vouchers and a trophy; Second Prize is £250 and a trophy and Third Prize £150 and trophy.

The Pedigree Chum Veteran Stakes Winner gets £200 voucher and trophy, Second £125 and trophy and Third £75 and trophy. Prize money is sometimes given at Open Shows, but very little and very seldom. Expenses of £5-£15 are sometimes given to return on a subsequent day for the BIS competition.

DOG SHOWS ABROAD

Eire

In Eire they have Green Stars and Reserve Green Stars. Each Green Star is worth a certain number of points, depending on the size of entry and popularity of the breed. Fox Terriers are now classed as a minority breed. These points are awarded by the Irish Kennel Club after the show and the value is printed on the card. Every Green Card is therefore deemed to be worth a number of points. It takes 40 points to make up a Champion. A five-point Green Star is equal in value to a British CC when counting awards. The Dublin show on St Patrick's Day offers a minimum five points win regardless of entries and there is a maximum of 10 points at any show. The win is related to the number of dogs or bitches that are beaten. In other words, if a bitch beats three bitches, she wins three points. If she then beats a dog in a class of three she wins an additional point. However, if a BOB winner goes on to win the group, that winner takes the number of points awarded to the highest winning dog that it has beaten, so that it may get the maximum of 10 points through a group win. Other grades of achievement are Honour, Diploma of Merit and Certificate of Merit.

United States of America

It is slightly similar in America. Because the country is so large the allocation of points is related to the number of exhibits of any particular breed in a given district.

To become a Champion a dog must earn 15 points, which must include two Majors of from three to five points awarded by two different judges. The Major requirements differ, depending upon how many of a particular breed and sex were shown in a geographical district in the past year for that particular breed. For example, in Michigan winning over an entry of six or seven bitches (or five dogs) will earn a three point Major. If there are not enough dogs for a Major, but enough bitches, the dog can go over the bitches to win 'Best of Winners', thereby winning a Major also. The same applies if there are more dogs and less bitches; the bitch can beat the winning dog and qualify for Best of Winners. Furthermore, if a dog that is not a Champion beats a Champion in the class, it earns an extra point. Having reached the position of Best of Winners they then compete in the Group.

Spain

To win a CC in Spain the dog must be at least 15 months old. There are four classes:

Puppy:	five to nine months.
Junior:	nine to 15 months.
Open:	15 months onwards. You can only win the National Challenge Certificate (CAC) from the Open class.
Champions:	at the International Shows the CACIB is awarded to the best of sex between the winners of the Open and Champions classes.

To become a Spanish Champion your dog must win four CACs under three different judges, and the Terrier must attend the National Terrier Championship Show of Spain in order to win at least an 'Excellent' grade. One of the CACs must be won at the Kennel Club of Spain International Championship Show, which is held in Madrid in May and November each year. This last show is the sticking point for most would-be Champions, because many Champions from other countries are also trying to become Spanish Champions and the competition is extremely fierce. Champions from other countries can still take two or three years to make it in Spain; in other words, six attempts at the Madrid show. A good Champion can continue to be shown to win BOB, Groups, and possibly BIS or RBIS.

Denmark

Puppies of both sexes are judged first in each breed, and then the other dogs and bitches, separated according to age and qualification. They are judged into groups of First Prize Red Ribbon (a typical dog with no significant faults and with worthy qualities); Second Prize Blue Ribbon (typical dog with neither significant faults nor qualities); and Third Prize Yellow Ribbon (a typical dog with some disqualifying faults). The Red group then compete further, and the four best dogs are selected.

15

Judging

Becoming a judge

The Breed Clubs have three Judging lists. Judges 'A1' List is a list of experienced members supported by the Association to award Kennel Club Challenge Certificates who have already been approved to award CCs in the breed by The Kennel Club. The 'A2' List is for members approved by the Association to award CCs, but who are not yet approved by The Kennel Club. The 'B' List is for members supported by the Association to judge the breed at shows where CCs will not be awarded.

Before approval is given, members need some years' experience of breeding and showing good quality dogs, and preferably to have bred a Champion or two. Apart from achieving a high standard in the preparation and showing of the dog, an in-depth knowledge of the Breed Standard is essential, as well as of the procedures to be followed in the ring. Next comes the ability to examine the dog efficiently and assess it accurately.

An eye for a good dog is a natural gift but the trade can be learned by experience, talking and listening to the experts, acting as a ring steward for a good judge, watching various breeds being judged from the ringside, watching Best in Show competitions and attending seminars and courses about judging. Whilst many people aspire to become judges, to become one you need considerable skill, time, energy and money; it is not usually a paid job, although something towards expenses is sometimes given.

Keeping records

A careful record needs to be kept of all dogs (numbers), breeds and classes judged in order to complete a questionnaire prior to judging Champions later on.

Challenge Certificates

Challenge Certificates (CCs) are Green Cards which are issued to the best dog and best bitch at a Championship show. The judge signs the Green Card which states 'I am clearly of the opinion that .... owned by .... is of such outstanding merit as to be worthy of the title of Champion.' The Reserve Challenge Certificate states 'is of such outstanding merit as to be worthy of being awarded the Challenge Certificate should the Challenge Certificate winner be disqualified.'

These cards are confirmed by The Kennel Club, which sends a certified Certificate about three weeks later. Once a dog has gained three CCs, The Kennel Club sends a formal card to the owner giving the dog's name as a Champion and a separate card to the breeder of the Champion. The Kennel Club allocates CCs to the various Championship Shows throughout the season.

Awarding CCs

All judges awarding CCs are approved by The Kennel Club at a special committee. The names are put forward by the breed societies for approval. The Championship Show Committee invites the person to judge their show. If he has not awarded CCs in the breed before, he has to complete a questionnaire sent by the Society. This provides the committee with complete and accurate information on the person's previous judging experience.

The questionnaire is returned to the committee that sent it and, if they are satisfied that the person is sufficiently competent and experienced to do the job, it is forwarded to The Kennel Club, who put it before the Judges' Sub-Committee. They may refer back to the breed club for further advice or opinion. If this is satisfactory they will advise the Canine Society that the person invited has been approved.

The Championship Show Committees either get the names of the judges from lists supplied by

The judge examines the line of neck into the shoulder

the breed clubs or they ask people within the breed whom they would like to see judge their breed. No examination has to be undertaken, although a Judging Diploma Course is run by the Canine Studies Institute.

There are two kinds of judges: the specialist who knows his own breed thoroughly and knows what type he likes, and the 'all rounder' who sees the dog from a more general angle and will not have such detailed knowledge of the breed standard. The breed specialist may fault judge against a particular point; the all rounder tends to look at the overall picture of the dog, specifically its conformation, outline, fitness for the job, angulation and movement. This may be important, as he wants a good sound dog, and will not worry so much about size or some other minor detail.

A judge needs to have knowledge of the dog and to be able to assess its qualities quickly. An experienced person with a good eye can often spot his winner the moment it walks into the ring. A further quality is the manner in which he goes over the dog. Some are a bit rough, but others chat to the dog and make him feel comfortable.

In the ring

When the judge arrives at the ring he has to decide with the steward where the line-up will be, where dogs that have been judged will stand and where the winners will go. There is a normal procedure for this, but some judges may adopt the US or some other procedure. Usually the dogs line up on the side of the ring to the left of the

The **final** line-up:
Ch Cumgarws Joint Venture
winning BOB at the Bath
Championship Show.

table. It is necessary to stand the dog on a mat so that he does not slip while being handled. Dogs from previous classes which have been judged usually stand on the opposite side of the ring, or where asked. Winners usually go in the centre of the ring, going from left to right of the judge.

What the judge looks for

The judge has one-and-a-half to two minutes to examine each dog. Sometimes you get an experienced judge who is very quick indeed.

The 'table' dogs are put on the table and 'stacked' to look their best. The judge looks at the general conformation, outline and overall balance. He looks at the head and expression, the shape and colour of the eyes, the placement and use of the ears.

He examines the teeth, the length of neck, and the line of neck into shoulder, then the bone in the leg and the feet, relating the point of

The winner: Ch Killick of the Mess, with handler Mr Lyn Snow and judge Mr V Mitchell, winning Terrier Group at The Leeds Championship Show.
Photo: Dave Freeman.

elbow to the brisket (depth of brisket). Next he looks at the line from brisket to belly; the muscle, angulation (bend of stifle) and length of first and second thighs of the back legs. He then goes over the body, looking for any slackness or dip in the back and at its length, seeing whether the dog is short coupled, and making sure it has the right tail set. The texture and condition of the coat and furnishings are also examined. He then has a general view of the whole outline, conformation and condition of the dog.

When he looks at the dog from the front he can see the position of the elbows, whether the toes turn in or out, and whether the dog is too close or too wide from this angle.

The judge has another look to see if the dog has that little extra something that he thought it had when it first entered the ring. Does it stand out in health and quality? The dog then moves, either in a triangle or straight up and down. It is then 'stacked' for a final look before returning to the side of the ring. Sometimes the dog may be required to walk up and down two or even three times. This is either to give him a chance if something went wrong the first time, or for the judge to confirm his initial assessment. Judges often use movement to make their final decisions, so in the final line up you may be asked to walk across the ring once more. Some judges use their hands as a measuring stick or even other parts of their body, knowing the knee (or whatever) is so many inches high. A dog is measured lengthwise from the point of shoulder to the buttock which should, in the Fox Terrier, equal the height from the withers to the ground, making a square.

Above: Am Ch Parkside Whitehall at Nethertonian with handler Judi Hallbeck and judge Col Purkhiser, winning BOB at the Platte Valley Kennel Club Show, 1995. (Owners: Ruth and Robert Libner, breeder: Diana Chads.)
Below: The same with judge Mildred K Bryant at the Chain o' Lakes Kennel Club Show, June 1995.

After looking at all the dogs the judge pulls out five dogs for placing in First, Second, Third, Reserve and Very Highly Commended. They go to the centre of the ring in order of merit from left to right of the judge. The steward calls the numbers and presents the cards. It is important the dog is shown to its best advantage until the card is actually in your hand, because the judge can change his mind at the last minute. This is regrettable for the exhibitors as there can be a considerable amount of tension at this time. The judge makes a note of the winning numbers and does a report on the attributes of the first two dogs. Some make critical remarks about the dogs they see, but most prefer to highlight the good points of the winners.

Judging abroad

English judges are often asked to judge Fox Terriers all over the world. The organisation making the request will usually have ascertained that the person concerned is approved by The Kennel Club to judge up to CC level. The procedures are different abroad, and the judge needs to be aware of what he has to do. For example, in Europe he is required to give a written critique to every exhibitor. The dogs are selected in groups of merit as described in Chapter 14.

Photo: Melia Photography.

16

A Few Common **ailments**

Your veterinary surgeon keeps a complete record of the medical history of your dog and he is the person to consult when the dog is ill or injured. The first essentials for a healthy dog are good food, daily grooming (watch ears and feet), clean bed, fresh air and exercise. Below are some remedies that breeders have successfully tried for less serious problems. Any stressful situation must be referred to the vet, who can usually sort it out very quickly.

Accident

If the dog suffers an accident keep him warm and calm and move him as little as possible to avoid further damage and pain. See the vet as soon as you can. When your dog is home again, keep him clean, warm, comfortable and quiet in a dark corner. A few drops of Rescue Remedy help the shock. Give a teaspoon of honey and water as necessary. Arnica also relieves shock and helps the healing process of the wounds. Wipe gums and teeth with cotton wool soaked in a mild solution of Dettol. Clean a dirty rectum with cotton wool soaked in olive oil or Vaseline. Use soapy water to clean off dirt from diarrhoea and dry with talcum powder. It can be difficult to feed a sick dog. Give him a little freshly-warmed food with gravy. Make soup out of chicken or rabbit, with carrots and other suitable vegetables. Sardines or salmon or an egg might be accepted.

Anal glands

If the dog drags his behind along the ground his anal glands may be full. These glands are just below the rectum. Using cotton wool, gently press the glands to clear out the surplus smelly brown liquid, which sometimes squirts out freely. If there is a problem see the vet.

Bites and stings

Bees and wasps pose a real threat to dogs. The bee sting is full of poison and remains in the skin, so pull it out at once. Apply bicarbonate of soda or a raw onion. If further treatment is needed, apply methylated spirits, or even neat brandy or whisky, to the affected area. Adder bites, usually occurring in heathland on a hot day, are very serious, and death could follow very quickly. Keep the dog still and, if possible, bandage it between the bite and the heart. Go to the vet at once.

Car rides

Apart from travel sickness (see below), some dogs are frightened of the motorway, concrete surfaces, or large lorries. A drive at a moderate speed on country roads to a favourite walk is tolerated happily.

Condition

Vetzyme tablets from the pet shop improve condition, and include Vitamin B. Alternatively use Abidec, following the manufacturer's instructions. Olive oil and Solvitax are good for the coat, and a dab of margarine also helps.

Conjunctivitis

The dog continually rubs his eye, which is weepy and bloodshot. Wash the eye in salty water (one teaspoon cooking salt to one pint water) using an eye dropper. Remove any foreign matter (dirt, grass seed or similar) using a drop of castor oil to loosen it. Acriflavian ointment or eye drops/ointment helps heal the eye.

Cuts and scratches

These normally heal very quickly. Clean the wound and apply iodine or powdered permanganate of potash crystals which stops any bleeding. An antiseptic cream may also be applied. A punctured wound should be cleaned with warm water containing a few drops of Dettol. Leave the wound open if possible because sometimes one bite can set up an infection. If this happens take the dog to the vet.

Diarrhoea

This is often caused by food, either something the dog has picked up while out or inappropriate diet. Eating grass usually makes the dog sick, which clears any indigestion. Diarrhoea could be the start of a streptococcal infection, however, so consult your vet if blood or mucus is present in the stools. In puppies, diarrhoea can result from eating too much, from a change of diet, or simply from excitement. Give the puppy plenty of water to drink. A teaspoon of castor oil should stop the trouble. Medicinal liquid paraffin will help or (the most usual remedy today) a teaspoon of Kaolin and Morphine. Do not give the puppy any milk or food for a day, then start on a plain diet of cottage cheese, boiled rice and perhaps a cooked egg or fish.

Ear canker

The dog will scratch his ear and put his head on one side. There will be either a dry brownish substance or a wet discharge in the external ear passage. There is often a smell to indicate trouble. This condition is usually treatable with Canaural Ear Drops or Canker Ointment. Canker can be caused by the blood overheating or by a parasite. Clean the ear carefully using cotton buds. Put antiseptic lotion or Benzyl Benzoate on the outside of the ear if it is sore. (This can be used for any sore parts of the skin.) Then give the dog Milk of Magnesia (four tablets a day to an adult, two to a puppy) for up to three weeks to cool the blood. Clean the ears of excessive hair fairly regularly and check there is no irritant.

Feet

Keep the feet clean, especially between the toes, to prevent the fur from matting and making the feet very sore. If the hair around the feet grows too thick and long the dog cannot walk properly. If the feet are sore, gently cut away the mats with round-ended scissors. Clean the feet with a few drops of Dettol added to warm water. Dry them off, then gently rub on an antiseptic cream. There is a condition called sweaty feet which is caused by the blood overheating or a fungoid infection. Give the dog Milk of Magnesia and SA37 or Vetzyme tablets to improve his overall condition.

Hot weather

I leave a baby bath in the garden as a swimming pool for the dogs. They love to jump in, get their tummies wet and then continue playing. They need plenty of water to drink, especially if they have been out for a walk. On a car journey it is essential to have plenty of water and a wet towel in case of any delays. However it is better not to travel at all with the dog in really hot weather.

Illness

A tablespoon of castor oil is always to be recommended at the first sign of sickness.

Inoculations

The vet will advise when to start inoculating the puppy, usually at six to eight weeks. Inoculations can be given against Canine Distemper, Canine Hepatitis (CAVI), Canine Adenovirus 2, Canine Parvovirus, Canine Parainfluenza (Kennel Cough) and Leptospirosis. This last one is a bacterial disease which affects the liver and kidneys and is transmissible to humans. These are all potentially lethal diseases against which the dog should be protected. They should then have an annual booster. Descriptions of the diseases and symptoms may be found on the vet's certificate.

Itching

Milk of Magnesia (tablets or liquid) cools the blood, cleans the system and cures tummy upsets and bad breath (see Skin).

Jaundice

Sickness and excessive thirst are the first symptoms, and then the white of the eyeballs goes yellow. Avoid fat and oils in the food and get the vet to treat quickly. It may be Leptospiral jaundice, carried by rats, which is contagious, or it may be simply a chill on the liver and kidneys. An old domestic remedy is to stop all food and give the dog 1 dessertspoon of sherry whey every hour. If there is no more sickness give two tablespoons four or five times a day. After two days the dog should be better and could have a little lean meat.
Sherry whey: Bring half a pint of fresh milk nearly to boiling point and add a wine glass of sherry. Leave it to stand and curdle. Reboil, strain through a fine cloth and throw away the curd. Add glucose to sweeten; and there is a clear liquid for use.

Nails

These need cutting regularly. Pavement walking usually keeps the nails on the back feet short, but movement can be faulty and painful if the nails are not trimmed on the front feet. Provided this is done regularly the dog will get used to it and not mind.

Parasites (internal)

Worms may be seen in the excreta. Other signs are that the coat may lack condition and the dog may go off its feed, lose weight and generally look rather miserable. All dogs should be wormed regularly, about twice a year. Canovel palatable worker has done the job effectively for me. The vet always keeps a supply of suitable wormers in stock.

Parasites (external)

This is a common problem and often difficult to solve. The suggestions below have been tried successfully, but should be tried one at a time. Then stick to the method that works. If the dog is very sore and distressed the vet can give an injection which gives prompt relief, but this only lasts a few days.

Fleas: These often invade the dog, especially in the summer months. An old remedy is to put a mixture of equal parts of paraffin oil and milk on the dog. This quickly kills the fleas and keeps them away. There are flea collars but they do not last very long. Flea powder and a bath usually does the trick. Sometimes one flea bite may cause a severe itching from dermatitis and the skin goes red and sore. Goat's milk helps to alleviate this condition and also Tetmolsol applied to the sore areas. Keep the dog away from grass areas; these are the most likely places to collect the fleas.

Lice: These are a dirty white colour and stick their heads deeply into the skin, often in clusters in the ears. Apply warm cow's milk and paraffin with a tooth brush. Afterwards wash with warm water and dry. This does not harm the skin and can be used on puppies. Otherwise use Blue Mercury Ointment (ask the chemist to make it up) and apply under the armpit, top of tail and top of head (occiput). Do not allow the dog to lick it.

Ticks: These are large, fat, white bugs that suck the blood from their host dog. They cause a considerable skin irritation and are hard to locate. Use the same paraffin mixture and pull out with tweezers. Iodine can be applied to the sore areas.

Skin mites: These live in the hair follicles and dig deep into the skin. This causes mange, which must be dealt with promptly by the vet. If the dog bites its paws or any other inflamed area the problem will be aggravated. The problem will not go away until treated effectively. The following remedies have been found effective:

- Vetzyme insecticidal shampoo (containing Permethrin) is excellent.
- Quellada is another good one obtainable from the vet. It was banned for containing Lindane (which can affect the chest and lungs) but is still on sale at the chemist for children.
- Aludex is a dip for mange, also obtainable from the vet.
- Malathion (one tablespoon to two gallons of water) is for garden use but it is also an effective dip for dogs and even other pets.

- Prioderm human shampoo/lotion can be obtained from the chemist and is an update to Tetmolsol.
  (**NB:** None of these dips should be allowed to get into the dog's eyes, nose or mouth, and all should be used with caution.)
- Tea Tree Oil (from homoeopathic shops) and lotion and shampoo (from The Body Shop). Put three drops of oil in half a teaspoon milk (optional) and half a pint warm water and use as a grooming spray daily. The shampoo cleans the coat, and the lotion applied neat heals scratches.
- Ointments containing goat's milk, honey or beeswax are beneficial.
- Thornit, which is used to treat ears, has also proved successful for itching feet and red sore patches on the skin.

Riff: This is a word used by terrier people to describe a skin problem in which the skin goes pink. It starts inside the back legs and under the front legs and becomes extremely sore. The hair also goes pink and eventually grows out. Wash the affected areas with soapy water every day for a week and apply a mixture of camomile and surgical spirit. Keep the bedding spotlessly clean.

Some suggestions to prevent skin problems:

- Garlic tablets, (or fresh garlic) in meals daily.
- Reduce the protein intake.
- Comb out any unwanted creatures.
- Smear the dog in one of the following before going out: flea powder, lemon juice, garlic spray, jungle formula or some similar spray.

Shock

If the dog suffers shock for whatever reason put him in a warm dark place to rest. Keep him warm with an infra-red lamp or hot-water bottle and put a blanket over him. Half an Aspirin might help calm him. Rescue Remedy is helpful or try arnica (see also Accident).

Skin Irritation   (See also Parasites (external))

Allergies of various kinds can cause skin irritation, and they are often related to diet. Test each type of food the dog has over a couple of months by omitting each in turn. Try white meat (chicken) with boiled rice or pasta instead of biscuit meal, which contains many different things. As you restrict the diet some deficiency in vitamins or fatty acids may result; these should be replaced by SA37 or some other nutritional supplement. Gradually add other items until the reaction worsens. Two to three days is enough to show the difference. A reduction in red meat will often help.

Skin irritation may also be due to thyroid or hormonal imbalance or some other clinical problem.

Teeth

Teeth usually keep clean in the younger dog. Dry biscuits and carrots help. Most useful is a good marrow bone from the butcher. There is usually a slight upset tummy afterwards, but nothing to worry about. If teeth have to be extracted, arnica helps the healing process. It is also said to be helpful to humans before and after the extraction. Nylabone manufactures a range of toys which help to prevent the build-up of tartar as the dog plays with them, thus promoting canine dental health.

Temperature

Normally 38.6°C (101.5°F). Put Vaseline on the end of the thermometer before inserting it into the rectum.

Travel sickness

This rarely occurs in dogs that have been taken out and about since they were six to eight weeks old. Once they get used to it (short journeys at first) they usually enjoy car rides. Do not feed a dog before travel or let him have a long drink. Human seasick pills (in smaller doses) the night before a trip calm the dog. Do not give one of these before a show, however, because he may then be too lethargic to show.

Alternative medicine/treatments for dogs

Homeopathy, reflexology, acupuncture and chiropractic treatment have all been used successfully. The practitioners usually work in association with the vet concerned. Acupuncture has been particularly successful for older dogs with spondylosis (when the intervertebral discs become worn) and it can also help in cases of incontinence.

Some homeopathic suggestions

Rescue Remedy:	To revive a fading puppy: two drops.
	To relieve stress, shock or following injury: four drops straight onto the tongue.
Evening Primrose Oil:	To get coat back from itchy skin.
	May help bitches' cycle problems.
Aconite:	For shock and cold.
Apis Mel:	Wasp or bee stings and arthritis.
Arnica:	Accidents, injury, shock, bruises, sprains and stress.
Arsen Alb:	Dandruff and ear infections.
Belladonna:	A major fever remedy.
Bryonia:	Kennel cough, painful joints.
Carbo Veg:	Flatulence.
Euphrasia:	Hayfever, conjunctivitis.
Graphites:	Smelly skin.
Hepar Sulph:	Infections, abscesses.
Rhus Tox:	Rheumatic remedy.
Sulphur:	Tummy troubles.
Urtkaurens:	False pregnancy, rashes.
Passiflora:	
Coclulus:	} Travel sickness.
Petroleum:	
Ustillago Haydis:	} Over-randy male dogs.
Testosterone:	
Calc Carb:	Eating own stools.
Nosodes:	Distemper.

For further guidance consult George MacLeod's book on the subject (see **Bibliography**).

A

The main Fox Terrier breed clubs in the United Kingdom are listed below. Addresses of current Hon Secretaries can be obtained from The Kennel Club.

The Wire Fox Terrier Association:
(They hold an annual Championship show in October.)

The Fox Terrier Club
(They hold an annual Championship show in July in Derbyshire.)

The Fox Terrier Club of Scotland

The Fox Terrier Club of South Wales

The Yorkshire Fox Terrier Association

The Bolton and District Fox Terrier Club

London Airedale and Fox Terrier Club

Kennel Clubs around the world:

The Kennel Club
1 Clarges Street
Piccadilly
London WC1Y 8AB
UK
Tel: 0181 493 6651

The American Kennel Club
51 Madison Avenue
New York
NY 10010
USA

The Australian National Kennel Club
Royal Show Grounds
Ascot Vale
Victoria
AUSTRALIA

The Canadian Kennel Club
111 Eglinton Avenue East
Toronto 12 Ontario
CANADA

The Irish Kennel Club
4 Harcourt Street
Dublin 2
EIRE

The New Zealand Kennel Club
PO Box 523
Wellington 1
NEW ZEALAND

USEFUL ADDRESSES

Other Useful Addresses:

The Council of Docked Breeds (CDB)
Secretary: Ginette Elliott
Marsburg Kennels
Whitehall Lane
Thorpe-Le-Soken
Essex CO16 OAF   Tel: 01255 830993

or   Anne Moore
Sprogmore Kennels
Main Road
Alresford
Colchester
Essex CO7 8AP   Tel: 01206 825302

Canine Studies Institute
London Road
Bracknell
Berks
RG12 6QN   Tol: 01344 420898

Our Dogs
5 Oxford Road
Station Approach
Manchester M60 1SX   Tel: 0161 236 2660

Dog World
9 Tufton Street
Ashford
Kent   TN23 1QN   Tel: 01233 22389

PRO Dogs
4 New Road
Ditton
Maidstone
Kent   M20 6A

For further information about the Wire Fox Terrier please contact:

Miss D R Chads
Corner Cottage
25 Brewery Road
Woking
Surrey GU21 4LL

B

Whelping table

Served Jan	01	02	03	04	05	06	07	08	09	10	11	12	13	14
Due to whelp Mar/Apr	05	06	07	08	09	10	11	12	13	14	15	16	17	18
Served Feb	01	02	03	04	05	06	07	08	09	10	11	12	13	14
Due to whelp Apr/May	05	06	07	08	09	10	11	12	13	14	15	16	17	18
Served Mar	01	02	03	04	05	06	07	08	09	10	11	12	13	14
Due to whelp May/Jun	03	04	05	06	07	08	09	10	11	12	13	14	15	16
Served April	01	02	03	04	05	06	07	08	09	10	11	12	13	14
Due to whelp Jun/Jul	03	04	05	06	07	08	09	10	11	12	13	14	15	16
Served May	01	02	03	04	05	06	07	08	09	10	11	12	13	14
Due to whelp Jul/Aug	03	04	05	06	07	08	09	10	11	12	13	14	15	16
Served Jun	01	02	03	04	05	06	07	08	09	10	11	12	13	14
Due to whelp Aug/Sep	03	04	05	06	07	08	09	10	11	12	13	14	15	16
Served Jul	01	02	03	04	05	06	07	08	09	10	11	12	13	14
Due to whelp Sept/Oct	02	03	04	05	06	07	08	09	10	11	12	13	14	15
Served Aug	01	02	03	04	05	06	07	08	09	10	11	12	13	14
Due to whelp Oct/Nov	03	04	05	06	07	08	09	10	11	12	13	14	15	16
Served Sep	01	02	03	04	05	06	07	08	09	10	11	12	13	14
Due to whelp Nov/Dec	03	04	05	06	07	08	09	10	11	12	13	14	15	16
Served Oct	01	02	03	04	05	06	07	08	09	10	11	12	13	14
Due to whelp Dec/Jan	03	04	05	06	07	08	09	10	11	12	13	14	15	16
Served Nov	01	02	03	04	05	06	07	08	09	10	11	12	13	14
Due to whelp Jan/Feb	03	04	05	06	07	08	09	10	11	12	13	14	15	16
Served Dec	01	02	03	04	05	06	07	08	09	10	11	12	13	14
Due to whelp Feb/Mar	02	03	04	05	06	07	08	09	10	11	12	13	14	15

WHELPING TABLE

15	16	17	18	19	20	21	22	23	24	25	26	27	28	29	30	31
19	20	21	22	23	24	25	26	27	28	29	30	31	01	02	03	04
15	16	17	18	19	20	21	22	23	24	25	26	27	28	(29)		
19	20	21	22	23	24	25	26	27	28	29	30	01	02	(03)		
15	16	17	18	19	20	21	22	23	24	25	26	27	28	29	30	31
17	18	19	20	21	22	23	24	25	26	27	28	29	30	31	01	02
15	16	17	18	19	20	21	22	23	24	25	26	27	28	29	30	
17	18	19	20	21	22	23	24	25	26	27	28	29	30	01	02	
15	16	17	18	19	20	21	22	23	24	25	26	27	28	29	30	31
17	18	19	20	21	22	23	24	25	26	27	28	29	30	31	01	02
15	16	17	18	19	20	21	22	23	24	25	26	27	28	29	30	
17	18	19	20	21	22	23	24	25	26	27	28	29	30	31	01	
15	16	17	18	19	20	21	22	23	24	25	26	27	28	29	30	31
16	17	18	19	20	21	22	23	24	25	26	27	28	29	30	01	02
15	16	17	18	19	20	21	22	23	24	25	26	27	28	29	30	31
17	18	19	20	21	22	23	24	25	26	27	28	29	30	31	01	02
15	16	17	18	19	20	21	22	23	24	25	26	27	28	29	30	
17	18	19	20	21	22	23	24	25	26	27	28	29	30	01	02	
15	16	17	18	19	20	21	22	23	24	25	26	27	28	29	30	31
17	18	19	20	21	22	23	24	25	26	27	28	29	30	31	01	02
15	16	17	18	19	20	21	22	23	24	25	26	27	28	29	30	
17	18	19	20	21	22	23	24	25	26	27	28	29	30	31	01	
15	16	17	18	19	20	21	22	23	24	25	26	27	28	29	30	31
16	17	18	19	20	21	22	23	24	25	26	27	28	01	02	03	

C

APPENDIX C: LIST OF CHAMPIONS

POST-WAR BRITISH WIRE FOX TERRIER CHAMPIONS FROM 1946

Name	Sex	Sire	Dam	Owner	Breeder	Born
1946						
Ch Weltona Revelation	D	Culverbrook Tuscan	Hoddlesden Lady	A Churchill	A Yates	7.12.43
Ch Crackley Straightaway	D	Ch Crackley Supreme Again	Crackley Sequel	J R Barlow	Owner	28.6.41
Ch Kirkmoor Carefree	B	Ch Miltona Mahmoud	Winkley Show Girl	W Mitchell	Mrs W Peel	3.8.41
1947						
Ch Foxdenton Sunstream	B	Ch Talavera Jupiter	Barries Vixen	J N Hilton	H Simpson	14.5.43
Ch Holmwire Hyperion	D	Weltona Axholme Barham	Woodstead Wish	Higginson & Staveley	W Woods	7.6.44
Ch Tescot Rita	B	Flexrona Futurist	Tescot Firefly	T Scott	Owner	23.7.44
Ch Chief Barmaid	B	Hotel Traveller	Chillie Sauce	R A Penny	Owner	1.4.45
Ch Drakehall Daisybelle	B	Brakehall Debonair	Bedlam Cristabelle	E Sharpe and A Butler	E Sharpe	22.7.45
Ch Travella Strike	B	Travella Sensation	Travella Gloria	Mrs B Cole	W B Cole	26.9.46
Ch Tinker Belle	B	Ch Weycroft Warfare	Princess Tan End	Mrs E Coton	F Lowe	2.5.45
Ch Stocksmoor Sharecroft Select	B	Blue Bird Emperor	Sharefield Surprise	Mrs J Creasy	J A Share	22.3.46
Ch Crackley Sailaway	D	Crackley Stowaway	Straightlace Susan	J R Barlow	Mrs E G Robinson	5.5.46
Ch Miltona Miss Martha	B	Miltona Magical	Warewell Darkie	W Hancock	Owner	30.9.42
Ch Weycroft Woolcomber	D	Ch Weycroft Warfare	Grendon Success	T Brampton	O Wright	25.7.44
Ch Wyretex Wyns Princess	B	Wyretex Wynstock	Wyretex Wyns Dainty	Mrs D White	Mr Fullbrook	11.12.43
Ch Clarington Contender	D	Wireford Colonel	Grenville Countess	W Seddon	A Smith	6.6.45
1948						
Ch Arley Miss Quality	B	Polo Fireaway	Penda Prize Packet	W Nelmes	Owner	1.8.46
Ch BlueBird Felicit Fireson	D	Tregolwyn Trademark	Dianes Selected	E Gray	T Hill	18.6.46
Ch Crackley Sunstorm	B	Crackley Satisfaction	Crackley Shelved	T Ganney	J R Barlow	1.11.46
Ch Glendoune Gavotte	B	Crackley Satisfaction	Crackley Shelved	R H McGill	J R Barlow	28.4.47
Ch Casfala Copyright	D	Hotel Traveller	Cawthorne Copyright	F M Hughes	J Roberts	16.6.45
Ch Cornwall Robecia Radiance	D	Bluebird Emperor	Robecia Streamlined	T Langley-Jones	T Goold	20.2.44
Ch Kirkmoor Anfield Patch-up	B	Ch Clarington Contender	Anfield Patchwork	M Seddon	J Bradley	26.4.47
Ch Roughsea Sparkle	B	Ch Holmwire Distinction	Deborah of Albernal	H Holden	J E Holden	20.2.45
Ch Secret Passionette	B	Miltona Magical	Secret Special Session	J Hudson	Owner	30.8.45
Ch Talavera Patch-Up	B	Eden Grenadier	Eden Juliet	Mrs H Graham	F Robson	28.6.43

LIST OF CHAMPIONS

Name	Sex	Sire	Dam	Breeder	Owner	Date
Ch Tonadic Burtona Bonanza Again	D	Burtona Beacon	Burtona Belona	T Ganny	C H Burton	3.3.45
Ch Weltona Exelwyre Dustynight	D	Middleforth Tuscan	Juliet of Exelwyre	A Churchill	J Yates	17.4.47
Ch Wynstead What's Wanted	D	Mahmoud Double	Nigels Sunshine	E Gray	T Dale	5.1.43
1949						
Ch Beaukrat Ritelsa Rightahead	D	Harrowhill Straightahead	Fitelsa Joy	C Webb & J R Charnley	Miss S Keenan	14. 2.47
Ch Bedlam Beau Ideal	D	Bedlam Wynstead Woolsack	Bedlam Guda	Mrs A Butler	A Butler	24.5.47
Ch Celtone Constance	B	Ch Weycroft Woolcomber	Celtone Cobnut	J Johnson	Owner	16.8.47
Ch Cockington Cock-a-Hoop	D	Cockington Gay Galliard	Cockington Cover Girl	Mrs M Cooper	Owner	10.9.47
Ch Drakehall Miss Banty	B	Axholme Newmaidley Paul	Axholme Delia's Folly	E Sharpe	G Burton	7.8.47
Ch Kirkmoor Cobler	D	Copledene Dante	Kingsbridge Selected	N Seddon	W B Edwards	2.11.47
Ch Knolbrook Keyman	D	Ch Clarington Contender	Kingsfield Debutante	J Greenhalgh	H Knowles	14.9.47
Ch Travella Skyliner	D	Ch Travella Strike	Travella Sunshine	W Browne-Cole	Owner	7.10.48
Ch Cornwall Lydbury Lady	B	Ch Cornwall Robecia Radiance	Crofton Contender	T Langley-Jones	Mr Mead	8.8.45
Ch Portbredy Party Piece	B	Penda Pompilius	Penda Prize Packet	Mrs E L Williams Beresford and Greaves	Owner	18.10.43
Ch Gedling Content	B	Gedling Contender	Brewson Patsy		F G Perks	18.10.44
Ch Drakehall Dairymaid	B	Drakehall Diplomat	Carniff Connie	E Sharpe	Mr G Hudson	4.11.47
Ch Kebser Whitwyre Mascot	D	Whitwyre Magnetic	Whitwyre Moti Mahal	G Hall	Mrs Whitworth	21.3.46
Ch Epping Ladycroft Trueform	D	Weltona Realstance	Weltona Ladybird	A A W Simmonds	K Twyford	14.2.48
Ch Bedlam Don Juan	D	Bedlam Wynstead Warrant	Nugrade Nublue	Mrs A Butler	J W Holmes	20.8.48
Ch Casfala Kepple Nobleman	D	Ch Casfala Copyright	Drakehall de Luxe	F M Hughes	A Barlow	28.2.49
Ch Winstan Wiswell	D	Ch Weltona Revelation	Winstan Wendy	E Winstanley	Owner	19.8.47
Ch Travella Quick Decision	D	Travella Sensation	Travella Rosebud	W Browne-Cole	J J Bath	14.2.49
Ch Weltona Realstance	D	Ch Weltona Revelation	Weltona Carnation	A Churchill	Owner	20.1.46
Ch Wycollar Duchess	B	Ch Crackley Sailaway	Wycollar Wonderous	J W Turner	Owner	29.5.49
Ch Waterton Maryholm Wendy	B	Eden Autocrat	Maryholm Dalfurn Delilah	L Hastings	A Clanachan	10.4.48
Ch Eden Kirkmoor Sunset	B	Ch Holmwire Hyperion	My Model Miss	F Robson	F W Sutton	20.6.47
Ch Yours & Mine	B	Stoneycrag Sensation	Lady Yvette	R F Harris	H Cheney	16.5.46
Ch Burntedge Besum	B	Ch Weltona Revelation	Talavera Return	J Hamilton	Owner	20.12.47

Name	Sex	Sire	Dam	Owner	Breeder	Born
Ch Roundway Rhapsody	B	Roundway Parody	Roundway Rhyming	Mrs J Creasy	Mrs E M Moseley	31.10.47
Ch Kirkmoor Vanity	B	Ch Clarington Contender	Wybury Wedlock	Mr & Mrs L S Rigby	W Berry	15.9.47
Ch Drakehall Delia	B	Drakehall Debonair	Drakehall Dreamgirl	E Sharpe	Owner	13.2.48
Ch Polo Fireaway	D	Ch Crackley Straighaway	Polo Minted	H W Hingle	C B Cole	21.7.45
1951						
Ch Drakehall Dandy	D	Danycraig Caich Have a Go	Bedlam Christabelle	H Harris	E Sharpe	13.2.50
Ch Epping Wyrevale Monogram	D	Wyretex Wynstock	Wyrevale Marguerite	A A W Simmonds	W Miles	29.11.48
Ch Meyrex Travella Reliable	D	Ch Travella Strike	Travella Stylist	Miss M Lloyd	W Browne-Cole	18.5.49
Ch Miltona Master Gunner	D	Miltona Marmaduke	Miltona Miss Maud	W E Hancock	Owner	13.9.48
Ch Newmaidley Hob	D	Newmaidley Ceasar	Rexine Fashion	Miss L G Beak	F Hobbs	10.9.48
Ch Travella Sizzler	D	Ch Travella Strike	Travella Sunshine	W Browne-Cole	Owner	19.4.50
Ch Travella Skyflyer	D	Ch Travella Strike	Travella Mannequin	W Browne-Cole	Owner	29.3.49
Ch Twynstar Accurist	D	Eden Commander	Twynstar Typist	L W Edmunds	Owner	23.11.46
Ch Arley Adorable	B	Ch Travella Strike	Polo Skylark	W Nelmes	C B Browne-Cole	29.3.50
Ch Newmaidley Cleopatra	B	Newmaidley Ceasar	Newmaidley Destiny	Miss L G Beak	Owner	16.12.46
Ch Penda Hieover Warrior	B	Penda Pompilius	Hieover Music	Mrs E Williams	R Penny	1.4.48
Ch Ravelly Perfect	B	Crackley Stowaway	Straightlace Susan	R A Floyd	Mrs E Robinson	1.4.47
Ch Roundway Cats Cradle	B	Ch Travella Strike	Ch Stocksmoor Sharecroft Select	Mrs J Creasy	Owner	1.5.48
Ch Summers Silhoutte	B	Summers Security	Foxite Miss	Capt F B Foy	Owner	19.7.49
Ch Travella Wildcroft Superb	D	Ch Travella Strike	Littlecroft Hopeful	W Browne-Cole	E T Best	17.12.48
Ch Tokard Susan	B	Castlecroft Cleanaway	Newmaidley Eve	A Francis	Owner	31.7.50
Ch Walldene Wysh	B	Newmaidley Ceasar	Walldene Waltztime	J Yates	Mrs E C Walls	1.4.48
Ch Westroad Lucky Charm	B	Ch Cornwall Robecia Radiance	Wyretex Wyns Dream Girl	D Evans	Owner	15.3.49
Ch Wyreholme Ember	B	Castlecroft Cleanaway	Wyreholme Entire	D Williams	Owner	10.3.49
1952						
Ch Casfala Colonist	D	Ch Casfala Kepple Nobleman	Casfala Careless	F M Hughes	Owner	10.10.50
Ch Castlecroft Contender Again	D	Castlecroft Cleanaway	Castlecroft Clean Cut	G A Prosser	Owner	10.6.49
Ch Rigwyre Royalist	D	Kirkmoor Connoisseur	Rigwyre Dorincourt Dinah	Mr & Mrs Rigby	Mrs Rigby	23.3.50
Ch Travella Starshine	D	Ch Travella Strike	Travella Crystal	W Browne-Cole	Owner	20.11.51
Ch Travella Superman	D	Ch Travella Skyflyer	Travella Carnation	W Browne-Cole	Owner	12.2.51

LIST OF CHAMPIONS

Champion	D/B	Sire	Dam	Breeder	Owner	Date
Ch Wyretex Wyns Tuscan	D	Culverbrook Tuscan	Wyretex Wyns Thralia	Mrs D White	Owner	23.11.45
Ch Burtona Beseem	B	Castlecroft Cleanaway	Burtona Briartul	C H Burton	Owner	14.10.50
Ch Dinglebank Debutante	B	Ch Weycroft Woolcomber	Dinglebank Wicked Lady	Mrs M B Gardner	Owner	10.1.49
Ch Graigydan Treacle	B	Ch Clarington Contender	Graigydan Olga	E G Jones	Owner	13.3.49
Ch Masterlea Lustre	B	Ch Travella Strike	Lyndoch Lovely Girl	E G Bowler	W Haslam	4.1.51
Ch Maryholm Mighty Good	D	Ch Knolbrook Keyman	Fair Pretender	A Clanachan	Owner	18.8.50
Ch Burtona Betoken	D	Burtona Bosun	Torkard Countess	C H Burton	Owner	14.4.50
Ch Wyrevale Monomark	D	Ebbw Swell Contender	Wyrevale Marguerite	W Miles	Owner	31.3.50
Ch Penda Blackwell Revelation	D	Ch Weltona Revelation	Elenholme Elfreida	Mrs E Williams	F Holliday	12.1.49
Ch True to Form	B	Ch Epping Ladycroft Truform	Write Start	Miss B Cliff	F Bates	5.8.50
Ch Newmaidley Dancer	B	Ch Newmaidley Hob	Newmaidley Kara	Miss L G Beak	Owner	24.1.50
Ch Miltona Miss Conduct	B	Miltona Marmaduke	Miltona Miss Maud	W Hancock	Owner	13.9.48
Ch Meyrex Travella Stella	B	Ch Travella Skyline	Travella Rosebud	Miss M Lloyd	J J Bath	3.10.49
Ch Castlecroft Contender Again	D	Castlecroft Cleanaway	Castlecroft Cleancut	A Francis	G Prosser	10.6.49

1953

Champion	D/B	Sire	Dam	Breeder	Owner	Date
Ch Quayside Drakehall Duncan	D	Drakehall Ardoch Advocate	Drakehall Dreamgirl	G E Rees	E Sharpe	4.1.52
Ch Weltona What's This	D	Ch Wyretex Wyns Tuscan	Full Dress of the Forces	A Churchill	W Davies	21.2.52
Ch Maryholme Northern Monarch	D	Ch Knolbrook Keyman	Newown Spitfire	A Clanachan	S E Chapman	20.10.51
Ch Axholme Double Strike	D	Ch Travella Strike	Axholme Miss Miranda	G Burton	Owner	16.8.51
Ch Caradochouse Fox Glove	B	Ch Bedlam Beau Ideal	Crowcroft Mermaid	P H Copley	T Page	12.3.50
Ch Burntedge Ballet Girl	B	Meritor Moorcrest Mac	Ch Burntedge Beaum	Miss B Cliff	J Hamilton	18.8.51
Ch Tindale Tina	B	Ch Knolbrook Keyman	Tindale Tay	W A Ewbank	Owner	15.12.51
Ch Travella Allure	B	Ch Travella Skyflier	Travella Carefree	W E Bellerby	W Browne-Cole	12.9.51
Ch Milne Reaghcastle Roberta	B	Hartleydene High Flight	Reaghcastle Romance	F & A Brooker	C McCoukey	10.10.51
Ch Burtona Ballet Girl	B	Ch Castlecroft Contender Again	Burtona Brunette	C H Burton	Owner	12.6.52
Ch Roundway Strike a Light	D	Ch Travella Strike	Roundway Wishbone	Mrs J Creasy	Owner	24.9.50

1954

Champion	D/B	Sire	Dam	Breeder	Owner	Date
Ch Karfree Captain	D	Whilwyre Mubarak	Konstallation Kebsir	Mrs M Aird	Owner	14.12.47
Ch Banwyn Welland Wendy	B	Tindale Taft	Welland Wedlock	W Hancock	L Jones	1.2.53
Ch Rawdon Rhoda	B	Ch Travella Strike	Fawdon Ruby	S Thorne	W Andrews	27.12.51
Ch Crackley Security	D	Crackley Splendid	Crackley Spectant	S Thorne	J R & J H Barlow	1.11.52
Ch Travella Suredo	D	Ch Travella Starshine	Travella Jasmine	W Browne-Cole	Owner	11.8.53
Ch Madam Moonraker	B	Ch Weltona Exelwyre Dusty Night	Eden Sunshine	J Stephenson	Owner	12.1.53

Name	Sex	Sire	Dam	Owner	Breeder	Born
Ch Striking of Laracor	D	Ch Travella Strike	Gloria of Laracor	Miss A Hope-Johnstone	Owner	13.11.51
Ch Wakesgreen Barry	D	Ch Knolbrook Keyman	Wakesgreen Falstaff Festival	J D Sellers	Owner	20.5.51
Ch Wybury Penda Quicksilver	B	Ch Penda Blackwell Revelation	Ch Penda Hieover Warrior	Mrs E L Williams	Owner	29.5.51
1955						
Ch Cawthorne Climax	D	Ch Burtona Betoken	Cawthorne Twynstar Actionette	Mr & Mrs Pardoe	Owners	26.6.53
Ch Caradochouse Spruce	D	Drakehall Ardoch Advocate	Caradochouse Rambler Rose	P H Copley	Owner	8.2.54
Ch Travella Sureset	D	Ch Travella Starshine	Travella Twinkle	W Browne-Cole	Owner	12.3.54
Ch Penda Callern Melody	B	Ch Wyretex Wyns Tuscan	Wyretex Wyns Gloria	Mrs E L Williams	E McCall	1.4.54
Ch Travella Silk	B	Ch Travella Starshine	Travella Jasmine	W Browne-Cole	Owner	11.8.53
Ch Lemonford Lullaby	B	Rhythmic Remus	Way Ahead	T Langley-Jones	J Donaldson	7.7.51
Ch Lemonford Lollipop of Roundway	B	Ch Roundway Strike a Light	Ch Lemonford Lullaby	Mrs J Creasy	J Donaldson	30.1.53
Ch Masterlea Sunspot	B	Ch Penda Blackwell Revelation	Masterlea Starturn	E G Bowler	Owner	2.12.52
Ch Arley Impressive	B	Ch Arley Topper	Aversham Lovely Lady	W Nelmes	G Ware	1.6.54
Ch Cawthorne Chloe	B	Ch Burtona Betoken	Clifton Pandora	Mr & Mrs Pardoe	J Armitage	16.6.54
Ch Wyrecliffe Kirkmoor Sunshine	B	Ch Castlecroft Contender Again	Ardoch Mansbrae Melody	Miss B Cliff	W Paul	1.7.52
Ch Arley Topper	D	Polo Prince	Polo Skylark	W G Nelmes	C B Cole	27.1.52
1956						
Ch Sunnybrook Special Choice	D	Ch Travella Wildcroft Superb	Sunnybrook Starry Model	Mrs E Hardy	Owner	12.9.54
Ch Wyrevale Monotype	D	Ch Cornwall Robecia	Wyrevale Marguerite Radiance	T Langley-Jones	W Miles	17.6.51
Ch Shoeman's Welland Winston	D	Ch Axholme Double Strike	Welland Wilwynne	F Pateman	L Jones	7.5.54
Ch Graig-y-Dan Fearnought	D	Ch Polo Fireaway	Graig-y-Dan Trophy	E G Jones	Owner	6.4.52
Ch Wyretex Wyns Wundar	D	Ch Wyretex Wyns Tuscan	Ch Wybury Penda Quicksilver	Mrs D White	Mrs E L Williams	4.5.55
Ch Whitwyre Field Marshall	D	Ch Striking of Laracor	Flyagain of the Forces	Mrs Whitworth	Owner	23.10.54
Ch Penda Peach	B	Ch Weltona Exelwyre Dusty Night	Ch Wybury Penda Quicksilver	Mrs E L Williams	Owner	19.8.54
Ch Crackley Standard	D	Crackley Splendid	Crackley Spectant	J H & J R Barlow	Owners	25.4.54

LIST OF CHAMPIONS

Name	Sex	Sire	Dam	Breeder	Owner	Date
Ch Bluebird Ruby of Radwyre	B	Robecia Romulus	Haybarus Harmony	E Gray	R W Southan	4.6.54
Ch Meritor Say Now	B	Ch Maryholm Northern Monarch	Moorcrest Model	N Seddon	Owner	12.4.55
1957						
Ch Emprise Sensational	D	Ch Cawthorne Climax	Twynstar Authoress	J Francis	J Moss	27.9.55
Ch Kenelm Supremacy	D	Ch Burtona Betoken	Barwyn Wildcroft Sunset	J Bywater	Owner	7.2.55
Ch Harrowhill Strike Again	D	Ch Travella Strike	Harrowhill Highlight	Miss Howles	Owner	30.7.52
Ch Sunnybrook Superjet	D	Ch Travella Wildcroft Superb	Sunnybrook Starry Model	Mrs E Hardy	Owner	1.7.56
Ch Newmaidley Treasure	B	Newmaidley Hannibal	Ch Newmaidley Dancer	Miss L G Beak	Owner	7.8.55
Ch Lyngarth Social Call	B	Ch Axholme Double Strike	Lyngarth Serenade	J Mayfield	Onwer	1.7.55
Ch Wyrecroft Whimsical	B	Wyrecroft Warrior	Wicklewood Twilight	Messrs Wells & Cartledge	Owners	18.10.55
Ch Falstaff Forever Amber	B	Ch Caradochouse Spruce	Mitre Miss Molyneaux	Mrs S Pinkett	F & A Booker	29.12.55
Ch Caradochouse Laurel	B	Drakehall Ardoch Advocate	Caradochouse Rambler Rose	P H Copley	Owner	8.2.54
Ch Mitre Miss Spruce	B	Ch Caradochouse Spruce	Mitre Miss Mavoureen	F & A Brooker	Owner	18.1.56
Ch Florate Fondah	B	Ch Whitwyre Field Marshal	Florate Fondant	J H Smith	Owner	30.9.56
1958						
Ch Anfield Contender	D	Ch Weltona What's This	Anfield Striking	J Bradley	J O'Donnell	4.8.56
Ch Roundway Bellbhoy	D	Ch Roundway Strike a Ligh	Roundway Wedding Belle	Mrs Creasy	Owner	14.10.55
Ch Gosmore Birthday Boy	D	Ch Caradochouse Spruce	Gosmore Zeloy Tiara	Mrs A B Dallison	Owner	10.5.56
Ch Steetonian Skipper	D	Ch Wyretex Wyns Wundar	Steetonian Suntan	A Francis	A G Dawson	24.1.57
Ch Crackwyn Corrector	D	Ch Axholme Double Strike	Mother's Pride	H Gill	H Bayles	5.1.57
Ch Penda Purbeck Repeat	B	Ch Axholme Double Strike	Tan Lady	Mrs E L Williams	J Sheasby	14.10.46
Ch Climax Token	B	Ch Cawthorn Climax	Regal Charmer	M Crawshaw	L Sanderson & A Murray	26.6.55
Ch Windlehurst Susan	B	Ch Cawthorne Climax	Twynstar Pretty Piece	H Gill & J Barlow	J Moss	1.4.55
Ch Crackwyn Caprice	B	Ch Crackley Standard	Crackwyn Cert	H L Gill	Owner	28.3.57
Ch Flying Alstir High Beamy	B	Ch Weltona What's This	Lovely Night	Baron van der Hoop	T C Walker	2.6.56
Ch Kirkmoor Crocus	B	Wyrecliff Sunnybrook Spitfire	Ch Burmadge Ballet Girl	W Mitchell	Owner	2.1.56
Ch Cudhill Kalypso	B	Ch Wyretex Wyns Wundar	Cudhill Christobel	Dr F Ogrinz & E Sharpe	R Thorpe	2.7.56

Name	Sex	Sire	Dam	Owner	Breeder	Born
1959						
Ch Seedfield Ardoch Aspiration	D	Al's Barbed Warrior	Ardoch Roundway Model Again	H M Harris	J Clifford	18.4.57
Ch Crackwyn Captivator	D	Ch Crackley Standard	Crackwyn Cert	H L Gill	Owner	28.3.57
Ch Wyretex Wyns Wundarful	D	Ch Wyretex Wyns Wundar	Purbeck Miss Rimfire	Mrs D White & D Stewart	J Sheasby	25.4.57
Ch Cornwell Odds On	D	Cornwell Cert	Ch Lemonford Lullaby	T Langley-Jones	Owner	27.9.55
Ch Zeloy Endeavour	D	Ch Wyretex Wyns Wundar	Supremacy's Smart Girl	E Robinson	S Naylor	21.8.56
Ch Steelholm Sheena	B	Ch Burtona Betoken	Clifton Pandora	J H Pardoe & E Sharpe	J Armitage	23.2.57
Ch Penda Ravena Snowdrift	B	Shoeman's Pattern	Millbourne Diedre	Mrs E L Williams	F Govier	7.4.57
Ch Mitre Miss Strike	B	Ch Gosmore Birthday Boy	Mitre Quicksilver	Mrs B Jull	F & A Brooker	20.5.57
Ch Penda Oregon Witchcraft	B	Ch Kenelm Supremacy	Oregon Queen	Mrs E L Williams	J Kirk	30.11.57
Ch Falstaff Lady Fayre	B	Mitre Advocate	Falstaff Frangrance	Mrs E Pinkett	Owner	18.12.57
Ch Crackwyn Correct	B	Ch Crackley Standard	Model Perfect	H L Gill	E G Lawson	1.6.56
Ch Penda Cawthorne Cobnut	D	Ch Cawthorne Climax	Cawthorne Ready Maid	Mrs E L Williams	J Pardoe	9.4.57
Ch Travella Supercatch	D	Ch Travella Sureset	Travella Sunflame	W Browne-Cole	Owner	31.10.56
1960						
Ch Helenstowe Pied Piper	D	Ch Wyretex Wyns Wundar	Helenstowe Pamela	Mr & Mrs P Robinson	Owners	23.4.58
Ch Extreal Realization	D	Extreal Revelation	Crawley Countess	S Mallam	W Warburton	30.3.58
Ch Crackwyn Cockspur	D	Ch Crackley Standard	Ch Windlehurst Susan	H L Gill	Owner	12.12.58
Ch Penda Peerless	D	Ch Penda Cawthorne Cobnut	Ch Wybury Penda Quicksilver	Mrs E L Williams	Owner	27.2.59
Ch Whitwyre Even Money	B	Ch Whitwyre Field Marshall	Whitwyre Maundy Money	Mrs M Whitworth	Owner	7.11.57
Ch Crackwyn Ardoch Artistic	B	Ch Anfield Contender	Ardoch Miss Conduct	H L Gill	J Clifford	7.7.58
Ch Gosmore Arberth Cyclamen	B	Ch Cornwell Odds On	Arberth Hyacinth	Mrs A B Dallison	F A Howell	24.9.58
Ch Weltona Miss Sundance	B	Weycroft Wonderboy	Woldlight Romance	A Churchill	W Richmond	11.11.55
Ch Clennon Chime	B	Ch Roundway Bellbhoy	Lady Simonetta	Miss N Fitz-Simons	Owner	11.4.58
Ch Wicklewood Candybar	B	Ch Crackley Standard	Wicklewood Flyaway	Miss J Long	Owner	1.6.58
1961						
Ch Wyrecliffe Satellite of Senganel	D	Exelwyre Mooroak Aristocrat	Smart Biddy of Senganel	Miss B Cliff	Mrs A Smith	16.7.59
Ch Lyngarth Scout	D	Ch Zeloy Crusader	Ch Lyngarth Social Call	J H Mayfield	Owner	12.3.60
Ch Weltona Platta Dainty Princess	B	Ch Anfield Contender	Mac's Model Wire	A Churchill	A Platt	16.5.59
Ch Kenelm Miss Supremacy	B	Ch Kenelm Supremacy	Kenelm Gloria	J Bywater	Owner	27.5.59
Ch Extreal Elegant	B	Ch Extreal Realization	Extreal Chorus Girl	S Mallam	Owner	8.2.60
Ch Kenelm Conquest	B	Kenelm Odds On	Kenelm Miss Quality	J Lejeune	J Bywater	19.2.60

LIST OF CHAMPIONS

Name		Sire	Dam	Breeder	Owner	Date
Ch Seedfield Brooklands Peeress	B	Ch Seedfield Ardoch Aspiration	Brooklands Coquette	H M Harris	H Johnson	8.5.59
Ch St Edmunds Sequel	B	Ch Cawthorne Climax	Sweet Simonetta	Miss E Home	Owner	29.6.59
Ch Oregon Highspot	D	Ch Kenelm Supremacy	Oregon Queen	J Kirk	Owner	17.2.59
1962						
Ch Crackley Cawthorne Compensation	D	Cawthorne Cocoanut	Cawthorne Conquest	Mrs J Lejeune	Mr A Tasker	1.4.51
Ch Zeloy Crusader	D	Ch Zeloy Endeavour	Zeloy Cinderella	Mr J Mayfield	Mr E Robinson	25.9.58
Ch Gosmore Harwire Hayday	D	Ch Wyrecliffe Satellite of Senganel	Matman Sunrise	Mrs A B Dallison	Mr Wall	30.5.51
Ch Taywell Tearaway	D	Ch Kenelm Supremacy	Taywell Threespire Tazard	Mr H Powell	Owner	2.12.59
Ch Zeloy Emperor	D	Ch Zeloy Endeavour	Zeloy Rhapsody	Mr E Robinson	Owner	10.3.60
Ch Penda Daleskirk Caress	B	Ch Penda Peerless	Purbeck Julie	Mrs E L Williams	Mr R French	5.7.60
Ch Meritor Baros Jewel	B	Ch Penda Cawthorne Cobnut	Irish Ch Baros Wyretex Lilactime	Mr N Seddon	Mr A G Barrett	30.5.60
Ch Gosmore Mariebel Tina	B	Ch Zeloy Endeavour	Mitre Miss Marie	Mrs A B Dallison	Messrs A & F Brooker	5.3.59
Ch Shoemans Stitcher	B	Kirkmoor Coachman	Shoemans Sciver	Mr F Pateman	Owner	17.3.61
Ch Baros Romance	B	Baros Gwenog Tuscan	Baros Storm	Mr A G Barrett	Owner	22.1.60
Ch Zeloy Moormaides Magic	B	Ch Zeloy Emperor	Moormaides Cha-Cha-Cha	Mr H M Harris	Mr J Morris	10.5.61
1963						
Ch Whitwyre Money Market	D	Mitre Advocate	Ch Whitwyre Even Money	Mrs M Whitworth	Owner	4.9.61
Ch Cademans Regent	D	Ch Axholme Double Strike	Cademans Fashion Queen	Mr E Massey	Owner	6.6.60
Ch Weltona Lyngarth Jamboree	D	Ch Lyngarth Scout	Lyngarth Love Call	Mr A Churchill	Mr J Mayfield	3.12.61
Ch Crackwyn Cock'On	D	Ch Crackwyn Cockspur	Ch Crackwyn Ardoch Artistic	Mr H L Gill	Owner	30.8.61
Ch Newmaidley Verdict	D	Newmaidley Barrister	Newmaidley Locket	Miss L G Beak	Owner	5.6.59
Ch Gosmore Empress Sue	B	Ch Zeloy Emperor	Crooklands Giftie	Mrs A B Dallison	Mr W Dodds	20.8.61
Ch Gosmore Kirkmoor Tessa	B	Exelwyre Mooroak Aristocrat	Erigston Carosel Miss Fonda	Mrs A B Dallison	Mr W Ratcliffe	9.2.62
Ch Dunwyre Countess	B	Ch Axholme Double Strike	Dunwyre Carbonetta	Mr D H Carse	Owner	21.4.61
1964						
Ch Ritelsa Sirius	D	St Erme Holmwire Simon	Ritelsa Happy Morn	Miss S Keenan	Owner	25.5.59
Ch Extreal Replica	D	Ch Extreal Relization	Extreal Chorus Girl	S Mallam	Owner	24.9.60

Name	Sex	Sire	Dam	Owner	Breeder	Born
Ch Penda Tavatina	B	Ch Penda Peerless	Tavaprim	Mrs E L Williams	R Davison	16.12.61
Ch Brooklands Elegance	B	Ch Zeloy Emperor	Brooklands Lola	Miss L Stella	H Johnson	29.11.61
Ch Travella Superstar	D	Travella Starraiser	Travella Serenade	W Browne-Cole	Owner	25.4.61
Ch Mitre Dusty Knight	D	Mitre Advocate	Mitre Quicksilver	A Brooker	Owner	25.2.61
Ch Wyrecroft War Bonus	D	Ch Penda Cawthorne Cobnut	Wyrecroft Warpaint	Mrs M Cartledge	Owner	29.7.62
Ch Seedfield Ernley Empress	B	Ch Zeloy Emperor	Townville Trinkett	H M Harris	C Whitham	9.5.62
Ch Wintor Townville Tuscan	D	Townville Traveller	Townville Trinket	Messrs A & G Shaw	C Whitham	10.1.63
Ch Gosmore Exelwyre Diamond	B	Exelwyre Mooroak Aristocrat	Exelwyre Donatella	V Mitchell	J Yates	15.4.63
Ch Moormaides Mandy	B	Ch Zeloy Crusader	Moormaides Melody	J Morris	Owner	8.8.62
Ch Holmwire Roxville Revision	D	Holmwire Paul Tudor	Roxville Mooremaides Moment	C H Higginson	Mr & Mrs W H Wright	15.7.63
Ch Crackwyn Connection	D	Ch Crackley Cawthorne	Crackley Spacer Compensation	H L Gill & J R Barlow	H Skan	23.3.63
1965						
Ch Bengal Ryburn Regent	D	Ch Zeloy Endeavour	Ryburn Radiance	Mrs Harmsworth	F H & F N Hopkinson	14.8.63
Ch Gosmore Kirkmoor Storm	D	Ch Zeloy Emperor	Model Taste	Mrs A Dallison	T Walker	10.10.63
Ch Wintor Caracus Call Boy	D	Ch Zeloy Crusader	Nugrade Nesta	A & G Shaw	J Woolley	18.5.64
Ch Zeloy Select	D	Ch Zeloy Emperor	Zeloy Tantalizer	E Robinson	Owner	2.1.62
Ch Seedfield Conqueror	D	Ch Zeloy Emperor	Townville Trinket	H M Harris	Owner	23.9.63
Ch Littleway Wakeful Rose Marie	B	Wakeful White Rajah	Wakeful Rosebud	J S Abbott	W Cobb	29.4.63
Ch Meritor Zeloy Sunflower	B	Ch Zeloy Endeavour	Zeloy Roxville Rainbow	N Seddon	E Robinson	2.5.63
Ch Penda Nugrade Zena	B	Ch Zeloy Emperor	Nugrade Nena	Mrs E Williams	J Holmes	15.9.63
Ch Platta Smart Susan	B	Ch Lyngarth Scout	Platta Susan's Princess	W E Bellerby	A Platt	14.3.64
Ch Rancourt Kirkmoor Cowslip	B	Ch Zeloy Emperor	Kirkmoor Cygnet	Mrs D Stewart	Mr & Mrs W Mitchell	9.9.63
Ch Sarabel Snapdragon	B	Ch Crackwyn Cockspur	Ch Mitre Miss Strike	Mrs B Jull	Owner	1.11.61
Ch Worsbro Oladar Royal Maid	B	Cawthorne Contender	Cawthorne Comfrey	F Robinson	Owner	2.4.62
1966						
Ch Hatta Boy	D	Ch Zeloy Emperor	Pride of Main Street	A S Booth	Owner	17.10.63
Ch Weltona Has It	D	Ch Holmwire Roxville Revision	Ch Weltona Platta Princess	A Churchill	Owner	16.1.65
Ch Wintor Statesman	D	Ch Wintor Townville Tuscan	Wintor Twilight	A & G Shaw	Owners	10.8.64
Ch Wyrecroft Monopoly	D	Wyreworth Justro	Miss Bingo	Mrs M Cartledge	E Bates	29.3.64
Ch Baros Marymount Cinderella	B	Ch Lyngarth Scout	Baros Delight	A G Barrett	L Pounch	30.6.64

LIST OF CHAMPIONS

Name	Sex	Sire	Dam	Breeder	Owner	Date
Ch Gosmore Emprise Elite	B	Emprise Epigram	Peerless Camelia	Mrs A Dallison	J Francis	24.2.66
Ch Gosmore Kirkmoor Content	B	Ch Zeloy Emperor	Kirkmoor Cygnet	Mrs A Dallison	Mr & Mrs W Mitchell	9.9.63
Ch Nedwar Misslyn	B	Ch Zeloy Emperor	Miss Delightful	R Ashworth	T C H Walker	25.9.64
Ch Sarabel Culswood Chanti	B	Ch Whitwyre Money Market	Nugrace Nannette	Mrs B Jull	Mrs M Cullis	28.4.64
Ch Wyrecroft Penda Pamela	B	Ch Zeloy Emperor	Exelwyre Diedre	Mrs M Cartledge	Mrs T Smith	5.1.64

1967

Name	Sex	Sire	Dam	Breeder	Owner	Date
Ch Gosmore Kirkmoor Satisfaction	D	Ch Zeloy Emperor	Gosmore Meritor Springtime	Mrs A Dallison	N Seddon	24.12.64
Ch Kirkdale Pirate	D	Exelwyre Mooroak Aristocrat	Mooremaides Merit	G Higgins	Owner	28.4.65
Ch Kirkmoor Speculation	D	Holmwire Contender	Platta Star Princess	Mr & Mrs W Mitchell	A Platt	1.5.66
Ch Meritor Sensation	D	Meritor Stringalong	Maryholm Winning Hit	N Seddon	Owner	11.5.63
Ch Penda Easelwood Totoplay	D	Ch Wyrecroft Monopoly	Our Jacynth	Mrs E L Williams	Mrs E Selwood	6.4.66
Ch Rumsam Rollo	D	Ch Lyngarth Scout	Cawthorne Catherine	F Critchley	Owner	29.8.65
Ch Seedfield Meritor Superflash	D	Ch Zeloy Emperor	Maryholm Wintersweet	H Harris	N Seddon	8.11.65
Ch Wyrecroft Woolcomber	D	Ch Zeloy Crusader	Seedfield Zeloy Zina	Mrs M Cartledge	T Brampton	21.2.65
Ch Wintor Extreal Invader	D	Ch Extreal Realization	Gussies Girl	S Mallam	Mrs Westerback	23.12.63
Ch Gosmore Emprise Elite	B	Emprise Epigram	Peerless Camelia	Mrs A Dallison	J Francis	24.2.66
Ch Littleway Junaken Viva	B	Ch Zeloy Emperor	Kirkmoor Cygnet	J S Abbott	Mr & Mrs W Mitchell	8.11.62
Ch Shoemans Worsbro Wistful	B	Worsbro Wayfarer	Worsbro Whisper	F Pateman	F Robinson	9.12.65
Ch Wintor Empress	B	Ch Wintor Townville Tuscan	Lyngarth True Call	Messrs A & G Shaw	Owners	5.4.65
Ch Wyrecliff Worsbro Whimsical	B	Anfield Betoken	Cawthorne Comfrey	Miss B Cliff	F Robinson	25.5.66

1968

Name	Sex	Sire	Dam	Breeder	Owner	Date
Ch Penda Worsbro Whistler	D	Worsbro Betoken Again	Choladar Royal Maid	Mrs E L Williams	F Robinson	1.6.67
Ch Townville Tally'O	D	Ch Wintor Statesman	Townville Teresa	C Whitham	Owner	4.6.67
Ch Whitwyre Market Day	D	Ch Whitwyre Money Market	Whitwyre Miss Elequence	Mrs M Whitworth	Owner	9.10.64
Ch Zeloy Exemplar	D	Ch Zeloy Emperor	Zeloy Ernley Edwina	E Robinson	Owner	27.6.66
Ch Zeloy Escort	D	Ch Zeloy Emperor	Zeloy Tantaizer	E Robinson	Owner	12.3.64
Ch Holmwire Tudor Regent	D	Ch Zeloy Emperor	Holmwire Suntan	W Prizeman	C Higginson	2.9.66
Ch Mooremaides Margo	B	Ch Zeloy Emperor	Mooremaides Zeloy Corona	J Morris	Owner	1.6.66
Ch Sarabel Seasprite	B	Ch Wyrecroft Woolcomber	Sarabel Silhouette	Mrs B I Jull	Owner	27.7.66
Ch Gosmore Geisha Girl	B	Exelwyre Mooroak Aristocrat	Exelwyre Empress	Mrs A Dallison	J Yates	21.9.66
Ch Penda Ritelsa Silver Spoon	B	Ch Zeloy Emperor	Ritelsa Radiant	Mrs E L Williams	Mrs Heginbotham	16.8.66
Ch Penda Peppermint	B	Wyrecroft Penda Popular	Ch Pricklewood Candybar	Mrs E L Williams	Mrs M Cartledge	28.5.67
Ch Wintor Countess	B	Ch Wintor Statesman	Winter Sue	A & G Shaw	Owners	8.3.67

Name	Sex	Sire	Dam	Owner	Breeder	Born
1969						
Ch Gosmore Kirkmoor Craftsman	D	Ch Kirkmoor Speculation	Kirkmoor Cygnet	Mrs A Dallison	Mr & Mrs W Mitchell	23.10.67
Ch Dimminsdale Crispin	D	Ch Lyngarth Scout	Dimminsdale Bellona	Mrs Y Braddock & Mr Nuttall	Mrs Y Braddock	1.9.67
Ch Jokyl Wyrecroft Gemini	B	Wyrecroft Penda Popular	Ch Wicklewood Candybar	Mrs O Jackson	Mrs M Cartledge	28.5.67
Ch Penda Worsbro Weasel	B	Worsbro Betoken Again	Ch Worsbro Oladar Royal Maid	Mrs E L Williams	F Robinson	1.6.67
Ch Cripsey Nedwar Matilda	B	Ch Seedfield Meritor Superflash	Ch Nedwar Miss Lynn	Mr & Mrs W Havenhand	R Ashworth	11.11.67
Ch Littleway Platta Miss Prim	B	Holmwire Contender	Platta Star Princess	J S Abbott	A Platt	1.5.66
Ch Holmwire Tudor Renown	D	Ch Zeloy Emperor	Holmwire Suntan	Mr & Mrs Higginson	Owners	2.9.66
Ch Alkara Mooremaides Bella	B	Ch Zeloy Emperor	Mooremaides Mayfair	Mr & Mrs Copcull	J Morris	5.1.68
Ch Mitre Belle Marie	B	Ch Holmwire Tudor Regent	Mariebel Countess	A Brooker	E Bellerby	16.4.68
1970						
Ch Littleway Haranwal Barrister	D	Ch Wintor Statesman	Sandwyne Roxville Revue	J S Abbott	H W Lewin	27.1.68
Ch Whitwyne Mighty Good	B	Crindu Thunderball	Whitwyre Marshaline	Mrs M Whitworth	Owner	27.10.68
Ch Rotherside Rather Lovely	B	Int Ch Penda Worsbro Whistler	Rotherside Rowena	Miss L Stella	J Ward	22.7.68
Ch Sarabel Mitre Sincerity	B	Ch Whitwyre Market Day	Mitre Irristible	Mrs B Jull	A Brooker	1.4.68
Ch Tarnwyre Witchcraft	B	Int Ch Baros Foxfinder	Parkgrove Marymount Candy	Mrs P Conway	D Clancy	14.1.68
Ch Townville Tantivy	B	Ch Wintor Statesman	Townville Traveeda	C Witham	Owner	9.7.69
Ch Vinoverita Kenwyre Suzette	B	Ch Seedfield Meritor Superflash	Kenwyre Mandy	Mrs J Chantelou	F Fisher	2.7.68
Ch Weltona Tiber Lady	B	Ch Weltona Has It	Weltona Scottish Maid	Mrs A Dallison	T Howie	19.11.69
1971						
Ch Cripsey Townville T'Other'Un	D	Ch Townville Tally'O	Townville Tamlyn	Mr & Mrs W Havenhand	C Whitham	4.10.70
Ch Dominus Double Day	D	Ch Whitwyne Market Day	Dominus Dolly Daydream	Mrs C Hunt	Owner	4.11.69
Ch Culswood Caress	B	Ch Seedfield Meritor Superflash	Nugrade Nanette	T V Willains	Mrs M Cullis	20.10.70
Ch Dominus Director	D	Ch Seedfield Meritor Superflash	Dominus Dolly Daydream	Mrs C Hunt	Owner	22.5.70
Ch Kathry Katie	B	Kathry Mooremaides Mercury	Kathry Krystal	Mrs K Hare	Owner	17.3.69

LIST OF CHAMPIONS

Name	Sex	Sire	Dam	Owner	Date
Ch Penda Patrician	B	Ch Penda Pied Piper	Ch Penda Worsbro Weasel	Mrs E L Williams	9.4.70
Ch Raynwyre Rebecca	B	Ch Zeloy Exemplar	Zeloy Countess	Mrs L Langley	26.9.68
Ch Sylvawire Personality	B	Roxville Realstar	Ashgate Wyrecroft Miranda	E Venables	19.1.69
Ch Tarnback Haranwal Diplomat	D	Ch Wintor Statesman	Sandwyre Roxville Revue	J S Abbott	27.1.68
Ch Penda Pied Piper	D	Int Ch Penda Worsbro Whistler	Wyrecroft Warpaint	Mrs E L Williams	5.9.68
1972					
Ch Mitre Beau Brummel	D	Ch Holmwire Tudor Regent	Mitre Irritable	A Brooker	9.9.69
Ch Jokyl Debutant	B	Ch Holmwire Tudor Regent	Ch Jokyl Wyrecroft Gemini	G Jackson	27.4.70
Ch Littleway Jenny Wren	B	Ch Wintor Statesman	Sandwyre Roxville Revue	J S Abbott	7.5.71
Ch Mitre Super Honey	B	Ch Seedfield Meritor Superflash	Mitre Miss Advocate	J Bywater	15.8.70
Ch Drakehall Dawn	B	Drakehall Dooley	Drakehall Symphony	E Sharpe	23.1.71
Ch Modern Millie of Jokyl	B	Ch Wintor Statesman	Sandwyre Roxville Revue	Mr & Mrs Jackson	7.5.71
Ch Brookewire Brandy of Layven	B	Ch Sunnybrook Spot On	Brookewire Wonderful	A Mills	4.12.71
Ch Sunnybrook Spot On	D	Ch Townville Tally'O	Sunnybrook Gosmore Fhotogenic	E Hardy	4.10.69
Ch Sarabel Penda Polly Perkins	B	Ch Penda Pied Piper	Ch Shoermans Worsbro Wistful	Mrs E L Wilhains	7.1.70
Ch Seawire Such A Spree	B	Brockly Easelwood Sun Up	Seawire Samantha	Mrs B Perry	25.4.70
1973					
Ch Axholme Townville Tarik	D	Ch Seedfield Meritor Superflash	Townville Taveeda	G Burton	8.10.70
Ch Exterminator of Emprise	D	Exelwyre Gold Dust	Exelwyre Golden Circle	J Francis	23.6.72
Ch Seawire Ellswyre Marksman	D	Ch Wintor Statesman	Ellisa Luyseta Backflash	Mrs B Perry	13.10.70
Ch Cripsey Camelot	D	Ch Cripsey Townville T'Other'Un	Cripsey Call me Madam	Mr & Mrs W Havenhand	22.2.72
Ch Townville Tieve Tara	B	Ch Cripsey Townville T'Other'Un	Townville Tyremo	C Whitham	25.4.70

Name	Sex	Sire	Dam	Owner	Breeder	Born
Ch Baglan Bertice	B	Ch Seawire Ellswyre	Baglan Benetta Marksman	G R Morris	Owner	24.9.71
Ch Sarabel Townville Treena	B	Ch Cripsey Townville T'Other'Un	Townville Traveeda	Mrs B Jull	C Whitham	24.4.72
1974						
Ch Townville Toastmaster	D	Ch Townville Tally'O	Townville Tamlyn	C Whitham	Owner	17.10.71
Ch Harrowhill Heroine	B	Ch Penda Pied Piper	Harrowhill Golden Aura	Miss E Howles	Owner	11.8.70
Ch Exelwyre Excelence of Jokyl	D	Exelwyre Gold Dust	Exelwyre Golden Circle	Mr & Mrs G Jackson	J Yates	31.1.73
Ch Littleway Harmil Vixen	B	Ch Townville Tally'O	Harmil Bounty Fair	J S Abbott	W Miller	29.7.72
Int Ch Talisman de la Noe aux Loupes	D	Ch Littleway Haranwal Barrister	Madam Fleure	J S Abbot	J Majorosi	25.12.70
Ch Harwire Hallmark	B	Ch Seedfield Meritor Superflash	Harwire Hazel	Mr & Mrs R Harris	Owner	7.5.71
Ch Harrowhill Supersonic	B	Ch Seedfield Meritor Superflash	Harrowhill Happy Talk	Miss E Howles	Owner	12.7.72
Ch Briartex Tavern	D	Ch Cripsey Townville T'Other'Un	Briartex Tania	Mr & Mrs A Taylor	Owner	6.1.73
Ch Bengal Emprise Ellerby	B	Ch Exterminator of Emprise	Exelwyre Margaret	Mrs M Harmsworth	J Francis	13.3.73
Ch Conock Carousel	B	Zeloy Majestic	Conock Holmwire	G A Hocking Tudor Vicki	Owner	31.7.72
1975						
Ch Jokyl Sandwyre Solomon	D	Ch Exelwyre Excelence	Sandwyre Sugar Puff of Jokyl	Mr & Mrs G Jackson	Mrs Sarginson	10.3.74
Ch Townville Tobias	D	Ch Wintor Statesman	Townville Tamlyn	C Whitham	Owner	27.7.73
Ch Cripsey Flashman	D	Bengal Cripsey Brigadier	Cripsey Call Me Madam	Mr & Mrs W Havenhand	Owners	11.1.73
Ch Harrowhill Huntsman	D	Ch Townville Tally'O	Harrowhill Happy Talk	Miss E Howles	Owner	15.8.74
Ch Harwire Hawk of Ryslip	D	Ch Cripsey Camelot	Harwire Holly	S Somerfield	Mr & Mrs R Harris	13.3.73
Ch Townville Trail	D	Ch Seedfield Meritor Superflash	Townville Traveena	C Whitham	Owner	20.10.73
Ch Weltona What A Girl	B	Ch Townville Tally'O	Weltona Has Its Princess	J Abbott	A Churchill	20.1.72
Ch Helenstowe Pearly Queen of Jokyl	B	Ch Sunnybrook Spot On	Helenstowe Parasol	Mr & Mrs G Jackson	Mr & Mrs P Robinson	29.9.72
Ch Tabortown Twilight	B	Ch Townville Tally'O	Tabortown Tina	D Lawton	Owner	25.2.73

LIST OF CHAMPIONS

1976

Name	Sex	Sire	Dam	Breeder	Owner	Date
Ch Holmwire Tudor Remarkable of Knollslane	B	Ch Exterminator of Emprise	Whitwyre Milady Tinkerbelle	N Hunt	Mr & Mrs Higginson	14.5.74
Ch Littleway McTavish	D	Int Ch Talisman de la Noe aux Loups	Ch Weltona What a Girl	J Abbott	J Majorosi	3.9.74
Ch Maythorn Mint	B	Hijack of Harwire	Whinlatter Alkara Avril	Mr & Mrs R May	A R May	11.12.72
Ch Sandwyre Lulu of Wilwyre	B	Bengal Cripsey Brigadier	Sandwyre Sugar Puff	S Wilson	Mrs Sarginson	5.7.73
Ch Seawire Such a Surprise	B	Ch Seawire Ellswyre Marksman	Seawire Shantung	Mrs B Perry	Miss F Peacock	23.9.73
Ch Harwire Hetman of Whinlatter	D	Ch Townville Tobias	Ch Harwire Hallmark	Mrs Fisher-May	Mrs M Harris	16.10.74
Ch Sandwyre Spindrift of Jokyl	B	Int Ch Talisman de la Noe Aux Loups	Ch Sandwyre Lulu of Wilwyre	Mr & Mrs G Jackson	Mrs Sarginson	20.12.74
Ch Bodiam Hoity Toity	B	Ch Briartex Tavern	Dimmimsdale Galatea	R McAdam	Owner	3.9.74
Ch Sandwyyre Mr Softy of Jokyl	D	In Ch Talisman de la Noe Aux Loups	Ch Sandwyre Lulu of Wilwyra	Mr & Mrs G Jackson	Mrs Sarginson	20.12.74

1977

Name	Sex	Sire	Dam	Breeder	Owner	Date
Ch Jarken Ballerina	B	Jarken Jeremiah	Jarken Janet	F Shaw	Owner	19.9.75
Ch Harwire Halidom of Whinlatter	D	Ch Townville Trail	Ch Harwire Hallmark	Mrs Fisher-May	Mrs M Harris	25.6.75
Ch Sarabel Jarken Bittersweet	B	Jarken Jeremiah	Jarken Janet	Mrs B Jull	F Shaw	19.9.75
Ch Cripsey Captain Poldark	D	Ch Cripsey Flashman	Cripsey Bobby's Girl	Mr & Mrs W Havenhand	Owners	24.9.75
Ch Turith Dear Daphne	B	Jarken Jethro	Turith Solitaire	Mr & Mrs Blower	Owners	19.9.75
Ch Telesia Head Boy	D	Ch Townville Tobias	Telesia Starlet	Mrs E Hart	Owner	12.4.75
Ch Townville Tara	B	Ch Townville Tobias	Townville Tillie	C Whitham	Mr Fox	14.7.75
Ch Maltman Sunny Smile	D	Worsboro Wideawake	Maltman Pride	G A Wall	Owner	15.9.75
Ch Seawire Statuette	B	Ch Cripsey Flashman	Ch Seawire Such-a-Spree	Mrs B Perry	Owner	31.7.75

1978

Name	Sex	Sire	Dam	Breeder	Owner	Date
Ch Bothwell Covenanter	B	Harmil Conquest of Littleway	Bothwell Lass	Miss Steel	T Weir	13.12.73
Ch Harwire Halyard of Whinlatter	D	Ch Townville Trail	Ch Harwire Hallmark	Mrs Fisher-May	Mrs M Harris	25.6.75
Ch Kathry Kesta	B	Emprise Extremist	Ch Kathry Katie	Mrs K Hare	Owner	20.11.75
Ch Alkara Ann Marie	B	Ch Townville Trail	Adeina of Alkara	Mr & Mrs Copcutt	Owner	14.6.76
Ch Harrowhill Hunters Moon	D	Ch Harrowhill Huntsman	Ch Harrowhill Golden Auriole	Miss E Howles	Owner	26.10.76
Ch Robelroy Delight	B	Ch Littleway McTavish	Roofwyre Princess Rebecca	Mrs E Baldwin	Owner	17.10.75
Ch Harwire Helmsmann of Whinlatter	D	Ch Townville Trail	Ch Harwire Hallmark	Mrs Fisher-May	Mrs M Harris	3.3.76

Name	Sex	Sire	Dam	Owner	Breeder	Born
Ch Townville Tristanian	D	Ch Harwire Halyard of Whinlatter	Townville Tillie	C Whitham	Owner	16.8.77
Ch Harrowhill Golden Aureole	B	Harrowhill Happy Day	Harrowhill Golden Aura	Miss E Howles	Owner	2.7.74
Ch Sandwyre Sportsman of Littleway	D	Ch Sandwyre Mr Softy of Jokyl	Sandwyre Sugar Puff	J Abbott	Mrs Sarginson	30.3.76
1979						
Ch Penda Pretty Perfect	B	Ch Harrowhill Huntsman	Ch Penda Worsboro Weasel	Mrs E Williams	Owner	21.11.76
Ch Sandwyre Daisy May	B	Ch Sandwyre Mr Softy of Jokyl	Suzanna Crimson	Mrs Stanfield	Miss Redman	20.3.77
Ch Blackdale Starbright	D	Procne Scout Boy	Foxy Thatch	H O'Donoghue	Owner	10.9.76
Ch Bodiam Topsy Turvey	B	Ch Townville Trail	Ch Bodiam Hoity Toity	R McAdam	Owner	23.3.78
Ch Kilnhill Kinsman of Purston	D	Ch Townville Trail	Kilnhill Goldcrest	D Jackson	Owner	18.8.77
Ch Leila v Adorna	B	Dark v d Bismarckquelle	Ziska v Dorneywald	C Mayorkas	H Schmiedner	21.6.77
Ch Seawire Successor	D	Ch Cripsey Captain Poldark	Ch Seawire Such a Surprise	Mrs B Perry	Owner	31.8.77
Ch Trucote Admiral	D	Ch Sandwyre Mr Softy of Jokyl	Ch Helenstowe Pearly Queen of Jokyl	H Atkinson	Mrs Urmston	19.4.76
Ch Tantaus Royal Lass	B	Ch Cripsey Captain Poldark	Manordale Melody	B Hadland	W Winkle	1.7.77
1980						
Ch Blackdale Consort	D	Int Ch Blackdale Starbright	Blackdale Gracious Princess	H O'Donoghue	Owner	12.1.78
Ch Seawire Such a Secret	B	Ch Cripsey Captain Poldark	Ch Seawire Such a Surprise	Mrs B Perry	Owner	31.8.77
Ch Sandwyre Scrooge	D	Ch Sandwyre Sportsman of Littleway	Ch Sandwyre Lulu of Wilwyre	Mrs Sarginson	Owner	8.2.78
Ch Townville Tradition	D	Ch Harwire Halyard of Whinlatter	Townville Tillie	C Whitham	Owner	28.6.78
Ch Wiredresst Jewel Price	B	Wiredresst Image	Wiredresst Bright White	W Joosse	Owner	11.4.78
Ch Jokyl Personality	B	Ch Trucote Admiral	Jokyl Show Off	Mr & Mrs G Jackson	Owners	25.1.79
Ch Dunlan Tipster	D	Townville Trail	Sandwyre Sparkle of Dunlan	Dr R Barbour	Owner	9.6.79
Ch Kathry Kottonsocks	D	Kathry Koronation	Ch Kathry Kesta	Mrs K Hare	Owner	3.7.78

LIST OF CHAMPIONS

1981

		Sire	Dam	Breeder	Owner	Date
Ch Blackdale Aristocrat	D	Int Ch Blackdale Starbright	Blackdale Honey	H O'Donoghue	Owner	25.2.79
Ch Barmaud Harvey Bannister	D	Int Ch Blackdale Starbright	Stepaside of Barmaud	J Barker	Owner	2.5.78
Ch Sandwyre Sunbeam	B	Ch Trucote Admiral	Sandwyre Shady Lady	Mr & Mrs Aguero	Mrs Sarginson	7.12.79
Ch Balmerino Javelin of Whinlatter	D	Ch Townville Trail	Whinlatter Solid Silver	Mrs Fisher-May	J Reekie	6.12.77
Ch Townville Texan	D	Ch Townville Tradition	Townville Tavrina	C Whitham	Owner	26.8.79
Ch Dunwyre Criterion	B	Int Ch Blackdale Consort	Ch Dunwyre Catriona	D Carse	Owner	6.9.79
Ch Camkin Dare Me	B	Seawire Suits Me	St Erme Pippa	A Jenkin	Owner	31.3.79
Ch Tava Wren	B	Ch Trucote Admiral	Tava Susan	Mr & Mrs Davison	Owners	13.5.79
Ch Sarabel Sailorman	D	Ch Townville Tristanian	Sarabel Sweet Talk	Mrs B Jull	Owner	8.5.79

1982

		Sire	Dam	Breeder	Owner	Date
Ch Dominus Daily Sun	D	Ch Telesia Head Boy	Dominus Droopy Drews	Mrs C Hunt	Owner	5.12.79
Ch Alkara Acushla of Whinlatter	B	Harwire Hallmarksman	Adelina of Alkara	Mrs Fisher-May	Mr & Mrs W Copcutt	14.5.79
Ch Wonderwyre Bunratty Bouquet	B	Ch Harwire Helmsman of Whinlatter	Vitoka Varica	M Kirby	Owner	27.2.80
Ch Treasure of Townville	B	Ch Townville Trail	Gavingae Natasha	C Whitham	Miss P Fox	6.8.80
Ch Penda Precision	B	Ch Townville Tradition	Ch Penda Pretty Perfect	G Pedersen	Mrs E Williams	4.1.80
Ch Gregdon Cora	B	Ch Trucote Admiral	Gregdon Crystal	J McGregor	Owner	10.5.80
Ch Procne Viceroy	D	Ch Harrowhill Huntsman	Procne Precision	F Sills	Owner	22.9.79
Ch Twynstar Accurist Again	D	Ch Balmerino Javelin	Miss Accurette of Whinlatter	L W Edmunds	Owner	31.5.80
Ch Sarabel Second Chance of Granemore	B	Ch Townville Tristanian	Sarabel Sweet Talk	McGeown & Parker	Mrs B Jull	8.5.79
Ch Bodiam Bizzie Lizzie	B	Ch Townville Trail	Ch Bodiam Hoity Toity	R McAdam	Mrs G Atkinson	5.5.79

1983

		Sire	Dam	Breeder	Owner	Date
Ch Conock Calypso of Sidewater	B	Ch Townville Tristanian	Ch Conock Carousel	G Hocking	Owner	21.6.71
Ch Blackdale Anticipation	D	Int Ch Blackdale Aristocrat	Blackdale Melba	H O'Donoghue	Owner	4.9.81
Ch Lazerbeam of Lynayon at Travella	D	Ch Harrowhill Huntsman	Tuxdene Tarantella	W Browne-Cole	L Tucker	4.5.80
Ch Ayewire Adam	D	Ch Townville Texan	Rotaroy Forever	M Lavender	Owner	16.2.81
Ch Louline Lord Fountleroy	D	Sw Ch Louline Horatio	Sw Ch Louline Lucy Lactic	S Somerfield	G Pedersen	23.8.81
Ch Saredon Charade	B	Int Ch Blackdale Aristocrat	Denidale Night Nurse	Mrs J Averis	D Anderson	3.7.81
Ch Blackdale Ambassador	D	Int Ch Blackdale Aristocrat	Blackdale Melba	H O'Donoghue	Owner	4.9.81

Name	Sex	Sire	Dam	Owner	Breeder	Born
Ch Wonderwyre Buttercup	B	Int Ch Blackdale Aristocrat	Vitoka Veronica	M Kirby	Owner	3.1.82
Ch Townville Tassie	B	Ch Penda Precision	Townville Token	C Whitham	Owner	9.7.82
Ch Sylair Star Leader	D	Ch Harrowhill Hunters Moon	Cub Hunter of Hendell	PG & L Potter	Owners	30.8.81
Ch Grambrae Prelude	B	Int Ch Blackdale Aristocrat	Rockport Caress	Mr Yates	Mr & Mrs Magill	27.6.81
1984						
Ch Maltman Country Life of Whinlatter	D	Int Ch Penda Precision	Maltman Waggon Girl	Mrs Fisher-May	G Wall	12.9.82
Ch Blackdale Carisma	B	Int Ch Blackdale Aristocrat	Blackdale Playgirl	H O'Donoghue	Owner	21.4.81
Ch Forchlas Cariad	B	Ch Harrowhill Huntsman	Twynstar Miss Accurist	Pedersen & Rikardson	R Roderick	11.9.81
Ch Tuxdene Tomputt of Sarabel	D	Whinlatter Prince Hal	Tuxdene Tarantella	B Jull & A Langley	L Tucker	23.9.81
Ch Penda Pin Up	B	Ch Townville Tradition	Ch Penda Pretty Perfect	Mrs E Hart	Mrs E Williams	4.9.82
Ch Dunwyre Candidate	D	Dunwyre Caesar	Dunwyre Catriona	Mrs A Stanfield	D Carse	7.7.82
Ch Barmaud Right Smart	B	Ch Townville Trail	Stepaside of Barmaud	J Barker	Owner	30.11.80
Ch Kilnhill Kate of Purston	B	Ch Townville Texan	Kilnhill Kristeena	J Collins	G Jackson	28.5.83
Ch Galsul Silver Charm	B	Ch Harwire Helmsman of Whinlatter	Galsul Institution	H O'Donoghue	J Galvin	3.5.83
1985						
Ch Townville Taveta	B	Ch Blackdale Anticipation	Ch Treasure of Townville	C Whitham	Owner	29.3.83
Ch Glanrob Crimson Velvet of Purston	B	Ch Louline Lord Fountleroy	Ch Glanrob Sanko Marina	M Collins	R Roberts	5.8.83
Ch Willowyre Wonder Boy	D	Sunnybrook Sebastian	Sprotboro Sweet Holly	Mrs S Nixon	Owner	9.6.82
Ch Galsul Excellence	D	Ch Harwire Helmsman of Whinlatter	Galsul Institution	H O'Donoghue	J Galvin	3.5.83
Ch Crindu Classic of Whinlatter	D	Int Ch Penda Precision	Crindu Rhosyn	Mrs Fisher-May	G James	26.4.84
Ch Pina Colada	B	Ch Kathry Kottonsocks	Kathry Kurtain Kall	Mr & Miss Lowe	Owners	4.9.82
Ch Rayne of Wryton	B	Ch Blackdale Ambassador	Milady Mandarin	Mrs C Halton	R & A Lomax	24.12.83
Ch Louline Heartstrain	B	Ir/Sw Ch Blackdale	Nor/Sw Ch Louline Hell Cat Commander	G Pedersen	Owner	10.12.83
1986						
Ch Killick of the Mess	D	Ch Sylair Star Leader	Molmik Cinderella	G & E Baxter	Owners	8.10.84
Ch Louline High'N'Magic	B	Int Ch Galsul Excellence	Louline High'N'Mighty	G Pedersen	Owner	6.11.84
Ch Penda Passion at Louline	B	Int Ch Galsul Excellence	Ch Penda Pretty Perfect	G Pedersen	Mrs E Williams	27.12.84
Ch Louline Limited Edition	B	Sw Ch Louline Horatio	Sw Ch Louline Lucy Lastic	Mrs Flyckt-Pedersen	G Pedersen	29.12.83
Ch Saredon American Pie	B	Int Ch Maltman Country Life of Whinlatter	Eskwyre Afternoon Delight	Havenhand Averis & Scawthorn	Mrs J Averis	27.8.84

LIST OF CHAMPIONS

Name	D/B	Sire	Dam	Breeder	Owner	Date
Ch Gavingale Diplomat	D	Ch Blackdale Ambassador	Gavingale Gemma	Miss P Fox	Owner	14.8.83
Ch Glanrob Sanko Marina	B	Ch Townville Texan	Glanrob Lillian Mandina	Collins & Roberts	Owner	11.8.81
1987						
Ch Conock Cornish Cream	B	Ch Townville Texan	Ch Conock Calypso of Sidewater	G Hocking	Owner	19.5.84
Ch Nethertonian Gayaity	B	Ch Penda Precision	Mischief Maker	A Westwood	Owner	2.11.84
Ch Louline Pickled Pepper	D	Am Ch Sylair Special Edition	Penda Picturesque	Mrs Flyckt-Pedersen	G Pedersen	10.4.85
Ch Easternvale Echo	D	Ch Harrowhill Huntsman	Easternvale Vixen	H Hingle	Owner	23.9.85
Ch Forchlas Cymro	D	Int Ch Maltman Country Life of Whinlatter	Forchlas Tania	R Roderick	Owner	26.10.84
Ch Louline Head Over Heels	D	Ch Louline Pickled Pepper	Ch Louline Heartstrain	G Flyckt-Pedersen	Owner	5.4.86
Ch Sylair Star Selection	B	Am Ch Sylair Special Edition	Sylair Senata	Mr & Mrs Potter	Mrs S Davison	28.2.85
Ch Whittingford Who Dares	D	Harrowhill Concorde	Whittingford Weal Zöe's Girl	Mr & Mrs Marshall	Owner	1.12.85
Ch Townville Terri	B	Int Ch Killick of the Mess	Ch Treasure of Townville	Y Yamada	C Whitham	31.8.86
Ch Louline Heartbreaker	D	Ch Louline Pickled Pepper	Ch Louline Heartstrain	G Flyckt-Pedersen	Owner	5.4.86
Ch Crindu Conan	D	Int Ch Penda Precision	Crindu Rhosyn	Y Yamada	G James	26.4.84
Ch Wonderwyre Wahine	B	Ch Louline Lord Fountleroy	Ch Wonderwyre Buttercup	M Kirby	Owner	8.5.86
1988						
Ch Aywire Ava	B	Ch Townville Texan	Roelroy Forever	Mr & Mrs Lavender	Owner	14.10.85
Ch Easternvale Envoy	D	Blackdale Patrol	Easternvale Sun Tan	H Hingle	Owner	27.8.86
Ch Townville Tarique	D	Ch Gavingale Diplomat	Townville Tempo	Y Yamada	C Whitham	16.1.87
Ch Louline Heartstrings	B	Ch Louline Pickled Pepper	Ch Louline Heartstrain	G Flyckt-Pedersen	Owner	10.2.87
Ch Townville Tarka	B	Ch Townville Texan	Ch Townville Tassie	Y Yamada	C Whitham	11.2.86
Ch Blackdale Charmer	B	Ch Blackdale Consort	Ch Balsul Silver Charm	H O'Donoghue	Owner	15.3.86
Ch Ammon Airs'N'Graces	B	Int Ch Killick of the Mess	Ammon Starshine	R Hoskins	Owner	23.9.86
Ch Baxee Jimmy the Won	D	Ch Harrowhill Hunters Moon	Molnik Cinderella	Mrs E Baxter	Owner	2.8.86
Ch Townville Tiller Girl	B	Int Ch Killick of the Mess	Ch Treasure of Townville	Mrs B Jull	C Whitham	31.8.86
1989						
Ch Easternvale Exalt	D	Blackdale Patrol	Easternvale Sun Tan	H Hingle	Owner	22.8.87
Ch Blackdale Special	B	Blackdale Prospect	Blackdale Limelight	H O'Donoghue	Owner	1.7.87
Ch Beauwire Bitter Sweet	B	Ch Townville Texan	Sarabel Sweet Mystery	Mesdames Jull & Steadman	Mrs S Steadman	22.12.86
Ch Townville Tradesman	D	Blackdale Prospect	Townville Tempo	C Whitham	Owner	5.10.87

Name	Sex	Sire	Dam	Owner	Breeder	Born
Ch Kathry Kurtis	D	Ch Kathry Kottonsocks	Sonorra Sugarpuff	Mrs K Hare	Owner	9.12.86
Ch Townville Tessa	B	Blackdale Prospect	Townville Tempo	C Whitham	Owner	5.10.87
Ch Nethertonian Sarah	B	Ch Louline Pickled Pepper	Mischief Maker	Mrs S Wiggins	A Westwood	6.8.87
Ch Easternvale Emblem	B	Blackdale Patrol	Easternvale Sun Tan	S Williams	H Hingle	22.8.87
Ch Cwmgarws Joint Venture	D	Blackdale Patrol	Easternvale Vixen	Mrs & Miss Frizell	Owners	5.7.87
Ch Brockly Mister Brocket	D	Int Ch Killick of the Mess	Brockly Sunberry	Miss M Coombes	Owner	28.7.86
Ch Aywire Astar	B	Kathry Krosby	Aywire Arlette	Mr & Mrs Lavender	Owner	29.4.88
1990						
Ch Blackdale Eurocrat	D	Blackdale Prospect	Blackdale Twighlight Girl	Y Yamada	H O'Donoghue	29.9.87
Ch Valken Skylark	B	Valken Skyrocket	Valken Tumbling Dice	Mr & Mrs Howe	Owners	1.5.88
Ch Garalex Dream Angus of Purston	D	Ch Blackdale Anticipation	Garalex May Queen	Mr & Mrs Howe	J Sneddon	9.4.83
Ch Louline Pemberton	D	Louline Highflier	Ch Penda Passion at Louline	G Flyckt-Pedersen	Owner	19.11.88
Ch Sonorra Silver Sparkle	B	Int Ch Louline Heartbreaker	Ch Pina Colada	Mr & Miss Lowe	Owners	18.10.87
Ch Seawire Silver Bell	B	Ch Brockly Mister Brocket	Seawire Sharlotte	Mrs B Perry	Owner	30.12.88
Ch Raynwyre Razzle Dazzle	D	Ch Sylair Star Leader	Westranch Rayne	Mrs L Gething	Owner	6.6.87
Ch Valken Downtown Boy	D	Ch Townville Tradesman	Valken Country Girl	Mr & Mrs Howe	Owner	6.3.89
1991						
Ch Fly the Flag for Rayfos	B	Can/Am Ch Flyover	Conock Candy at Rayfos	E Allen	Mr & Mrs Siddon	18.10.88
Ch Blackdale Going for Gold	D	Int Ch Blackdale Aristocrat	Blackdale Amanda	H O'Donoghue	Owner	7.1.89
Ch Wonderwyre Honeysuckle	B	Int Ch Louline Heartbreaker	Ch Wonderwyre Buttercup	M Kirby	Owner	13.10.87
Ch Louline High Tide	B	Int Ch Louline Heartbreaker	Louline Highty-Tighty	G Flyckt-Pedersen	Owner	11.12.87
Ch Stagwire Samurai	D	Ch Townville Tradesman	Maryholm Warrior Trail	Mr & Mrs Everard	Owners	18.5.89
Ch Nedella Wot a Fella	D	Int Ch Killick of the Mess	Dominus Daily Star of Nedella	J & M Morris	Owners	3.11.87
Ch Easternvale Evita of Wiredot	B	Ch Townville Tradesman	Ch Easternvale Emblem	R Taylor	H Hingle	14.1.90
Ch Louline Head On	B	Ch Blackdale Eurocrat	Ch Louline Heartstrings	G Flyckt-Pedersen	Owner	13.11.89
Ch Blackdale Superstar	D	Int Ch Blackdale Aristocrat	Blackdale Caroline	H O'Donoghue	Owner	29.1.89
Ch Burrenbrook Keyman	D	The Swagman of Townville	Burrenvale Tinkerbell	Wakefield & May	M Thompson	26.7.89
Ch Townville Tiptoes	B	Ch Blackdale Autocrat	Townville Tempo	Mrs B Whitham	C Whitham	5.6.89
Ch Sonorra Star Splendour	D	Kathry Krosby	Sonorra Show Stopper	Mr & Miss Lowe	Owners	15.8.89
1992						
Ch Wyndam The Boss	D	Ch Townville Tradesman	Brookside Delight-Imp	Mrs W Porteous	H Atkinson	13.4.90
Ch Whittingford Welcome	B	Porthvale Beaula	Whittingford Weal Zöe's Girl	Mrs J Marshall	Mr & Mrs Marshall	27.11.89
Ch Rayfos Fair Enough	B	Ch Louline Pickled Pepper	Conock Chance of Rayfos	Mr & Mrs Greenway	Owners	28.2.88
Ch Aywire Arlena	B	Kathry Krosby	Aywire Arlette	Mr & Mrs Lavender	Owners	5.3.90
Ch Blackdale Queen of Dreams	B	Int Ch Blackdale Going for Gold	Blackdale Caroline	H O'Donoghue	Owner	12.4.91

LIST OF CHAMPIONS

Name	Sex	Sire	Dam	Breeder	Owner	Date
Ch Townville Triona	B	Ch Valken Downtown Boy	Ch Townville Tiller Girl	Mrs E Whitham	C Whitham	21.4.91
Ch Fenfox Uptown Girl	B	Ch Valken Downtown Boy	Townville Tina	Mrs P Wallman	Owner	4.12.90
1993						
Ch Cwmgarws Lady Trish	B	Blackdown Sundown	Cwmgarws Surprise Packet o Cwmgarws	Mrs & Miss Frizell	Owners	2.12.88
Ch Megastar of Minerstown	D	Ch Stagwire Samurai	Princes Tara Star	Mr & Mrs F Kellett	D Mason	23.9.91
Ch Valken Charlie's Girl at Sarabel	B	Ch Valken Downtown Boy	Valken Bootiful Dreamer	Mrs B Jull	Mr & Mrs Howe	27.4.91
Ch Burrencombe Select of Fairway	D	Ch Valken Downtown Boy	Burrenlea Starlight	Stanfield & Berlaque	M Thompson	21.6.91
Ch Travella Strike Twice	D	Cont Ch Travella Strike Force	Cont Ch Travella Same Girl	W Browne-Cole	Owner	2.9.91
Ch Baglan Some Boyo	D	Ch Blackdale Eurocrat	Baglan Bellah	G Morris	Owner	5.1.89
Ch Parkside Regale	B	Ch Cwmgarws Joint Venture	Drumsheugh Jaiti Mania	Miss D Chads	Owner	31.1.90
Ch Sceftesbr Chianti	B	Int Ch Louline Pemberton	Newmaidley Christmas Eve	Mrs J Kennedy	Owner	30.9.90
Ch Rayfos Ringmaster	D	Ch Valken Downtown Boy	Christmas Rose of Rayfos	Mr & Mrs Greenway	Owners	9.10.91
Ch Burrenhill Advocate	D	Ch Wyndam The Boss	Burrenlea Starlight	M Thompson	Owner	29.8.92
Ch Valken Tumblebug	B	Ch Valken Downtown Boy	Ch Valken Skylark	Mr & Mrs Howe	Owners	15.3.92
1994						
Ch Burrenedge Marksman	D	Ch Valken Downtown Boy	Burrenlea Starlight	Mr & Mrs Stansfield	M Thompson	21.6.91
Ch Parkside Vanity Fair	B	Ch Valken Downtown Boy	Parkside Treasure	Miss D Chads	Owner	17.10.91
Ch Sarabel Just Susie	B	Ch Cwmgarws Joint Venture	Beawire Britannia	Mrs B Jull	Owner	2.10.92
Ch Beemaid Tyson	D	Ch Stagwire Samurai	Sceftesbr Trumpington	Mrs M Forman	Owner	25.1.92
Ch Cripsey Trammer from Minerstown	D	Ch Stagwire Samurai	Valken Dusky Maiden	W Havenhand	Mrs E Hart	18.12.92
Ch Burrendon Heather of Fairwyre	B	Ch Wyndham The Boss	Burrenlea Starlight	Miss A Stansfield	M Thompson	29.8.92
1995						
Ch Travella Special Strike	D	Ch Travella Strike Twice	Travella Striking Image	Mrs S Browne-Cole	Owner	28.10.93
Ch Willowyre Wisecrack	D	Kathry Krosby	Spotcoro Sensation at Willowyre	Mrs S Nixon	Owner	21.5.90
Ch Brocolitia Storm Force	D	Ch Stagwire Samurai	Harm Sequence at Brocolitia	Mrs A Maughan	Owner	22.3.92
Ch Burrendale Escort of Purston	D	Ch Valken Downtown Boy	Burrenlea Starlight	M Collins & J Coutts	M Thompson	21.6.91
Ch Cripsey Trammer from Minerstown	D	Ch Stagwire Samurai	Valken Dusty Maiden	Mr & Mrs E Hart	W Havenhand	18.12.92
Ch Beemaid Trouble	B	Ch Travella Strike Twice	Sceftesbr Trumpington	Mrs M Forman	Owner	27.8.93
Ch Sceftesbr Cabinet	B	Ch Baglan Some Boyo	Ch Sceftesbr Chianti	Mrs J Kennedy	Owner	6.1.94
Ch Glanrob Bayly Belle	B	Am Ch Caspar Libra	Am Ch Glanrob Gazeebo	R Roberts	Owner	12.2.93
Ch Larchstream Rula of Saredon	B	Ch Stagwire Samurai	Harm Sylvia	Mrs J Averis	H Rogers	27.12.92
Ch Corriecote Willow o' Fiona	B	Ch Cwmgarws Joint Venture	Whynacraege Mystique of Corriecote	Mrs J Heathcote	Owner	27.9.91
Ch Valken Wild Orchid	B	Ch Valken Downtown Boy	Valken Bootiful Dreamer	Mr & Mrs K Howe	Owners	17.4.93

POST-WAR BRITISH SMOOTH FOX TERRIER CHAMPIONS FROM 1946

Name	Sex	Sire	Dam	Owner	Breeder	Born
1946						
Ch Boreham Belsire	D	Boreham Bedad	Boreham Belmalva	The Maharajah of Pithapuram	Dr R M Miller	20.10.43
Ch Lethal Weapon	D	Lethean Waters	Smeatonwood Girlie	L C Wilson	T George	2.7.43
Ch Leslow Lunette	B	Molton Moonlighter	Danesgate Gwenny	J Armstrong	Miss E Smith	1.9.43
Ch Olton Holdfast	B	Preco Prelude	Ladyship Queen	B Gradwell	A Bearsley	4.1.43
1947						
Ch Abberdale Audacity	D	Abberdale Admiral	Lady Clare	Mr & Mrs Ludford	Mrs E Wilson	21.1.44
Ch Flying Fairstead Pilot	D	Stewton Skipper	Fairstead Trixis	Baron van der Hoop	C H Fairs	2.3.45
Ch Hampole Tinkler	D	Ch Boreham Belsire	Tidser Tranquil	Miss E Lindley-Wood	Miss E Sparrow	15.3.46
Ch Laurel Wreath	D	Ch Lethal Weapon	Parthings Lassie	L C Wilson	G E Hurrell	26.2.46
Ch Twentygrand Avon Joystick	D	Westwood Wizard	Kipyard Miss Marine	N A Nicholson	B Bale	9.10.44
Ch Cream of Andely	B	Landmark of Andely	Andely Lovely Lady	Mrs B Lowe-Fallas	Owner	5.7.44
Ch Darkie Princess	B	Darkie Monarch	Fox Lass	Mr & Mrs E Mantle	Owners	19.12.43
Ch Fortuna of Ballig	B	Lethean Waters	Silver Snapper	W Bateson	Owner	7.10.44
Ch Wags Dignity	B	Burmar Dan Russel	Zilph	S Wagstaff	L Morby	2.11.45
1948						
Ch Black Andrew	D	Ch Selecta Rich Reward	Selecta Golden Rule	H R Bishop	Owner	30.7.46
Ch Blyboro Spotlight	D	Molten Moonlighter	Santuzza	J G Reynolds	W Newman	17.9.44
Ch Full Pay	D	Ch Selecta Rich Reward	Normstress	G Mann	Owner	9.7.46
Ch Reansway Havanap	D	Saltaire Subaltern	Patchwork	S C Flint	Mr & Mrs T James	16.10.47
Ch Solus Gold Ore	D	Burmar Dan Russel	Gradley Betty	C H Bishop	M Houghton	27.7.44
Ch Benmoir Pierette	B	Bournedale Pierrot	Benmoir Exquisite	J Bendall	Owner	27.12.46
Ch Blyboro Sunmaid	B	Blyboro Molten Moonseed	Blyboro Melody	N Bown	I Guest	16.11.45
Ch Brooklands Ebony Girl	B	Brooklands Ebony	Glamour Girl of Yealand	H Johnson	S Jury	1.10.45
Ch Farleton Florette	B	Farleton Flyaway	Farleton Fuchsia	Mrs D R Richardson	Owner	4.7.47
Ch Flying Brooklands Venus	B	Wychway Fanfare	Brooklands Queen Bee	Baron van der Hoop	H Johnson	13.10.46
Ch Moorside Mannequin	B	Molton Monarch	Molton Merriment	J Dobson	W Bright	13.12.46
Ch Wright Smart	B	Ch Travelling Fox	Burmar Bridget	H M Harris	M Houghton	27.7.44

LIST OF CHAMPIONS

1949

Ch Flying Revised Line	D	Ch Hampole Tinkler	Barrowby Belle	Baron van der Hoop	A Nicholson	1.6.48
Ch Maryholm Spun Gold	D	Ch Laurel Wreath	Maryholm Sweetbit	A Clanachan	Owner	25.1.48
Ch Selecta Rich Reward	D	Golden Spur of Sker	Lucky Strike	H R Bishop	P Davenport	21.8.43
Ch Sorreldene Barrowby Bahram	D	Molton Moonlighter	Barrowby Temptress	T Morris	W Ducker	14.9.46
Ch Watteau Midas	D	Ch Laurel Wreath	Brooklands Ebony Belle	Mrs A Blake	Owner	21.1.48
Ch Wychway Quintessence	D	Wychway Fanfare	Wychway Delight	W Snape	Owner	12.10.47
Ch Brooklands Black Narcissus	B	Wychway Fanfare	Brooklands Queen Bee	H Johnson	Owner	13.10.46
Ch Charnworth Sea Storm	B	Ch Lethal Weapon	Charnworth Liberty Boat	Miss A D Cole	Owner	28.6.47
Ch Chosen Dinah of Notts	B	Dunedil of Notts	Cast Iron of Notts	Her Grace, Kathleen Duchess of Newcastle	Owner	16.1.48
Ch Flying Dream	B	Ch Laurel Wreath	Ch Flying Brooklands Venus	Baron van der Hoop	Owner	30.7.48
Ch Hampole Tinkle	B	Ch Boreham Belsire	Tidser Tranquil	Miss E Lindley-Wood	Miss E C Sparrow	15.3.46
Ch Lanneau Jewel	B	Firstmonsieur	Lanneau Victoria	J Lowe	Owner	28.6.47
Ch Rush Gleam	B	Ch Lethal Weapon	Rush Modeste	G Truman-Hewitt, JP	Owner	2.4.48

1950

Ch Boreham Bendigo	D	Ch Lethal Weapon	Boreham Between	Capt T Ashcroft	Dr R M Miller	31.7.47
Ch Lavish Warpaint	D	Ch Laurel Wreath	Boreham Bequile	Mrs L C Wilson	F W Mills	20.2.48
Ch Sheresta Malbrue Monarch	D	Ch Selecta Rich Reward	Ian's Own	H R Bishop	E Robins	2.5.49
Ch Maryholme Simon	D	Ch Maryholme Spun Gold	Maryholme Soucie	A Clanachan	Owner	4.6.49
Ch Sheresta Monogram	D	Ch Selecta Rich Reward	Selecta Golden Rule	H R Bishop	Owner	6.1.49
Ch Touchwood Tribute	D	Ch Selecta Rich Reward	Wisecion Coronet	Mrs MacLeod Smith	Owner	1.4.49
Ch Bournedale Charm	B	Bournedale Rush Recorder	Wintonian Precise	J S Smith	W Bradley	7.5.49
Ch Farleton Farina	B	Ch Lethal Weapon	Farleton Fuschia	Mrs D R Richardson	Owner	30.3.48
Ch Kingswood Scroggy Sylphides	B	Clondara Code	Scroggy Princess	A H Newbrook	J Stevenson	15.5.49
Ch Rosemorder Firefly	B	Ch Hampole Tinkler	Rosemorder Dainty Lady	F Furnier	Owner	15.5.48
Ch Sheresta Miss Andrew	B	Ch Black Andrew	Emsway Diana	H R Bishop	A W Wilkinson	14.1.49
Ch Watteau Lustrous	B	Ch Full Pay	Watteau Waitress	Mrs A Blake	Owner	12.12.47

1951

Ch Brooklands Black Prince	D	Ch Watteau Midas	Ch Brooklands Black Narcissus	H Johnson	Owner	18.10.49
Ch Farleton Oxhill Bahram	D	Rory of Doury	Abbercale Prim	Mrs R D Richardson	Miss D J Beardsley	12.4.50
Ch On Parade	D	Guns of Victory	Marigold Little Princess	W Foster	W McAuley	17.11.49
Ch Solus Smasher	D	Solus Maryholm Showman	Solus Aprille	C H Bishop	Owner	23.7.49
Ch Brooklands Happy	B	Ch Watteau Midas	Brooklands Queen Bee	H Johnson	Owner	3.10.49

Name	Sex	Sire	Dam	Owner	Breeder	Born
Ch Flying Larks Wing	B	Ch Lethal Weapon	Hunston High Jinks	Baron van der Hoop	Mrs K Southwick	10.6.48
Ch Hewshott Joyful Light	B	Hewshott Juno	Chosen Light of Notts	J F C Glover	Owner	10.5.49
Ch Maryholm Sugar Plum	B	Ch Maryholm Spun Gold	Benmoir Begonia	A Clanachan	J Bendall	29.6.49
1952						
Ch Beechbank Klesby Heritage	D	Ch Laurel Wreath	Swisscot Sirag Caress	W Hepwood & Rev I D Knowles	Capt A G Hucklesby	7.5.49
Ch Brooklands Black Knight	D	Ch Watteau Midas	Brooklands Queen Bee	H Johnson	Owner	23.4.51
Ch Brooklands Lucky Wishbone	D	Ch Brooklands Black Prince	Burham Bint	H Johnson	Mrs L Wilson	22.12.50
Ch Correct Wartax of Notts	D	Ch Lavish Warpaint	Chiffney of Notts	Her Grace, Kathleen Duchess of Newcastle	Owner	11.9.49
Ch Full-o-Pep	D	Ch Lavish Warpaint	Pandora's Pet	J Gough	Owner	16.2.50
Ch Hampole True Ring	D	Ch Hampole Tinkler	Hampole Bellrosa	Mrs G Leatt	Miss E Lindley Wood	21.6.49
Ch Sheresta Model	D	Sheresta Marlbru Marquis	Selecta Golden Rule	H R Bishop	Owner	30.5.50
Ch Broughton Victory Princess	B	Guns of Victory	Marigold Little Princess	Mrs A G Boggia	W McAuley	26.8.50
Ch Dunold Highland Cream	B	Bournedale Rush Recorder	Dunold Head Barmaid	J Ellison	Owner	7.9.50
Ch Hewshott Joyful Lark	B	Hewshott Juro	Chosen Light of Notts	J F C Glover	Owner	10.5.49
Ch My Lady of Rivazdal	B	Ch Hampole Tinkler	Rosemorder Dainty Lady	Mrs H Haworth	Owner	25.9.50
Ch Sheresta Borman Vesta	B	Ch Sheresta Monogram	Borman Victoria	H R Bishop	Miss I Beale	20.8.50
Ch Watteau Stealaway	D	Ch Watteau Midas	Brooklands Ebonetta	Mrs A Blake	H Johnson	18.5.50
1953						
Ch Brooklands Black Mask	D	Ch Brooklands Black Prince	Brooklands Milady	H Johnson	Owner	1.12.51
Ch Guisboro Spotlight	D	Ch Hampole Tinkler	Defiant Jill	D Holmes	Owner	19.12.50
Ch Hermon Parthings Loyal Lad	D	Parthings Laddy	Amber Solitaire	Miss K Emery	Mrs H Terrell	20.6.51
Ch Kingswood Kozy Kole	D	Ch Lethal Weapon	Charnworth Sea Storm	A H Newbrook	Miss A D Cole	20.7.52
Ch Scroggy Sophocles	D	Ch Lethal Weapon	Scroggy Sultana	J Stevenson	Owner	15.1.51
Ch Sheresta Mighty Fine	D	Ch Sheresta Marlbru Monarch	Sheresta Harmony	H R Bishop	Owner	2.2.51
Ch Stubbington Matinee Idol	D	Ch Laurel Wreath	Ryden's Danesgate Daisychain	Misses A Beale & V B Sodenberg	Owners	27.4.52
Ch Charnworth Patched Sails	B	Charnworth Matelot	Ch Charnworth Sea Storm	Miss A D Cole	Owner	18.10.50
Ch Defray	B	Clondara Code	Stockman's Magnet	P J McNamee	Owner	11.8.51
Ch Gosmore Rosemorder Fireaway	B	Ch Farleton Oxhill Bahram	Ch Rosemoreder Firefly	Mr & Mrs Dallison	F Furniss	4.8.52
Ch Harkway Lille	B	Ch Lethal Weapon	Harkaway Likeable	Miss B Stapley	Owner	2.9.50
Ch Watteau Songstress	B	Ch Lavish Warpaint	Wildflower	Mrs A Blake	D Kay	24.4.51

LIST OF CHAMPIONS

1954

Name	Sex	Sire	Dam	Breeder	Owner	Date
Ch Brooklands Black Ace	D	Ch Brooklands Lucky Wishbone	Brooklands Black Tulip	H Johnson	Owner	9.11.52
Ch Hampole Housemaster	D	Ch Hampole Tumbler	Hampole Home Chat	Miss E Lindley Wood	Owner	29.5.53
Ch Lanneau Jerrod	D	Lanneau Hayespark Topnotcher	Kentucky Teddibar Aileen	J Lowe	E Barnard	22.10.52
Ch Rush Pegasus	D	Ch Watteau Midas	Rush Modeste	G Truman-Hewitt JP	Owner	23.12.52
Ch Barwyn Princess	B	Bournedale Rush Recorder	Blyboro Barley	T F Lewin	Owner	14.8.52
Ch Burmar Dawn	B	Burmar Lance	Burmar Adriana	Mrs E Marshall & Miss E G Burton	Owners	9.8.52
Ch Farleton Gay Florentina	B	Ch Farleton Oxhill Bahram	Ch Farleton Florette	Mrs D Roy Richardson	Owner	8.3.53

1955

Name	Sex	Sire	Dam	Breeder	Owner	Date
Ch Brooklands Lucky Dip	D	Ch Brooklands Lucky Wishbone	Ch Brooklands Black Narcissus	H Johnson	Owner	28.9.53
Ch Hewshott Jaguar	D	Hewshott Javelin	Hewshott Joy's Wish	J F C Glover	Owner	13.5.53
Ch Oxhill Band Leader	D	Farleton Fine Fellow	Oxhill Bridesmaid	A Baldwin	Owner	8.6.53
Ch Samarium Jan	D	Ch Beechbank Klesby Heritage	Princess Priceless J Cropper	Miss A K Keats &	J Cropper	20.5.53
Ch Wychway Buccaneer	D	Wychway Newsboy	Wychway Tinker Belle	W Snape	Owner	12.2.53
Ch Farleton Amber Gaiety Girl	B	Ch Farleton Oxhill Bahram	Thealelands Jill	Mrs D Roy Richardson	Owner	13.12.53
Ch Hermon Palmist	B	Ch Hermon Parthings Loyal Lad	Crystal Lady	Miss K Emery	Owner	18.7.54
Ch Kenelm Bellechien Pirouitte	B	Ch Lethal Weapon	Bellechien Ballerina Girl	J W Bywater	Mr & Mrs R Kiesekoms	4.4.53
Ch Lady Fox of Tutbury	B	Ch Sheresta Monogram	Cannily of Notts	C E Ballance	Owner	20.9.51
Ch Maryholm Sweetmeat	B	Ch Farleton Oxhill Bahram	Maryholme Sweetbit	A Clanachan	Owner	24.3.54
Ch Wenn of Ballig	B	Ingham Racket	Beltuna of Ballig	W Bateson	Owner	20.5.53

1956

Name	Sex	Sire	Dam	Breeder	Owner	Date
Ch Burmar Warrior	D	Burmar Lance	Burmar Adriana	Mrs E L Marshall & Miss S G Burton	Owners	21.11.53
Ch Farleton Barrowby Barney	D	Ch Oxhill Bandleader	Lady Jewel	Mrs D R Richardson	W Ducker	26.4.54
Ch Lanneau Jeremy	D	Ch Lanneau Jerod	Lanneau Jenta	Mr & Mrs J Lowe	J Lowe	20.12.54
Ch Solus Rosemorder Fire Alarm	D	Ch Hermon Parthings Loyal Lad	Rosemorder Yes Milady	C H Bishop	F Furniss	24.9.54
Ch Watteau Chorister	D	Ch Brooklands Lucky Wishbone	Ch Watteau Songstress	Mrs A Blake	Owner	3.11.54

Name	Sex	Sire	Dam	Owner	Breeder	Born
Ch Hampole Housewife	B	Hampole Campsmount	Hampole Homechat Warbond	Miss E Lindley Wood	Owner	22.5.54
Ch Harkway Eliza	B	Ch Hermon Parthings Loyal Lad	Harkaway Lilli	Miss B Stapley	Owner	24.8.54
Ch Parkend Druscilla	B	Parkend Director	Parkend Diana	N Bown	Owner	17.3.54
1957						
Ch Hewshott Juggler	D	Ch Hewshott Jaguar	Hewshott Jigsaw	J F C Glover	Owner	5.3.56
Ch Last o' Weapon	D	Ch Lethal Weapon	Lesser Waxbill	Mrs L C Wilson	Owner	31.8.55
Ch Maryholm Sailaway	D	Maryholm St Patrick	Maryholm So Sweet	A Clanachan	Owner	15.5.55
Ch Parkend Delegate	D	Parkend Director	Parkend Diana	N Bown	Owner	8.2.56
Ch Parkend Director Again	D	Parkend Director	Parkend Diana	N Bown	Owner	25.6.55
Ch Charnworth Sea Nymph	B	Ch Kingswood Kozy Kole	Ch Charnworth Patched Sails	Miss A D Cole	Owner	14.12.53
Ch Farleton Saltholme Saucy	B	Ch Rush Pegasus	Saltholme Sally	Mrs D Roy Richardson	A M Simpson	31.7.55
Ch Harkaway Emma	B	Ch Hermon Parthings Loyal Lad	Ch Harkaway Lilli	Mrs E L Marshall & Miss E G Burton	Miss Stapley	24.8.54
Ch Maryholme Silver Lady	B	Ch Maryholme Sailaway	Maryholme Silver Mist	A Clanachan	Owner	7.6.56
Ch Parthings Land Girl	B	Parthings Laddie	Amber Solitaire	G E Hurrell	Mrs H Terrell	4.4.53
Ch Shaftmoor Sundew	B	Farleton Fine Fellow	Platoon Commander	A Lloyd	E Sandland	31.8.56
1958						
Ch Auchencrosh Jack Boot	D	Hunt Master	Auchencrosh Antigone	Mr & Mrs H J Hewetson	W Platten	28.8.56
Ch Brooklands Royal Tan	D	Brooklands Decorator	Brooklands Sparkle	H Johnson	Owner	25.12.56
Ch Charneth Choir Boy	D	Charneth Call Boy	Charneth Gipsy	C K Bowden	Owner	7.4.57
Ch Glascoed Gangster	D	Ch Wychway Buccaneer	Glascoed Garland	S A Wheeler	J J Lynch	4.5.55
Ch Hermon Rebel	D	Ch Hermon Parthings Loyal Lad	Crystal Lady	Miss K Emery	Owner	1.10.56
Ch Solus Marilyn	B	Ch Solus Rosemorder Fire Alarm	Wraysdale Enterprise	C H Bishop	Mrs V Gold	10.10.56
Ch Watteau Sonata	B	Ch Watteau Chorister	Watteau Marilyn	Mrs A Blake	Owner	16.3.57
1959						
Ch Brooklands Happy Wish	D	Ch Brooklands Lucky	Ch Brooklands Happy Wishbone	H Johnson	Owner	10.10.56
Ch Glascoed Guinea Gold	D	Ch Maryholme Spun Gold	Glascoed Glitter	S A Wheeler	J J Lynch	22.6.57
Ch Maryholm Sureline	D	Laurel of Din	Ch Maryholm Sweetmeat	A Clanachan	Owner	22.4.58

LIST OF CHAMPIONS

Name	Sex	Sire	Dam	Breeder	Owner	Date
Ch Watteau Madrigal	D	Ch Watteau Chorister	Watteau Marilyn	Baron van der Hoop	Mrs A Blake	4.5.58
Ch Watteau Merry Thought	D	Ch Brooklands Happy Wishbone	Watteau Skylark	Mrs A Blake	Owner	27.9.57
Ch Burmar Snocat	B	Ch Burmar Warrior	Ch Harkaway Emma	Mrs E L Marshall & Miss E G A Burton	Owners	11.2.58
Ch Forthill Fascination	B	Barrack Bandlader	Molton Melia	J Smyth	Owner	16.1.58
Ch Hampole Fidelity	B	Ch Hermon Parthings Loyal Lad	Ch Hampole Housewife	Miss E Lindley Wood	Owner	15.12.57
Ch Lanneau Jessica	B	Ch Brooklands Black Ace	Lanneau Jente	Mr & Mrs J Lowe	Owners	10.4.56
Ch Silver Mannequin	B	Laurel of Din	Joans Gem	J Magill	Owner	3.9.57
Ch Watteau Rhapsody	B	Ch Watteau Chorister	Watteau Marilyn	Madam M Soudee	Mrs A Blake	4.5.58
1960						
Ch Solus Soloist	D	Ch Watteau Chorister	Ch Solus Marilyn	C H Bishop	Owner	11.2.59
Ch Hermon Card Trick	B	Ch Burmar Warrior	Ch Hermon Parmist	Miss K Emery	Owner	15.11.58
1961						
Ch Ellastone Gold Nugget	D	Ch Watteau Chorister	Brooklands Lady Alice	K Dickinson	Owner	15.12.59
Ch Foremark Festive	D	Brooklands Decorator	Watteau Skylark	Mrs W Newbury	Mrs A Blake	21.12.59
Ch Maryholm Nornay Mainsail	D	Ch Maryholm Sailaway	Maryholm Shamrock	A Clanachan	Mrs M Coward & Mrs F M Soubrey	15.10.59
Ch Brooklands Spice	B	Ch Watteau Chorister	Brooklands Joybelle	H Johnson	Owner	12.7.60
Ch Flying Hermon Diamond	B	Ch Hermon Parthings Loyal Lad	Crystal Lady	Baron van der Hoop	Miss K Emery	29.4.59
Ch Watteau Cantata	B	Ch Watteau Chorister	Watteau Marylyr	Mrs A Blake	Owner	16.5.59
1962						
Ch Maryholm Ship Ahoy	D	Maryholm Nornay Mainsail	Ch Maryholm Silver Lady	A Clanachan	Owner	9.2.61
Ch Lanneau Jekyll	D	Lanneau Jeweller	Lanneau Jezebel	Mr & Mrs J Lowe	Owners	18.11.60
Ch Mattocline	D	Ch Maryholme Sureline	Keyworth Pagegil	P H Ireson	Owner	2.9.59
Ch Viaduct Beau Brummel	D	Viaduct Golden Rod	Viaduct Carmen	Miss S Langstaff & E Lockey	Owners	12.6.59
Ch Newmaidley Jehu	D	Ch Brooklands Lucky Wishbone	Newmaidley Destiny	Miss L G Beak	Owner	8.5.60
Ch Burmar Emily	B	Burmar Arrow	Ch Harkaway Emma	Mrs Marshall & Miss Burton	Owners	1.8.60
Ch Hermon Fantasy	B	Ch Hermon Rebel	Hermon Witchcraft	Miss K Emery	Lady Gooch	14.5.60
Ch Hermon Blacklands Sophia	B	Ch Solus Soloist	Blacklands Jane	Miss K Emery	Lt-Col & Mrs D Yate-Lee	22.11.60

Name	Sex	Sire	Dam	Owner	Breeder	Born
Ch Nornay Topsail	B	Ch Maryholm Sailaway	Maryholm Shamrock	Mesdames M Coward & F M Soubrey	Owners	24.11.60
Ch Maryholm Royal Surepay	B	Roylan Rich Reward	Roylan Golden Gem	H Thomas	J Morton	27.5.59
1963						
Ch Watteau Snuff Box	D	Watteau Sculpture	Beechbank Olive	Mrs A Blake	Owner	1.2.62
Ch Lesterley Starliner	D	Ch Mattocline	Hermon Stargazer	Miss M E Lambert	Owner	16.2.61
Ch Solus Sidewater Seahawk	D	Ch Watteau Chorister	Sidewater Snow Fairy	C H Bishop	Mrs V J Goold	18.10.60
Ch Brooklands Present	B	Ch Watteau Chorister	Watteau Marylyn	H Johnson	Mrs A Blake	16.5.59
Ch Astonabbotts Fair Dinkum	B	Burmar Major George	Aston Sally	P Kempster	Owner	11.6.60
Ch Maryholm Silver Snowflake	B	Ch Maryholm Sureline	Ch Maryholm Silver Lady	A Clanachan	Owner	1.9.59
Ch Hewshott Jennie Jerome	B	Hewshott Jerome	Hewshott Jane Eyre	J F C Glover	Owner	16.2.62
Ch Harkaway Holly	B	Ch Solus Soloist	Harkaway Dinah-Mite	Miss B Stapley	Owner	5.12.60
1964						
Ch Newmaidley Vodka	D	Ch Watteau Snuff Box	Newmaidley Destiny	Miss L G Beak	Owner	18.1.63
Ch Shaftmoor Bellechien White Heather	B	Ch Hermon Rebel	Bellechien Songstress	A Lloyd	Mr & Mrs Kiesekoms	24.9.62
Ch Spaceman	D	Debough	Wynnor's Fancy	J Russell	N Simpson	14.5.61
Ch Casterbridge Starlight	B	Ch Lesterley Starliner	Casterbridge Fairy Snow	C N Rippingale	Owner	28.10.63
Ch Greenbelt Coppernob	D	Lanneau Jerome	Greenbelt Autumn Tint	Mrs L Brady	Owner	20.4.61
Ch Conformable Benjamin	D	Ch Glascoed Guinea Gold	Conformable Sexta	S A Wheeler	Owner	23.6.62
Ch Hermon Snow White	B	Hiya Harbourmaster	Hiya Hanwen	Miss K Emery	Mrs A M Tomlinson	28.6.62
1965						
Ch Ellastone Lucky Nugget	D	Ch Ellastone Gold Nugget	Ellastone Lucky Dip	K Dickinson	Owner	7.6.62
Ch Foremark Ebony Box	D	Ch Watteau Snuff Box	Watteau Gay Bird	Mrs W Newbury	Owner	9.10.63
Ch Harkaway Lancashire Lad	D	Ch Watteau Snuff Box	Harkaway Mandy	Miss B Stapley	Owner	26.1.63
Ch Newmaidley Joshua	D	Ch Watteau Snuff Box	Newmaidley Kala	Miss L G Beak	Owner	9.10.63
Ch Hampole Hero	B	Ch Hermon Parthings Loyal Lad	Ch Hampole Housewife	B Walker	Miss E Lindley Wood	30.6.59
Ch Hermon Mirage	B	Ch Watteau Snuff Box	Ch Hermon Fantasy	Miss K Emery	Owner	24.8.63
1966						
Ch Fernery Grand Duke	D	Fernery Viscount	Honeysweet of Fargreen	T Fennyhough	Owner	15.10.61
Ch Lanneau Jevron	D	Lanneau Jepcot	Lanneau Jeminy	Mr & Mrs J Lowe	Owners	10.6.65
Ch Parkend Democrat	D	Ch Parkend Director Again	Parkend Donna	N Bown	Owner	19.9.64

LIST OF CHAMPIONS

Name		Sire	Dam	Breeder	Owner	Date
Ch Viscum Voluntary	D	Hampole Tatler	Ch Hampole Hero	B Walker	Owner	30.3.64
Ch Foxformee Spots	B	Ch Harkaway Lancashire Lad	Foxformee Burmar Unity	Mrs M Greenslade	Owner	18.2.65
Ch Lanneau Jessie	B	Ch Watteau Madrigal	Lanneau Jezebel	Mr & Mrs J Lowe	Owners	11.1.64
Ch Maryholm Gelston Impala	B	Ch Maryholm Sureline	Solus Tanis	A Clanachan	The Hon A Oakshott	22.10.64
1967						
Ch Ellastone Firecrest	D	Ch Ellastone Gold Nugget	Martag Maytud	K Dickinson	Mr & Mrs E R Davies	30.6.65
Ch Lesterley Starliner	D	Ch Mattocline	Herron Stargazer	Miss M E Lambert	Owner	16.2.61
Ch Foxformee Adelaide	B	Ch Harkaway Lancashire Lad	Foxformee Burmar Unity	Miss M Bagot	Mrs M Greenslade	27.3.66
Ch Hermon Snow Drift	B	Ch Harkaway Lancashire Lad	Ch Hermon Snow White	Miss K Emery	Owner	16.6.65
Ch Watteau Last Word	D	Watteau S'nufsed	Lingrove Linnet	Mrs & Miss A Blake	Owners	4.4.66
Ch Hermon Snow Fall	B	Ch Harkaway Lancashire Lad	Ch Hermon Snow White	Miss K Emery	Owner	16.6.65
Ch Maryholm Siller Belle	B	Ch Maryholm Sureline	Ch Maryholm Silver Lady	A Clanachan	Owner	31.10.65
Ch Nornay Windward	B	Nornay Conviction	Ch Nornay Topsail	Mrs M Coward & Mrs F M Soubry	Owners	5.8.64
1968						
Ch Nornay Navigator	D	Nornay Conviction	Ch Nornay Topsail	Mrs M Coward & Mrs F M Soubry	Owners	6.1.67
Ch Lanneau Jethro	D	Ch Lanneau Jevron	Ch Lanneau Jessie	Mr & Mrs J Lowe	Owners	3.8.67
Ch Hermon Snowman	D	Ch Harkaway Lancashire Lad	Ch Harmon Snow White	Miss K Emery	Owners	31.10.66
Ch Davesfame Kompliment	B	Burmar Major George	Hampole Chitchat	Master David Kitchen	D Kitchen	1.7.66
Ch Watteau Happy Talk	B	Watteau S'nufsed	Lingrove Linnet	Mrs & Miss A Blake	Owners	4.4.66
Ch Hermon Snowball	B	Ch Harkaway Lancashire Lad	Ch Hermon Snow White	Miss K Emery	Owner	31.10.66
Ch Newmaidley Naomi	B	Ch Newmaidley Vodka	Newmaidley Kala	Miss L G Beak	Owner	20.3.65
Ch Spritely Chorus Girl	B	Ch Newmaidley Vodka	Spritely Lady	A Thomson	Miss Robinson	12.12.64
1969						
Ch Barrowby Martha	B	Barrowby Consul	Barrowby Daphne	W Ducker	Owner	22.6.67
Ch Thermfare Inca	B	Thermfare Elegance	Andersley Arbess	J Pitcairn	Owner	23.1.68
Ch Hermon Snowflake	B	Ch Harkaway Lancashire Lad	Ch Hermon Snow White	Miss K Emery	Owner	23.1.68
Ch Newmaidley Cossack	D	Ch Newmaidley Vodka	Newmaidley Leira	Miss L G Beak	Owner	7.12.69

Name	Sex	Sire	Dam	Owner	Breeder	Born
1970						
Ch Newmaidley Black Admiral	D	Newmaidley Black Diamond	Newmaidley Black Queen	Miss L G Beak	Owner	3.3.68
Ch Casterbridge Mariner	D	Int Ch Nornay Navigator	Ch Casterbridge Starlight	C Rippingale	Owner	20.2.69
Ch Newmaidley Whistling Jeremy	D	Ch Newmaidley Vodka	Newmaidley Dew	Miss L G Beak	Mrs Burbridge	28.4.69
Ch Laurel Drive	D	Ch Watteau Madrigal	Lanneau Jexas	Messrs Downes & Hollinrake	L Downes	1.1.69
Ch Hiya Hush	B	Hiya Hanaper	Witfylde Whisper	Miss K Williams	Owner	21.9.66
Ch Lesterley Bequest of Dingley Dell	B	Ch Lesterley Starliner	Ir Ch Molten Market-Value	F Taylor	Miss M E Lambot	14.3.68
Ch Pittlea Carousel	B	Pittlea Centaurus	Pittlea Charmer	Mrs P Robinson	Owner	1.1.69
Ch Ebony Enterprise	D	Ch Ellastone Firecrest	Trinket Box	J G Ord	Owner	29.6.68
1971						
Ch Ellastone Jolly Roger	D	Ch Ellastone Firecrest	Duckaway Dainty Lass	K Dickinson	P Davenport	19.8.69
Ch Sprotboro Rebel	D	Sprotboro Sir Ivor	Hermon Icicle	Mrs J Langstaff	Owner	2.10.69
Ch Boreham Ballerina	B	Ch Lesterley Starliner	Boreham Bacchante	Mrs J T Winstanley	Owner	12.1.68
Ch Ellastone Carousel	B	Ch Ellastone Firecrest	Hopleys Gold Petal	K Dickinson	Mrs Lakin	7.10.68
Ch Maryholm Siller Venture	B	Maryholm Viscom Venture	Ch Maryholm Siller Belle	A Clanachan	Owner	14.8.69
Ch Watteau Lyrical	B	Ch Watteau Madrigal	Ch Watteau Happy Talk	Mrs A & Miss A Blake	Owners	11.4.70
Ch Huddfield Surprise	D	Viscum Vogue	Viscum Vivian	H Senior	B Walker	1.1.68
1972						
Ch Burmar Ted	D	Ch Harkaway Lancashire Lad	Ch Burmar Snowcat	Misses Marshall & Burton	Owners	10.9.66
Ch Harkaway Matador	D	Ch Ellastone Firecrest	Ch Hermon Snowfall	Miss B Stapley	Owner	9.2.70
Ch Karnilo Chieftain	D	Ch Laurel Drive	Karnilo Cavalena	Mrs E Hollinrake	Owner	1.3.71
Ch Pittlea Chortle	D	Pittlea Centaurus	Pittlea Gay Imp	Mrs P Robinson	Owner	23.11.70
Ch Casterbridge Amber Star	B	Int Ch Nornay Navigator	Ch Casterbridge Starlight	C N Rippingale	Owner	20.2.69
Ch Gabryl Greta	B	Ch Newmaidley Vodka	Gabryl Girlie	Mrs M D Gabriel	Owner	4.10.69
Ch Newmaidley Cinnamon	B	Ch Newmaidley Cossack	Newmaidley Diana	Miss L G Beak	Owner	29.4.70
Ch Northill Melody	B	Ch Newmaidley Cossack	Northill Gold Leaf	K Johnson	Owner	2.1.69
Ch Windley Black Tarquin	B	Maryholm Viscom Venture	Liberty Jasmine	W Tong	Mr & Mrs J Cotter	21.3.70
Ch Newmaidley Florence	B	Ch Newmaidley Whistling Jeremy	Newmaidley Echo	Miss L G Beak	Owner	13.10.71

1973

	Sex	Sire	Dam	Owner	Owner	Date
Ch Boreham Burlesque	D	Ch Newmaidley Whistling Jeremy	Ch Boreham Ballerina	Mrs J T Winstanley	Owner	27.4.72
Ch Chelston Passaford Piper	D	Passaford Part Song	Passaford Brengun Bernadette	Mrs E C Carter	Mrs H R White	19.8.69
Ch Coniebroom Pixie	B	Ch Spaceman	Int Ch Sidewater Mary Poppins	Mrs G E Eady	N Simpson	9.12.67
Ch Harmac Prim Rose	B	Ch Spaceman	Etyne Leda	Messrs Harrison & MacDonald	Owners	2.10.71
Ch Sprotboro Sincerity	B	Hampole Home Master	Sprotboro Viscarm Velociu	Mrs M Newman	Mrs J Langstaff	25.10.69
Ch Sunspot of Greenbelt	B	Greenbelt Copper Coin	Locksheath Mitzi	Mrs L Brady	Mrs V Hartley	16.1.72
Ch Watteau Ballad	B	Ch Ellastone Firecrest	Ch Watteau Lyrical	Mrs A & Miss A Blake	Owners	6.3.72

1974

Ch Riber Ramsey	D	Riber Rockafella	Riber Sioe Sadoe	Mr & Mrs P Winfield	Owners	23.10.72
Ch Jonwyre's Galaxy	D	Ch Spaceman	Jonwyre's Space Girl	E Jones	Owners	19.2.73
Ch Gaybryl Glenda	B	Ch Burmar Ted	Ch Gaybryl Greta	J Gabriel	Owner	29.8.72
Ch Astona Sioux	B	Astona Boysie	Astona Goldy	Mr & Mrs P Kempster	Mrs J Timms	12.10.70
Ch Sprotboro Sparkel of Townville	B	Ch Sprotboro Rebel	Sprotboro Surprise	C Whitham	Mrs J Langstaff	25.9.73

1975

Ch Newmaidley Laura	B	Ch Newmaidley Whistling Jeremy	Newmaidley Lustre	Miss L G Beak	Owner	13.4.73
Eng/Nor/Am Ch Watteau Chief Barker	D	Eng/Am Ch Karnilo Chieftain	Ch Watteau Happy Talk	Mr & Mrs A Blake	Owners	1.11.72
Ch Harkaway Lively	B	Ch Harkaway Lancashire Lad	Harkaway Lisa	Miss B Stapley	Owner	22.9.73
Ch Duckaway Dell	B	Ch Burmar Ted	Duckaway Dana	D J Daly	Owner	27.12.72
Ch Brengun Moonraker	D	Ch Newmaidley Whistling Jeremy	Brengun Bracelet	Miss B Gough	Owner	8.5.71
Ch Newmaidley Soap Box	D	Ch Watteau Snuff Box	Newmaidley Anthee	Miss L G Beak	Owner	28.8.73
Ch Brengun Force Ten Gail	B	Ch Newmaidley Whistling Jeremy	Brengun Brolie	Miss B Gough	Owner	18.1.74
Ch Newmaidley Jacko	D	Ch Newmaidley Whistling Jeremy	Newmaidley Orange Blossom	Miss L G Beak	Owner	8.12.73
Ch Black Emperor of Ellastone	D	Ch Ellastone Jolly Roger	Marteg Maybelle	K Dickinson	Mr & Mrs Davies	29.3.72
Ch Boreham Ballet Star	B	Int Ch Jonwyre's Galaxy	Ch Boreham Ballerina	Mrs J T Winstanley	Owner	4.7.74

Name	Sex	Sire	Dam	Owner	Breeder	Born
1976						
Ch Maryholm Starry	D	Ch Riber Ramsey	Burnaun Princess of Maryholm	A Clanachan	Owner	27.10.73
Ch Mosvalley Marksman	D	Ch Riber Ramsey	Mosvalley Magpie	C M Day (Davies)	Owner	20.7.75
Ch Wat-U-May-Callit	D	I'm Robinson	Silver Seal	Mr Deacon	Owner	26.9.73
Ch Riber Apple Blossom	B	Riber Rockafella	Riber Side Saddle	Mr & Mrs P Winfield	Owners	23.10.72
Ch Sprotboro Serenade of Northill	B	Ch Sprotboro Rebel	Sprotboro Surprise	K Johnson	Owner	25.9.73
Ch Strondour Ginger	B	Ch Riber Ramsey	Burnaun Princess of Maryholm	A Clanachan	W Walker	27.10.73
Ch Jonwyres Galore	B	Greenbelt Tri-star	Reflection of Jonwyre	F Jones	Owner	17.6.75
1977						
Ch Newmaidley Mapleden Laurel	D	Newmaidley Eden	Newmaidley Candybox	Miss L G Beak	Mrs Manolsen	2.4.76
Ch Boreham Briar Rose	B	Ch Riber Ramsey	Ch Boreham Ballerina	Mr & Mrs P Winfield	Owners	24.9.75
Ch Teesford Trier	B	Teesford Tartar	Teesford Twink	B Brown	Owner	12.11.75
1978						
Ch Gavingale Joshua	D	Gavingale Black Pirate	Gavingale Nerissa	P Fox	Owner	31.3.75
Ch Maryholm Stockmark	D	Am Ch Boreham Black Domino	Ch Strondour Ginger	A Clanachan	Owner	18.12.76
Ch Burnaun Rascal of Maryholm	D	Ch Maryholm Starry	Maryholm She's Sound	A Clanachan	R McNeish	1.7.76
Ch Hewshott Jessie	B	Ch Burmar Ted	Hewshott Julie	J F C Glover	Owner	23.8.76
Ch Harkaway Good Gracious	B	Harkaway Hallmark	Harkaway Harmony	B Stapley	Owner	4.2.74
Ch Maryholm She's Sweet	B	Maryholm Ship Ahoy	Maryholm Sprig	A Clanachan	Owner	10.8.72
Ch Duckaway Dapple	B	Ch Riber Ramsey	Ch Duckaway Dell	D Daly	Owner	4.6.76
Ch Roxway Eclat	B	Roxway Elite	Waikaremoana Tinkerbelle	Mrs P & Miss P Strong	Owner	9.5.76
Ch Sprotboro Straight Lace	B	Hampole Homemaster	Sprotboro Sensation	J Langstaff	Owner	23.12.74
1979						
Ch Newmaidley Esau	D	Newmaidley Eden	Newmaidley Venus	Miss L G Beak	Owner	24.4.78
Ch Watteau Ploughman	D	Ch Maryholm Stockmark	Ch Watteau Lyrical	Mr Blake & A Thornton	Owners	26.12.77
Ch Boreham Blueprint	B	Ch Riber Ramsey	Ch Boreham Ballet Star	Mrs E Winstanley	Owner	27.8.76
Ch Noble Gesture of Beechdene	B	Grandmaster of Grambrae	White Blossom of Grambrae	H Fairley	J A Magill	6.1.78
Ch Maryholm Siller Jewell	B	Ch Maryholm Stockmark	Ch Maryholm Siller Venture	A Clanachan	Owner	11.11.77
Ch Mosvalley Maytime	B	Ch Mosvalley Marksman	Boreham Blossom Time	Mrs C Davies	Owner	12.4.77

LIST OF CHAMPIONS

Name	Sex	Sire	Dam	Breeder	Owner	Date
Classicway Crack of Dawn	B	Ch Riber Ramsey	Crazy Gift of Classicway	Mrs E Darby	Owner	17.4.77
Ch Casterbridge Bay leaf	B	Ch Newmaidley Mapleden Laurel	Casterbridge Celeste	C Rippingale	Owner	27.10.77
1980						
Ch Karnilo Comanche	D	Karnilo Chief Whip	Karnilo Chrissie	H & E Hollinrake	Owner	6.11.78
Ch Riber Ricochet	D	Ch Watteau Ploughman	Boreham Briar Rose	Mr & Mrs P Winfield	Owners	5.2.79
Ch Newmaidley Industry	D	Ch Newmaidley Mapleden Laurel	Newmaidley Merciful	Miss L G Beak	Owner	16.7.79
Ch Astona Sukie	B	Ch Burmar Ted	Ch Astona Sioux	Mrs G Kempster	F Sills	23.7.76
Ch Astona I'm Sure To	B	Ch Burmar Ted	Ch Astona Sioux	Mrs G Kempster	Owner	16.4.77
Ch Higrola Harriet of Britlea	B	Ch Mosvalley Marksman	Teesford Teaser	L Cowen	J Noble Eddy	6.3.78
Ch Boreham Bagatelle	B	Astona Georgie	Ch Boreham Ballet Star	Mrs E Winstanley	Mrs K Evans	21.9.78
Ch Stockinette of Sufredon	B	Ch Maryholm Stockmark	Viscum Valmar	Mrs S Laws	Owner	24.11.78
Ch Travelling Time of Classicway	B	Ch Riber Ramsey	Tiedam Burmar Star	Miss J Darby	Maj Forsyth-Forrest	16.1.79
1981						
Ch Boreham Blueblack	D	Ch Maryholm Stockmark	Ch Boreham Blueprint	Mrs E Winstanley	Owner	15.9.79
Ch Brengun Billabong	D	Brengun Boomerang	Brengun Cathy	Mrs E B Gough	Owner	18.5.78
Ch Gavingale Sherpa	D	Gavingale Black Pirate	Gavingale Tina	P Fox	Owner	17.10.79
Ch Newmaidley Glider	D	Ch Newmaidley Whistling Jeremy	Newmaidley Nimble	Miss L G Beak	Owner	2.7.79
Ch Karnilo Corolla	B	Karnilo Chief Whip	Karnilo Chrissie	H & E Hollinrake	Owners	21.5.79
Ch Gramgrae Quest	B	Foylewood Tobia	Idyll of Grambrae	J & S Magill	Owners	21.2.80
Ch Crooksmoor Chantilly Lace	B	Ch Sprotboro Rebel	Sprotboro Sheer Vanity	R Crooks	Owner	20.1.80
Ch Newmaidley Dutiful	B	Ch Newmaidley Mapleden Laurel	Newmaidley Merciful	Miss L G Beak	Owner	4.2.78
Ch Newmaidley Transit	B	Ch Newmaidley Mapleden Laurel	Newmaidley Merciful	Miss L G Beak	Owner	18.12.79
1982						
Ch Sirandra of Maryholm	D	Fieldron Finnegan	Maryholm She's A Honey	A Canachan	A Taylor	19.2.81
Ch Eclipse of Roxway	D	Roxway Encore	Roxway Enterprise	Mr & Mrs E Christisson	W R Davey	2.4.80
Ch Riber Rosemead	B	Ch Watteau Ploughman	Ch Boreham Briar Rose	Mrs C M Davies	P Winfield	20.9.80
Ch Grambrae Replica	B	Foylewood Tobia	White Blossom of Gambrae	J & S Magill	Owners	22.6.80
Ch Astona Dinki Doo	B	Ch Boreham Blueblack	Ch Astona I'm Sure To	P & G Kempster	Owners	26.9.80
Ch Gaybril Glimma	B	Ch Maryholm Stockmark	Ch Gaybryl Glenda	M Gabriel	Owner	11.10.79
Ch Vertway Sweet Sue	B	Harmac Black Boy	Vertway Black Princess	J Greenway	Owner	26.7.80

Name	Sex	Sire	Dam	Owner	Breeder	Born
1983						
Ch Britlea Bizet	D	Ch Newmaidley Glider	Ch Higrola Harriet of Britlea	J Cowen	Owner	24.6.81
Ch Sufredon Inkling	D	Ch Boreham Blueblack	Ch Stockinette of Sufredon	Mrs S M Laws	Owner	13.6.81
Ch Vertway Bothy Boy	D	Ch Watteau Ploughman	Vertway Sweet Girl	J Greenway	Owner	6.5.82
Ch Canterwey Cavaletti	B	Ch Riber Ricochet	Ch Boreham Bagatelle	N Dams	Mrs K Evans	24.10.80
Ch Roxway Extreme	B	Ch Boreham Blueblack	Ch Roxway Eclat	Mrs P M & Miss P A Strong	Owner	11.11.81
Ch Liareb Bolder Blaze	B	Jonwyre's Quazer	Jonwyre's Star Bird	Miss R L Beales	Mr & Mrs J Hurst	26.6.82
Ch Manorstate Melody at Bannerdown	B	Ch Sprotboro Rebel	Sprotboro Staybright	P Creed	S Taylor	11.12.80
Ch Rarity of Riber	B	Ch Riber Ricochet	Ch Canterwey Cavaletti	Mr & Mrs P Winfield	Owners	15.9.82
Ch Maryholm Spring Mannequin	B	Maryholm Stockwhip	Maryholm Sweeny	J Smith	A Clanachan	1.3.81
1984						
Ch Maryholm Siller Star	B	Ch Sirandra of Maryholm	Maryholm Siller Pearl	A Clanachan	Owner	10.5.82
Ch Roxway Evita	B	Roxway Encore	Boreham Belinda	Mrs P M & Miss P A Strong	Miss R L Beales	16.2.82
1985						
Ch Glenure Theo	D	Ch Britlea Bizet	Ch Travelling Time of Classicway	R Marples	Owner	29.10.83
Ch Paulanna Pilgrim	D	Ch Sufredon Inkling	Gema of Paulanna	Mr & Mrs R Baxter	Owners	11.10.82
Ch Newmaidley Plant	D	Newmaidley Industry	Newmaidley Laurel Leaf	Miss L G Beak	Owner	12.11.82
Gedstar Petronella	B	Ch Sirandra of Maryholm	Gedstar Copper Rise	Mrs E Geddes	Owner	7.11.82
Ch Glenure Myrtle	B	Ch Britlea Bizet	Ch Travelling Time of Classicway	R Marples	Owner	29.10.83
Ch Mosvalley Mimosa	B	Ch Sufredon Inkling	Mosvalley Maytime	P Horspool	Mrs C Davies	27.4.83
1986						
Ch Riber Reckless	D	Ch Paulanna Pilgrim	Ch Canterwey Cavaletti	R Henry	Mr & Mrs P Winfield	1.10.84
Ch Mullantean Master Joe	D	Ch Sirandra of Maryholm	Mullantean Miss Ella	J McDowell	Owner	8.8.83
Ch Conductor of Karnilo	D	Ch Karnilo Comanche	Happy Streak	M Hollinrake	Mr Firth	23.12.83
Ch Glenure Arthur	D	Ch Britlea Bizet	Travelling Time of Classicway	H Derwent	R Marples	29.10.83

LIST OF CHAMPIONS

	Sex				Owner	Date
Ch Burgla Poacha	D	Landscove Rustla	Brown Cardy	M s C M Wilcox	Mrs G Ferguson	6.3.82
Ch Glenure Amy of Hansom	B	Ch Britlea Bizet	Ch Travelling Time of Classicway	R M Finch	R Marples	29.10.83
Ch Riber for Real	B	Inkspot of Fieldron	Ch Rarity of Riber	Mr & Mrs P Winfield	Owners	2.2.85
Ch Noehew Blazeaway of Ursron	B	Ch Sirandra of Maryholm	Ch Liareb Bolder Blaze	R Foskett	Mr & Mrs J Hurst	9.9.84
Ch Tanreel Fox Trot	B	Ch Sirandra of Maryholm	Maryholm Spring Mannequin	T Weir	J Smith	4.3.84
1987						
Ch Mosvalley Mirage	D	Ch Sufredon Inkling	Ch Mosvalley Maytime	Mrs C Davies	Owner	12.10.85
Ch Mosvalley Spice	D	Inkspot of Fieldron	Ch Riber Rosemead	Mrs M Rose	Mrs C Davies	23.3.85
Ch Noehew Blazing Scot	D	Ch Sirandra of Maryholm	Ch Liareb Bolder Blaze	Mr & Mrs J Hurst	Owners	9.9.84
Ch Vertway Stable Lad	D	Ch Sirandra of Maryholm	Vertway Sweet Kate	Mrs J Thornton	J Greenway	13.11.84
Ch Gedstar Sun Boy	D	Ch Newmaidley Glider	Marshan Sunshine Girl at Gedstar	Mrs E Geddes	Owner	12.9.84
Ch Darlaur Director	D	Ch Paulanna Pilgrim	Karnilo Candy Tuft	K Jones	Owner	11.10.85
Ch Sufredon Cracknel	D	Sufredon Cream Cracker of Glendraterra	Ch Stockinette of Sufredon	Mrs S M Laws	Owner	21.5.84
Ch Yarrum Dixie Dapper	B	Redcap of Riber	Faberge of Fieldron	M Murray	Owner	18.5.85
Ch Traffox Tara	B	Ch Glenure Theo	Karnilo Chief Joy	Mrs F Blondon	Owner	25.8.85
Ch Eskwyre Exquisite	B	Ch Noehew Blazing Scot	Gallinach Daddies Girl of Maryholm	Mrs E Peet	M Vickers	26.2.86
Ch Maryholm So Nice	B	Ch Sirandra of Maryholm	Ch Maryholm Spring Mannequin	A Clanachan	Owner	6.10.85
1988						
Ch Watteau Black Magic	D	Ch Vertway Bothy Boy	Watteau Witchcraft	Mesdames M Blake & A Thornton	Owners	23.6.85
Ch Riber Mint Imperial	D	Inkspot of Fieldron	Ch Rarity of Riber	Miss K Turner	Mr & Mrs P Winfield	2.2.85
Ch Smooth Touch at Travella	D	Ch Sufredon Inkling	Saleden Sincerity	W Browne-Cole	K W Rundle	12.2.87
Ch Noehew Noel's Gift at Eskwyre	D	Ch Noehew Blazing Scot	Bo Donna o Noehew	H Rickford & Son	Mr & Mrs J Hurst	26.12.86
Ch Chemonmon of Karnilo	D	Ch Conductor of Karnilo	Zebedy of Ronell	H Hollinrake	R Whyte	3.12.87
Ch Black Satin of Sufredon	B	Ch Sufredon Inkling	Sufredon Penny Black	Mrs S M Laws	J Jones	16.6.85
Ch Gaybryl Gabriella	B	Ch Riber Reckless	Gaybryl Gayna	M Gabriel	Owner	3.10.85
Ch Astona Duskie Doo	B	Astona Paleface	Astona Georgette	Mr & Mrs P Kempster	Owner	4.10.86
Ch Bothwell Snowdrop	B	Ch Sufredon Inkling	Ch Tanreel Fox Trot of Bothwell	T Weir	Owner	12.3.87
Ch Tamerisha Untouchable	B	Am Ch Foxmooor Field Marshall	Bollingate Melody	F Rundle	Mr & Mrs Graham	17.1.87

Name	Sex	Sire	Dam	Owner	Breeder	Born
1989						
Ch Alkell Legionary	D	Ch Sufredon Inkling	Ch Glenure Myrtle	W H Kellett	R Marples	31.1.81
Ch Dambuster at Glendraterra from Sufredon	D	Ch Sufredon Inkling	Glendraterra Cassandra	Mrs S M Laws	Mesdames Laws & Thornton	22.8.85
Ch Gavingale Leo Dandy	D	Ch Sufredon Inkling	Little Damsel at Gavingale	Miss P Fox	Owner	6.2.87
Ch Sweet Dream at Vertway	B	Ch Sirandra of Maryholm	Dairymaid of Vertway	Mrs J Thornton	S Malone	23.10.86
Ch Bothwell Rosebud	B	Ch Sufredon Inkling	Ch Tanreel Fox Trot of Bothwell	J Moore	T Weir	12.3.87
Ch Riber Shindig	B	The Maverick of Riber	Ch Riber for Real	M Gabriel	Mr & Mrs P Winfield	18.8.88
Ch Bizzie Lizzie from Sufredon	B	Ch Sufredon Inkling	Glendraterra Cassandra	Mrs S M Laws	Mesdames Laws & Thornton	22.8.85
Ch Emblem of Dunlossit	B	Ch Sufredon Inkling	Ch Glenure Myrtle	P Donaldson & H & J Pickford	R Marples	31.1.88
Ch Noehew Zelba Cost	B	Ch Noehew Blazing Scot	Liareb Bolder Blaze	Mr & Mrs J Hurst	Owners	27.10.87
1990						
Ch Fieldron Phoenix	D	Fieldron Forger	Fieldron Fontaine	J Watson	Owner	26.12.86
Ch Darlaur Duellist	D	Darlaur Dempsey	Darlaur Destiny	K Jones	Owner	22.12.88
Ch Bothwell Bright Spark	B	Ch Sirandra of Maryholm	Ch Bothwell Snowdrop	T Weir	Owner	22.1.89
Ch Vertway Sweet Gem	B	Ch Sirandra of Maryholm	Vertway Sweet Katie	R Bebbington	J Greenway	17.11.87
Ch Fieldron Saintly Lady	B	Sufredon the Saint of Fieldron	Ebony of Fieldron	J Watson	Owner	12.8.89
1991						
Ch Crooksmoor Cheeky Chappie	D	The Maverick of Riber	Ch Crooksmoor Chantilly Lace	R Crooks	Owner	20.8.88
Ch Roxway Embargo	D	Ch Sufredon Inkling	Ch Roxway Evita	Mrs P M & Miss P A Strong	Owners	12.12.88
Ch Bothwell Tan Boy	D	Ch Sufredon Cracknel	Ch Bothwell Snowdrop	I & F Thompson & T Weir	T Weir	12.1.90
Ch Lanyon's Rondelet	D	Ch Smooth Touch at Travella	Lanyon's Limerick	P Julian	Owner	7.3.89
Ch Astona Dowie	D	Astona Dudley	Tenruh Tickety Boo at Astona	Mr & Mrs P Kempster	Owners	15.10.88
Ch Laurelvale Gesture	B	Laurelvale Mystery Man	Beechdene Small Virtue	A & S Magill	M Graham	25.4.89
Ch Adaires Debonair	B	The Maverick of Riber	Mustard of Mosvalley	P Horspool	Owner	20.10.89
Ch Bothwell Sweet Cindy	B	Ch Sufredon Cracknel	Ch Bothwell Snowdrop	T Weir	Owner	12.1.90
1992						
Ch Boreham Benedict	D	Ch Sufredon Inkling	Boreham Belladonna	Mr & Mrs P Freeman	Mrs J T Winstanley	26.11.88
Ch Wynneville Charlie Boy	D	Bollingate Minstrel	Bollingate Mysterious	R Griffiths	Owner	31.5.91
Ch Dunlossit Inklination	D	Ch Sufredon Inkling	Ch Emblem of Dunlossit	P Donaldson & H & J Pickford	Owners	6.9.90
Ch Sufredon Diplomat	D	Ch Darlaur Duellist	Sufredon Black Ribbon	Mrs S M Laws	Owner	29.10.90

LIST OF CHAMPIONS

Name	Sex	Sire	Dam	Breeder		Date
Ch Gavingale Loveme Do	B	Ch Vertway Stable Lad	Little Damsel at Gavingale	Miss P Fox	Owner	11.5.90
Ch Shillelagh Party Animal	B	Sufredon the Saint of Fieldron	Bannside Just a Wee Drop	M & C Gavin	Delmar & Rose	9.10.89
Ch Bankend Superlass	B	Clongoes Superflash	Riber Crystal	H & J & H Kelly	D Kearney	7.11.90
Ch Mosvalley White Orchid	B	The Maverick of Riber	Ch Mosvalley Mimosa	Mrs C Davies	Owner	18.3.89
Ch Riber Masquerade	B	The Maverick of Riber	Ch Riber for Real	Mrs R Turner	Mr & Mrs P Winfield	18.8.88
Ch Two Steps to Larchenwald	B	Ch Glenure Theo	Sanamaris Foxtrot	J Thornton & R Bebbington	Managed	8.10.88
1993						
Ch Wilkates Solomon	D	Ch Astona Dowie	Riber Real Choice	Mr D G W & Mrs C M Wilkes	Owners	5.8.91
Ch Saleden a Winter's Tale at Jetstream	D	Ch Sirandra of Maryholm	Saleden Flash Imp	M Sargeant	Mrs V Gray	24.11.90
Ch Roxway Elgatere	B	Roxway Encore	Roxway Egeria	Mesdames P Strong & P Broom	Owners	23.4.91
Ch Boreham Ballad	B	Ch Sufredon Inkling	Boreham Belladonna	Mrs J T Winstanley	Owner	26.11.88
1994						
Ch Watteau Dominic	D	Ch Boreham Benedict	Pearl Culture from Watteau	Mesdames M Blake & A Thornton	Owners	16.7.92
Ch Mosvalley Dessert Orchid of Roxway	D	Ch Wilkates Solomon	Ch Mosvalley White Orchid	Mesdames P Strong & P Broom	Mrs C Davies	2.1.93
Ch Glendraterra Dancing Brave	D	Glendraterra Rock and Roll	Ch Sweet Dream at Vertway	Mrs J Thornton	Owner	16.10.91
Ch Paulanna Pot Luck of Sanamaris	D	Inkspot of Fieldron	Paulanna Promise	Mrs S Morris	Mr & Mrs R Baxter	14.7.92
Ch Watteau Painted Lady	B	Ch Boreham Benedict	Pearl Culture from Watteau	Mesdames M Blake & A Thornton	Owners	16.7.92
Ch Mosvalley Snow Orchid	B	Ch Wilkates Solomon	Ch Mosvalley White Orchid	Mrs C Davies	Owner	2.1.93
Ch Pagister Luvme Luvme Not	B	Ch Sufredon Inkling	Pagistar Northern Rocket	S A Bull	Owner	29.4.92
Ch Gaybryl Galina	B	Ch Wilkates Solomon	Ch Riber Gundig	M D Gabriel	Owner	28.11.92
1995						
Ch Jetstream Front Page	D	Ch Roxway Embargo	Saleden Sneak Penny at Jetstream	M J Sargeant	Owner	13.3.93
Ch Brindfield the Best	D	Glendraterra Dancing Brave	Ch Laurelvale Gesture	S Clarke	Owner	4.1.94
Ch Dunlossit Murphy at Sufredon	D	Ch Sufredon Inkling	Ch Emblem of Durlossit	Mrs S M Laws	Donaldson & Pickford	22.1.93
Ch Boreham Bay Domino	D	Ch Astona Dowie	Boreham Bellavista	E Winstanley	Owner	4.10.93
Ch Crooksmoor Commotion	B	Ch Wilkates Solomon	Crooksmoor Confetti	R Crooks	Owner	15.11.93
Ch Rotur Witchcraft	B	Rotur Repertoire	Ch Riber Masquerade	Mrs R Turner	Owner	3.11.92
Ch Gavingale Living Doll	B	Glendraterra Rock and Roll	Little Damsel at Gavingale	Miss P Fox	Owner	4.11.92
Ch Rockenhart Tiber	B	Inkspot of Fieldron	Rockenhart Chelidonium	J Hartigan	Owner	31.10.91

BIBLIOGRAPHY

Further information about the breed can be found at The Kennel Club in London.

- **BEAK**, Linda **Fox Terriers** W & G Foyle Ltd, London: 1960.

- **BRUCE**, *Rev Dr* Rosslyn, *DD (Oxon)*, *FLS* **Fox terrier breeding.** Eastbourne: Strange.

- **BRUCE**, *Rev Dr* Rosslyn, *DD (Oxon)*, *FLS* **The popular fox terrier.** London: Popular Dogs, 1950.

- **CAVILL**, David **All about mating, whelping and weaning.** Pelham, 1981.

- **DALZIEL**, Hugh **The Fox Terrier.** London: The Bazaar, Exchange &Mart

- **DANGERFIELD**, Stanley **The Wire-haired Fox Terrier.** Nicholson & W, 1958.

- **JONES**, Rowland **Our friend the Fox Terrier.** 1932, 1933 and 1934.

- **LEE**, Rawdon B **Modern Dogs** Horace Cox.

- **MACDONALD**, Daly **The Fox Terrier.** London: W & R Chambers.

- **McLEOD**, George **Homeopathy for pets.** The Homeopathic Development Foundation Ltd, 1981.

- **MILLER**, Evelyn **Fox Terriers.** TFH, 1990

- **NAYLOR**, L E **The modern Fox Terrier.** London: H G & G Witherby.

- **NICHOLAS**, Anna Katherine **The Fox Terrier Smooth and Wire.** TFH, 1990.

- **PARDOE**, J H **Fox Terriers** Morrison and Gibb Ltd, London.

- **PERRINS**, Leslie **Showing your dog.** London: W & G Foyle Ltd.

- **WILLIAMS**, Elsie **The Fox Terrier.** Popular Dogs Publishing Co Ltd, London: 1965.

- **WOOD**, Lindley E **The Smooth Fox Terrier.** (Foyles handbook).

CONCLUSION

I hope all Terrier enthusiasts reading this book will find something useful in it. I have tried to provide an insight into the delights of owning a Fox Terrier for those not familiar with Terrier breeds. It has proved impossible to include all information on all relevant topics (especially History and Breeding) but I have done my best to include the essentials. I have tried very hard to have every detail correct, but I apologise to my reader for any minor discrepancies or omissions in the text. Researching dates has been particularly difficult, as authorities differ. I hope you will bear with me in this.

My prime object in writing this book has been to help people understand and love the breed and to encourage old and new Fox Terrier enthusiasts to meet together and enjoy each other's company. English books on the breed have been out of print for 20 years now, and I hope my research will help you in your journey with Fox Terriers. The List of Champions at Appendix C will give you the opportunity to research the top dogs and breeders at any given time. Many thanks again to all who have helped me to write this book, and to all who have read it.

Ch Crackley Stormer 1934

Ch Wakeful Lady 1929

Keresley Pandy 1928

Ch Crackley Society 1934